DRUMS
OF
REDEMPTION

Recent Titles in
Contributions to the Study of Religion

DRUMS
OF
REDEMPTION

An Introduction
to African Christianity

Harvey J. Sindima

Contributions to the Study of Religion,
Number 35

GREENWOOD PRESS
Westport, Connecticut • London

Library of Congress Cataloging-in-Publication Data

Sindima, Harvey J.
    Drums of redemption : an introduction to African Christianity /
Harvey J. Sindima.
        p.   cm.—(Contributions to the study of religion, ISSN
0196–7053 ; no. 35)
    Includes bibliographical references and index.
    ISBN 0–313–29088–1 (alk. paper)
    1. Christianity—Africa.   2. Christianity—Africa—History.
I. Title. II. Series.
BR1360.S564   1994
209.6—dc20   93–31637

British Library Cataloguing in Publication Data is available.

Library of Congress Catalog Card Number: 93–31637
ISBN: 0–313–29088–1
ISSN: 0196–7053

First published in 1994

Greenwood Press, 88 Post Road West, Westport, CT 06881
An imprint of Greenwood Publishing Group, Inc.

Printed in the United States of America

The paper used in this book complies with the
Permanent Paper Standard issued by the National
Information Standards Organization (Z39.48–1984).

10 9 8 7 6 5 4 3 2 1

Copyright Acknowledgements

The author and publisher gratefully acknowledge permission to reprint the following material:

The Gospel and the African by Alexander Hetherwick. Edinburgh: T & T Clark, pp. 108–109, 112–113, 117. Used with permission.

From Charity to Liberation by Jean-Marc Ela © CHR, London 1984. Reproduced by permission.

African Theologies Now: A Profile by Justin S. Ukpong. From *Spearhead No. 80*, 1984. Eldoret: Gaba Publications. Used with Permission.

"Theological Trends in Africa" by Gabriel M. Setiloane. From *Missiolania*, vol. 8, 1980, pp. 47, 50, 65. Used with Permission.

Hope and Suffering by Desmond Tutu. Johannesburg: Skotaville Publishers, 1984, pp. 26–27, 75, 76. Used with Permission.

"Africa's Christian Heritage: Some Notes on the Ethiopian Church" by Harvey J. Sindima. From *Africa Theological Journal*, vol. 2, no. 2, 1991.

From Orbis Books, permission was granted to reproduce extracts from the following material:

Christianity Without Fetishes: An African Critique and Recapture of Christianity. F. Eboussi Boulaga, Robert R. Barr, trans., 1984.

African Theology en Route, Appiah-kubi and Sergio Torres, eds., 1979.

The Will to Arise: Women and the Church in Africa, Mercy Oduyoye and Musimbi R. A. Kanyoro, eds., 1992.

With Passion and Compassion: Third World Women Doing Theology. Mercy Amba Oduyoye and Virginia Fabella, eds., 1989.

My Faith as an African. By Jean-Marc Ela. John P. Brown and Sussan Perry, trans., Maryknoll, 1989.

African Cry. By Jean-Marc Ela, Robert Barr, trans., 1986.

The Emergent Gospel. Sergio Torres and Virginia Fabella, eds., 1978.

Kwa wokondeka, Anaphiri.
Muzigona kutali ndi moto.

Contents

Acknowledgements

Parts of this book developed during 1984 through 1988 from mission lectures I delivered at Haddonfield First Presbyterian Church, Haddonfield, New Jersey. I thank Dr. Robert L. Veon, former senior minister of the Church, for his vision for mission. He invited me to be Missionary in Residence. I thank the Mission Committee of the Church for supporting Dr. Veon's idea and giving me the opportunity to share my experience and knowledge of African Christianity. I am very grateful to the committee and the Deacon's Board for their support. My gratitude also goes to the members of the congregation and the Men's Bible Class for attending my lectures. My wife and I very much appreciate the love and kindness received from individuals and families who took interest in us.

I am indebted to my fellow struggler in faith, a partner in work and companion in life, my wife, Gertrude. She proofread the manuscript at its various stages of development.

Introduction

Christianity is growing in Africa. According to the Center for African Christianity in Nairobi, there are over 205 million Christians in Africa today. Some statistics show that every day there are approximately 13,000 to 16,000 people becoming Christians.[1] By the turn of the century, the Christian population in Africa will be over 350 million. Africa will then have the largest Christian concentration in the world. Africa embraces Orthodox (Coptic, Ethiopian and Greek) and the Roman Catholic tradition, as well as various branches of Reformed tradition— Adventist (both Seventh Day and Baptists), Anglicans, Baptists of all kinds, Lutherans, Methodists, Pentecostals, Presbyterians, and other less common ones. In addition, there are over six million indigenous Churches of various sizes. The largest of the African indigenous Churches is the Kimbaguist Church, which has a membership of over ten million. The smaller ones may have as few as a household. David Barrett, who has conducted extensive research on indigenous Churches across Africa, has shown that the membership of these Churches shows no sign of decreasing.[2] My own research, done on a national scale, agrees with Barrett's conclusion that these Churches of African origin are a power to be reckoned with, and that they are growing at a greater rate than generally thought.[3]

Africa's connection with Christianity is as old as Christianity itself; but many people know very little of this early connection because of a lack, or a distortion, of general knowledge concerning Africa's past. This situation is perpetuated by the tendency to separate the southern regions of Africa from the north, treating the latter as part of Western culture and civilization. This ideological separation make the Tertullian, Cyprian, Augustine and other like people, non-Africans; yet these great Christian thinkers of the Church were born or worked in Carthage, the present day Tunis! Indeed we do not find their writings in the local language, Berber, but Latin, and this is because Latin had become the *lingua franca* of the Roman empire as well as of the

Church. The result of using Latin was that some of the theological categories developed or used did not reflect the thought forms of the local culture; but this is typical of a colonized situation. In an uncolonized situation, language defines a people. It orders and describes the world and way of life of the people, it mediates a culture as well as enables communication.[4]

The distorted knowledge about the south of Africa is also observed in what is not mentioned in Church history books and mission chronicles. Such documents are silent about the fact that Christianity has always grown under the influence of a dominant imperial power—the Early Church expanded with imperial protection and help. In the 15th century, Christianity was brought to Africa under the expansion program of a dominant European power, and throughout the colonial period it was protected by the State.[5] So, we see that what is often given as Church history is actually the history of the expansion and domination of Western civilization.[6] Since Church history is equated with the activities of conquest and domination of Western culture, mission chronicles trim all stories to fit the goals and purposes of Western culture and civilization.

In light of the foregoing discussion, this book attempts to transcend ideological distortions of the history of African Christianity by recounting its story from the first century to the present. I have highlighted Africa's contributions to the development of Christian thought and practice during the first five hundred years of Christianity. From the glory of the Early African Church, I have discussed a less known period in the history of African Christianity: the period covering the eighth century through medieval times to the fifteenth century. The reason for the obscurity of facts concerning African Christianity during this period is mainly ascribed to Islamic conquests and influence in North Africa, which began in the seventh century with the fall of Egypt. Luckily, a few Moslem travelers and scholars documented the presence of strong Christian kingdoms beyond the Coptic communities in the Nile valley. These documents, covering the period from the seventh century through the medieval period, reveal that there were many monasteries—big and beautiful Churches—in Nubia (Sudan) and Ethiopia. These writings help us to link the history of the Early African Church to the medieval period and beyond—the era of Western missionary enterprise.

Chronicles have documented the work of Western missionaries, their societies, or agencies from the fifteenth century to the present. On the other hand, such histories of Christian missions in Africa often say little or nothing about two groups of missionaries: the Africans of the diaspora and the early African evangelists. The work of the Africans of the diaspora was often beset by financial problems, as well as lack of moral support both at home and on the mission field. In spite of the many obstacles faced, they rendered a significant and commendable service to the land of their ancestors. While Church history books are filled with names of missionaries, one searches in vain for names of African evangelists who opened new fields of mission work and set up mission stations. In this book I have called attention to the work of African evangelists.

The book is in two parts. The first focuses on the historical development, while the second examines responses to the missionary enterprise and the theological work that followed. The second section begins by re-examining missionary thought and practice, focusing on mission strategy for evangelization of Africa. Missionaries came to Africa after the Enlightenment, that intellectual climate which changed Europeans' concept of the world, values, and self-understanding. These concepts influenced the way missionaries thought of others and what they perceived as the nature of the missionary enterprise. The problems of African Christianity today cannot be fully appreciated unless they are seen against the background of the clash between two different concepts of the world—Western (as informed by the Enlightenment) and African.

The problem of different world concepts and value systems pressed hard on African converts to Christianity. After baptism, they found that their new faith and the African way of life belonged to two irreconcilable worlds. Faced with the dichotomy between faith and culture, some Christians started to find ways of grounding the new faith in the African way of life. This attempt produced new types of Churches that attempted to incorporate African way of life into Christianity. These Churches, commonly referred to as Independent Churches, have generated a lot of scholarly interest concerning their origin, nature, and the kind of things they emphasize from Christianity and African tradition. The book discusses the independency phenomenon and its theological orientation.

The accomplishment of Christian authenticity has been a task taken seriously by African theologians. Western modes of theology do not respond to African needs and conditions. Challenged by the condition of their people, African theologians have sought to develop paradigms which express the gospel in a truly African mode of thought, language, and way of life. A number of theological approaches and themes have emerged from their exercise, namely, indigenization or inculturation, Black theology, and African Liberation Theology. African theologians are discovering that theology is basically a cultural phenomenon even when it claims to be dogmatic. Indeed, theology can be no other since it is the interpretation of people's experience of the divine as expressed by their cultural symbols.

The book presents an overview of Christianity in Africa from the first century to the present day. Books on African Christianity tend to have one perspective—historical, theological, or sociological. In this book I have included various perspectives and issues. There are certainly a lot of issues that could be covered, but only the major points have been tackled here. I hope beginners as well as advanced readers will find this brief introduction informative and helpful in their work.

NOTES

1. This figure was estimated by David Barrett, an Anglican researcher based in Nairobi. *Cf.* David Lamb, *The Africans* (New York: Vintage Books, 1984), 143. A figure of 15,000 was cited in *New Blackfriars*, Jan. 1984, 3, which also stated that Europe has a decrease of 7,500 Christians per day.

2. David Barrett, *Schism and Renewal in Africa* (Nairobi: Oxford University Press, 1968).

3. Harvey Sindima, "A General Survey of Independent Churches in Malawi 1900-1976," *All Africa Conference of Churches Bulletin*, 1977.

4. Ngugi wa Thiong'o, *Decolonizing the Mind: The Politics of Language in African Literature* (Nairobi: Heinemann, 1986), 13-15.

5. I have discussed the Church-State relation in colonial Africa in *Christianity and Political Crisis in Africa*, chap. 1 (forthcoming).

6. This point has been argued at length by Walbert Buhlmann in *The Coming of the Third Church* (Maryknoll, N.Y.: Orbis Books, 1977).

I

HISTORY

1

The Early African Church

Christianity has existed in Africa as long as the religion has existed, but it is not the first religion to have adherents on the continent—Judaism can make that claim. The story of the Pentecost lists Africans among "devout men" who were in Jerusalem—presumably they were there to worship. Libya and Egypt are mentioned by name (Acts 2:5,10). Other sources say that Ethiopians were also present on the day of Pentecost. For example, John Chrysostom in his Epiphany Homily says that "the Ethiopian also understood."[1] This is an indication that there were at least a few Ethiopians present on the day of Pentecost. It may be there were too few Ethiopians for Luke to mention them in his list of those who were in Jerusalem on the day of Pentecost. This chapter is devoted to the life and work of the Church in North Africa, beginning with Egypt.

THE CHURCH IN EGYPT

According to oral tradition of the Coptic Church in Egypt, one of the first evangelists is said to have come to that land. The Coptic Church attributes the coming of Christianity to Egypt to John Mark, the writer of the first Gospel—the Gospel according to Mark. Eusebius (260-339), the learned historian of the Early Church, agrees with the Egyptian oral tradition that the writer of the Gospel according to Mark was indeed a missionary to Alexandria. This learned historian from Caesaria is believed by contemporary Church historians to be accurate in his reports, so for him to testify to this oral tradition, makes the story a more probable history.

Egyptian christianity grew from the urban areas (e.g., Alexandria). Jews who had been converted to Christianity and Greek-speaking Gentiles were found in these cities. Historical evidence is scanty about Christianity in the first century, but it is established that cities served as the basis for the evangelization of Egypt. The first written documents about Christianity in Egypt dates back to the time of Bishop Demetrius of Alexandria (189-232). According to the documents he wrote in 189, he had jurisdiction over the whole of Egypt. The Church grew in the years following the bishopric of Demetrius. The Gospel spread into the Nile valley, where it was to find its lasting stronghold. By the year 260, many Copts in the valley had begun joining the Church. The Copts have held on to Christianity to this day.

Egypt was not only the home of the Coptic Church, but the origin of missionary activity south into Nubia; it was also the center for both the Christian Church and Jewish dispersion. In Alexandria, a quarter of the city was occupied by Jews. No wonder that it was there that the Old Testament was translated into Greek for the first time. This translation, commonly known as the *Septuagint* (a Greek word meaning translation of or by the seventy—referring to the number of translators) was, done in 250. Alexandria was important to the Jewish community. It was there, too, that Jewish intellectual life flourished in the person of Philo, the famous Jewish philosopher. Philo lived from 20 B.C.E. (Before the Common Era) to 40 C. E. (in the Common Era). For Christians, Alexandria was the home of two famous intellectuals—Clement and Origen. It was within this academic atmosphere that Christianity first developed systematic catechetical instructions. It was natural, then, that this center of knowledge also became the center of the controversy over the nature of the person of Christ. Here theologians debated the identity of Jesus. Did Jesus embody both divine and human qualities, and to what extent were these two natures present? Alexandrian theologians maintained that the two natures became one. Thus they were known as *monophysites*, a Greek term meaning of one (*mono*) substance (*phusis*). It was also in Alexandria that Christianity developed respect for the Virgin Mary.

Before delving into the development of Christianity south of Egypt, it is important to mention a few things about the strength of the Egyptian Church in the first five centuries. The Egyptian Church was well established, having survived numerous persecutions under different Roman emperors in the first three centuries. It was strong enough to send missionaries up into Nubia and later, upon invitation, into the area of King Alodia (the region where the Blue and White Nile meet) and into the Abyssinia region. Eusebius, again testifies to the strength of the Egyptian Church. He has recorded that at one synod meeting in 320, there "were close to 100 bishops in Egypt, the Thebais (an area five hundred miles up the Nile), Kibyae and Pentapolis." At another synod meeting held at Sardica in 343, there were 94 bishops who signed their names. Eusebius also reports of persecutions suffered by Christians in Egypt and Thebais: "Thither, as to some great arena, were escorted from Egypt and the whole of Thebais God's champions, who, through their most steadfast endurance in divers tortures and modes of death, were wreathed with crowns laid up with God."[2]   He also gives an eyewitness account of martyrdoms in Thebais. "We also, being on the spot ourselves, have observed large crowds in one day; some suffering decapitation, others torture by fire . . . . As soon as sentence was pronounced against the first, one after another rushed to the judgment seat, and confessed themselves Christians."[3]

The Egyptian Church grew stronger in each century and by the year 300, it had one million adherents.[4] This growth allowed the Church to enter missionary work. By the sixth century such work spread well into the south. Between the years 543-580 Christianity had reached the three kingdoms of Nobatia, Mukurra, and Aloa, going onto the island of Philae.[5] The first missionary to go south from Alexandria was Julian. He was a presbyter (elder) of the Church who preached the Gospel to Nubians (Sudanese). In 543 Julian of Alexandria got permission from Empress Theodora of Constantinople to evangelize the Nubians. The empress was happy with Julian's mission because it lessened border conflict and at the same time brought the Nubians into her empire. Julian was such a missionary for two years.

Twenty years after Julian's missionary work in Nubia, the Egyptian Church commissioned Longius to the King of Alodia. The king had invited Longius to come and preach the "Good News" to his people. With the coming of Longius to the kingdom of Alodia, Christianity was established among the three kingdoms of today's Sudan: Nobatia to the north, Makurra in the middle, and Alodia in the south.

Again, upon invitation, the Egyptian Church went beyond Nubia into Abyssinia (or the region now known as Ethiopia). It was this move to the south, as opposed to the west, which gave witness to the missionary enterprise of the Egyptian Church; this witness has remained. Expansion into Nubia brought the Egyptians closer to the Abyssinian people among whom a strong Church emerged. While Christians already existed in Abyssinia, they had not organized themselves into an institution with a structured hierarchy, a Church.

THE CHURCH IN LIBYA AND THE WEST

The Egyptian Church expanded in two directions westward along the Mediterranean seaboard and south along the Nile valley. To the west, it reached as far as Pentapolis or Cyrenaica (Libya). In Libya Christianity was preceded by Judaism. Although Jews in Libya were few in number, a visible Jewish community existed. These Libyan Jews were recorded to have gone to Jerusalem to worship and, according to Luke, the writer of the Book of

Acts of the Apostles, Libyans were present on the day of Pentecost (Acts 2:10). He also says that Libyans in Antioch reported having heard the Greeks preach of the Lord Jesus (Acts 11:19-20). Luke records that there were some Libyans at Antioch; two of them are mentioned by name: Lucius and Niger. The name, Niger, suggests that the person may have been a Berber (Acts 13:1-3).

Tertullian, the great North African theologian of the second century, was right when he said: "The ofter we are moved down by you, the larger grow our numbers. The blood of Christians is a seed. . . . That very obstinacy which you reprobate is our instructress."[6] This was indeed true of the growth of the Church in the Roman Province of Cyrene or Carthage, Numidia, Proconsular, and Mauritania—the whole of North Africa. The growth of the Church in Libya seems to have been slow until the Scilitan martyrdom when twelve Christians (seven men and five women) at Scill refused to sacrifice to the Roman gods; on July 16, 180, Proconsul Vigellius Saturninus condemned the 12 to death.[7]

Although records are not available on the evangelization of North Africa prior to 180, the persecution is sure testimony of Christian presence in the region in the second century. By 200 there were ten Churches in Libya, and by the third century the Church had reached the Atlantic coast with hundreds of Churches in between. It was a growing presence which, toward the end of the second century had its own bishop, Agrippinus, in Carthage. Christianity continued to grow so that by the beginning of the third century Carthage commanded authority over North Africa. As early as 220 Agrippinus showed the power and authority of Carthage by summoning a Council of North African bishops to debate the rebaptism of those baptized by heretics; the Council agreed to the rebaptism.

The rapid growth of the Libyan Church was achieved during the persecutions of Decian (249-251) and Valerian (253-259). When this period of persecutions began, Dionysius, known as the "Great," was Bishop of Alexandria. The bishop and other Christians were arrested upon imperial order and sent to the oasis of Kufra in the Libyan desert. Dionysius wrote that he and the others saw this as an opportunity to preach the "Good News."

> And there God opened unto us a door for the word. And at first we were pursued, we were stoned, but afterwards not a few of the heathens left their idols and turned to God. Then for the first time was the word sown through our agency among those who had not formerly received it. It was, as it were, for this that God took us away to them, and when we had fulfilled this ministration, took us away again.[8]

Men and women throughout North Africa died in the persecutions. Accounts of anguish and pain from torture abound, but there are not many about women suffering persecution. There is one account of Vibia Perpetua and her servant friend Felicitas. Vibia was a woman of high standing who had a suckling child when she was put in prison in Carthage. Her father often brought her baby to her cell and implored her to offer to the Roman gods so that she could be let free to nurse her baby. Vibia would not reject her faith, nor would Felicitas. Since they would not offer to the gods, they were both condemned to death. With her friend Felicitas, they were led into the arena where some Christian men were torn to pieces by animals as a public spectacle. The women were stripped naked, but when the crown was offended by the authorities exposing the ladies' nakedness, Vibia and Felicitas were given over to a bull which was let loose into the arena. The bull tossed and wounded the women but did not kill them, so gladiators were ordered to kill them with swords. This persecution took place on February 2, 203.

Many Christians would not sacrifice to the gods, however some did for fear of their lives. The trial of Pionius gives us an idea of the court proceedings of those who refused to practice civil religion.

Judge: Will you sacrifice?
Pionius: No.
Judge: What is your religion?
Pionius: The religion of God the Father, who made all things.
Judge: We all worship gods-heaven, the gods in heaven, Zeus, the king of the gods.
Pionius: Silence.
[The warders then tortured him by stretching his body with ropes.]
The Warders: Now sacrifice.
Pionius: No.
[The warders then tore his flesh with iron claw.]
The warders: Change your mind. What madness is this?
Pionius: Not madness, it is fear of the living God.
Proconsul: Others have sacrificed, and are alive. Think about it to yourself a moment and change your mind.
Pionius: Not I, sir.
Proconsul: Why are you so determined upon death?
Pionius: Not upon death, upon life.[9]

During the persecutions Church leaders also suffered martyrdom. Eusebius describes how these leaders went through their martyrdom: "they. . . suffered deaths illustriously at Alexandria and throughout Egypt and Thebais."[10] Among those leaders who suffered martyrdom was Cyprian, Bishop of Carthage. Earlier, Cyprian had fled into the wildness for fear of his life because he would not sacrifice to the gods or the emperor and get a certificate of Sacrifice. (Emperor Decius ordered these certificates.) However, under the persecution of Valerian, the bishop of Carthage accepted martyrdom. When his sentence was pronounced, Cyprian is recorded to have said: "Thanks be to God." He died in 258. Bishop Dionysius of Alexandria (247-64) also went into hiding during the persecutions of Decius and Valerian, but in both cases he was restored to his episcopal office, which he occupied until his death in 264. Earlier, Dionysius himself lamented Christians turning apostate. Calling those Christians "by nature cowards in everything, cowards both to die and to sacrifice."[11]

During the persecutions of Decius and Valerian, Cyprian took a strong position against readmission into the fellowship of the Church of those who had sacrificed during persecution. Except for those who sacrificed under torture, he condemned the rest to live in penitence all their lives. Those who had sacrificed under torture would have to perform a period of penance before being received again into the fellowship of the Church. A man called Novatus led a party of those who believed the Church should show leniency toward those who had lapsed during persecution. The problem of the lapsed also aroused controversy at the Church in Rome. There a presbyter, by the name of Novatian (not to be confused with Novatus of Carthage), led the opposition against the no-readmission policy of the Church. When Novatus went to Rome to appeal his case to the Church leaders there, he did not get any support. Because his views were similar to those of Novatian, he decided to join a Novatian Church. Upon his return home to Carthage, he founded a Novatian Church opposing Cyprian's strict policy.

There were many persecutions in the first three centuries of the early African Church. The story of the Egyptian and North African Churches is filled with persecutions, one after another. North African Christians suffered persecutions under Emperor Marcus Aurelius (161-180), Septimus Severus (202-203), Decius and Valerian (249-259), and Diocletian, Galerius, and Maximian (303-312). The persecutions arose because of Christians' refusal to worship or sacrifice to the emperors. The earliest written protest of North African Christians towards Roman (civil) religion and morals is *The Acts of the Scilitan Martyrs* (180). The document rejects the popular assumption that the problems of the empire were caused by Christians refusal to offer to the Roman gods.

Persecutions had an adverse effect for they failed to create fear or deter people from becoming Christians. The gruesome scenes of torture and death of martyrs did nothing to stop the growth of Christianity. Indeed, the blood of the martyrs was the seed of Christianity, for the religion continued to grow in Libya where it had its own bishops, but not a Patriarch. According to the Canon (Church law) of Nicaea, Libya was under the jurisdiction of the Patriarch of Alexandria. Thus, Libyan bishops attended Church councils in Egypt and were present at the Alexandrian council that condemned Arius for his teachings.

CONTRIBUTIONS OF THE EARLY AFRICAN CHURCH

The contributions that Africa has made toward the Christian faith have been great. One has only to look at the multitude of volumes on the Christian thought, faith, and practice written by early African theologians to confirm their tremendous contribution to the Christian faith. Names of lay and ordained theologians, Church leaders, and others whose work or writings shaped Christian thought are too many to be discussed in one chapter. We will mention only a few of the leading thinkers—the Church Fathers: Tertullian, Cyprian, Origen, Athanasius, Cyril, and Augustine. Innumerable volumes have been written about the life and work of each of these men. We will also briefly discuss the work of Victor 1, Melchiades, and Gelasius—three Africans who became bishops of Rome, thereby Popes of the Catholic Church.

Carthage

Carthage was the largest and most influential city in the Roman empire; it was *the* city of the third century. It was also the most Christian city, producing such important ecclesiastical figures as Tertullian, Cyprian, and Augustine. Carthage was only second to Alexandria as center of Christian thought, and its Christian library was one of the largest in the Christian world.

Tertullian

Quintus Septimius Florend Tertullianus (or usually referred to as Tertullian), born in Carthage in 150, was the first great theologian of the Early Church. His education was in Greek and Latin. He studied law and became one of the most noted lawyers of Rome. His training in law and classical languages, along with his competency in philosophy, were to prove of extreme help in defending the Christian faith. For his work in defense of the Church he is known as the greatest apologist (defender of the faith). After Tertullian became a Christian in 193, he lived a very strict and disciplined life; he was an ascetic. He advocated purity of the Church and high moral standards of its members. It was for this reason that in 207 he joined a puritanical sectarian movement called Montanism. This movement taught that Christians should completely separate themselves from the world and wait for the coming of the Holy Spirit at Mount Pepuza. In other words, the kingdom of God would be coming soon. (Montanism was started in 156 by a man named Montanus who lived in Phrygia, Central Asia Minor). Tertullian joined a Montanist Church and remained there until his death in 220. He is also remembered for his position on the issue of the nature of Jesus. Tertullian argued that Jesus embodied in himself two natures, human and divine—united, full, and complete. Therefore, Jesus was fully human and fully God.

The great north African theologian wrote numerously on apologetics, theology, and ethics. He wrote in defense of Christianity against Jews as well as people of other religions, but he also wrote against Gnostics who taught that knowledge was the way to salvation. Further, he defended Christianity against the teaching of the Marcionites who believed that the God of creation and law, that is, the God of the Old Testament, was inferior to the God of love and redemption, the God of the New Testament. When the Roman government started persecuting Christians, Tertullian did not retreat into piety but wrote in defense of Christianity; his training in law is evident in such works as *On Testimony of the Soul, Prescription Against Heretics, and Apology*. In the first work, he places the soul of a non-Christian on the witness stand, and through a process of cross-examination, reminiscent of the style of the time, he forces that soul to confess the rationality of Christian faith. Then Tertullian in a statement of summation, concludes: "Every soul is a culprit as well as a witness: in the measure that it testifies for truth, the guilt of error is in it."[12]

The most significant of Tertullian's work is the *Apology*, written in defense of Christians against the persecution of the Roman state. In this work, Tertullian exposes the unfair nature of Roman policy on dealing with Christians. The policy, stated by emperor Trajan in his instructions to Pliny, Governor of the province of Bithynia in Asia, was that Christians should not be sought out, but if someone were accused of being a Christian, the authorities should investigate the matter and attempt to convince the accused to deny Christ. If the accused did not change, then death penalty should be applied. In *Apology* Tertullian exposes the contradictions within this practice.

> O miserable deliverance—under the necessities of the case, a self contradiction! It forbids them to be sought after as innocent, and it condemns them to be punished as guilty. It is at once merciful and cruel; it passes by, and it punishes. Why dost thou play a game of evasion upon thyself, O Judgment? If thou condemnest, why dost thou not also inquire? If thou dost not inquire, why dost thou not absolve?[13]

Tertullian's theological reflections included such subjects as baptism, the person of Christ, resurrection, and penitence. The issues that he reflected on in ethics included virginity, monogamy, chastity, fasting, and even on dress code and public shows. These works on ethics reflected Tertullian's own sense of the purity worthy of a Christian. His idea of purity also appears in his theological writings, especially on baptism. In *De Baptismo*, Tertullian connects the purity of the sacraments with the sanctity of the priest and the Church. He begins by arguing that in baptism the Holy Spirit is actually present in the water,[14] and since a heretic does not have the Spirit, his baptism, as that of a person in mortal sin, is invalid.[15] Therefore anyone baptized by a heretic or someone in mortal sin must be rebaptized. According to Tertullian, a priest is worthy of the divine office if "he knew how to administer in sanctity."[16] The works of Tertullian may be divided into two groups—(a) defense of Christianity; and (b) teaching and practice of Christianity—both of which had a great impact upon the course of Christianity.

Cyprian

Caecilius Cyprian was a bishop of Carthage from 248-258. He was born in 200 in the city and became a Christian in 246. In 250, during the persecution of Decius, he went into hiding and returned from exile in 251. He was arrested on August 30, 257 during the persecution of Valerian and was taken to Curubis (Kurba) on the Gulf of Hammamet; then he was transported back to Carthage where he was tried and condemned to death. He was executed on September 14, 258.

His theology was clearly influenced by Tertullian whom he called "the Master." Some of his works look like revisions of Tertullian's writings. Those works included: *On the Dress of Virgins, On the Lord's Prayer, On the Vanity of Idols*, and *On the Advantage of Patience*. He also made original contributions which discussed the nature of the Church and its sacraments and the office of the bishop. His works were more pastoral, which is to say they were a response to what Christians were going through. Responding to the question of what should be done with the lapsed, Cyprian wrote two treatises: *On the Unity of the Church* and *On the Lapsed*. In 250 there was a plague in North Africa. A certain Demetrianus blamed the epidemic on the Christians—the gods were angry. Cyprian responded to the accusation with a brief treatise: *To Demetrianus*. But he also wrote *On Mortality*, an address to the people to help them face death. To encourage them to practice the works of charity, he wrote: *On Works and Alms*. He was one of the first theologians to struggle with the question of the relationship between Church and State. His work concerned itself with showing how Christianity was opposed to sacrificing to secular powers. Cyprian was the first to strongly advocate for the episcopate; he based his argument on the words of Jesus: "You are Peter, and upon this rock I will build my Church" (Matt. 16:18,19).

Thence age has followed age and bishop has followed bishop in succession, and the office of the episcopate and the system of the Church has been handed down, so that the Church is founded on the bishops and every act of the Church is directed by the same presiding officers.

. . .[17] Hence you should know the bishop is in the Church and the Church in the bishop, and that if any one be not with the bishop he is not in the Church.[18]

While he argued for the episcopate, the primacy of Peter and Rome as "the chief Church whence priestly unity takes its source," Cyprian was against granting the bishop of Rome any power over the internal matters of his diocese. Cyprian advocated a federated episcopacy, in which every bishop would have a certain autonomy and yet would listen to fraternal recommendations of other bishops and would obey decisions of Church councils. Nevertheless, Cyprian was for the unity of the Church; in his autumn 251 tract, "The Unity of the Catholic Church," Cyprian emphasized the idea of one bishop, one see but also that "he cannot have God for his Father who has not the Church for his mother," an idea which he had emphatically expressed in his *Epistle*—there is no salvation outside the Church.

Augustine

Perhaps the most outstanding of Africa's children was Aurelius Augustine, son of Monica and Patricius. Augustine (354-430) is most often referred to as Augustine of Hippo. He was born at Thagaste in Numidia on November 13, 354. At sixteen he left home to continue his education at Madaura in the plains of Numidia and then on to the university at Carthage. There he studied oratory or law, took a concubine, with whom he stayed for thirteen years, and had a boy with her. In Carthage, Augustine joined the Manichean religion in 373. This religion from Persia taught that all life is to be understood in terms of a struggle between good and evil, light and darkness, and that there is a spark of light in every person but it is encased in the body. Salvation, therefore, is freeing this light from the body. Augustine remained a Manichee until 383 when he went to Rome to seek employment as a teacher. There he got interested in neo-Platonist philosophy. His search for employment took him to Milan where he was impressed by the preaching of Ambrose, the bishop of the city. He sent his concubine away and asked Ambrose to instruct him in the Christian faith; he received baptism in the summer of 386. After his conversion, Augustine decided to return to Africa and serve. Very quickly he became a church leader: he was ordained a presbyter in 389, in 395 Augustine became assistant bishop of Hippo, and a year later was consecrated full bishop.

Augustine was a great theologian. He was involved in two major controversies: the Donatist and Pelagian. The Donatists were orthodox members of the Church who did not agree with the Catholic Church.

Donatists broke away from the Catholic Church because it allowed Felix Amptunga, a man who had surrendered the scriptures to the authorities during persecution, to participate in the ordination of a bishop, Caecilian. Donatists, so called after their leader Donatus, maintained that sacraments administered by unworthy priest, or by one who was ordained in unworthy manner, were invalid. Augustine wrote a book, *Against the Donatists*, in which he made a historic theological response that the power of the sacraments does not lie in the character of the priest but in the holy apostolic nature of the Church.

The second controversy, advanced by an Irish monk, Pelagius, stated that God created every person with a possibility of living a sinless life and that humans have the will to accept this divine gift (sinless life). Augustine's response to this, in his book *Against the Pelagians*, elaborated on the teaching of original sin, arguing that sin does not consist of evil actions but in an evil nature inherited from Adam; therefore sin cannot be removed, it is part of the human. Humans are only able to do good things with the power of God working in their hearts; he called this power grace. Today the Catholic Church follows Augustine in its teaching of sin and grace; and it also maintains Augustine's view that the efficacy of the sacraments is not dependent on the character of the celebrant (priest) but in the holy nature of the Church.

Augustine left numerous writings on many subjects including philosophical treatises, apologetics, religious and theological works, devotionals, homilies, and ethical and autobiographical works. Of the two autobiographical books he wrote, the *Confessions* and the *Retractation*, the *Confessions* (written about the year 400) is the most widely read and has inspired many people throughout the ages. A major part of the *Confessions* is a continuous prayer and confession before God, a general sketch of his earlier life, of his conversion, and of his return to Africa at the age of 34. The last part of the book is on speculative philosophy addressing such topics as the possibility of knowing God, the nature of time and space, and cosmology of Moses.

The City of God is another popular book by Augustine. In this book, he sets forth his view of history and its meaning. Augustine acknowledges the greatness of earthly cities, in particular Rome. As great as Rome was, it had to pass, for all cities and nations must follow this course, therefore, humanity must look to the city of God, New Jerusalem. This book, and the one entitled *On Trinity*, has had a great impact on the Christian Church across the centuries.

Egypt

Pantaenus and Clement

Egypt, with its 700,000 volume library, was the center of Christian and Jewish learning. It was in Alexandria in 180 that the first organized catechetical instructions were given at a school set up by Pantaenus, about whom nothing much is known, except that he was the teacher of Clement. Of him Clement said, "[in power he was the first] I met and found him, when I had caught him, hidden away in Egypt." Pantaenus was a (Stoic) philosopher and a Christian. Using his house, he instructed people in Christian teachings, that is, prepared them for baptism and Christian life. The school also provided a higher level of philosophical and theological training. Pantaenus charged no fees and lived off gifts from well-to-do students. The school grew and became known as the Catechetical (Greek for oral instruction) School. Upon his death in 200, Pantaenus was succeeded by his student Clement as head of the school.

The background of Clement himself is obscure; scholars differ about his origin. Some say he was born in Athens, while others say in Egypt but not in Alexandria. Whatever the case may be, scholars agree that Clement was certainly shaped by and he contributed to Alexandrian thought. Clement (150-215) was Alexandria's first famous Church leader and theologian. Having studied and worked with Pantaenus, Clement continued the tradition of the catechetical school of providing higher philosophical and theological training. Under his leadership the school trained African and Greek students. Great Church leaders were trained there, among them Origen and Alexander, bishop of Jerusalem. Clement was forced to leave Alexandria during the persecution of Septimius Severus and nothing much more of his life is known except that he visited Cappadocea and Antioch and that he died in 215.

Clement was an intellectual giant who emphasized that Christianity was not anti-intellectual or against philosophy; he believed people could be both intellectuals and Christians. He demonstrated this in his own career; he undertook the task of interpreting the gospel to educated Greeks. He argued that "philosophy," which the Greeks loved, "was a preparation, paving the way towards perfection in christ."[19] Clement did not see a contradiction between faith and philosophy. He argued, "philosophy, being the search for truth; not as being the cause of comprehension, but a cause along with other things, and cooperator; perhaps also a joint cause."[20] Clement's position was that truth is one and it comes from God, therefore Christians should see in philosophy a reflection of the same truth that has been revealed to them. If some Christians feared that this would lead them into error, it meant they did not have faith in the power of truth. In summary, Clement maintained that "knowledge is to be believed;" and "faith is to be known." Clement was one of the early thinkers to address the relation of philosophy and faith.

Another contribution Clement made was in the reading and understanding of the scriptures. Important to him was the manner in which God speaks in the scriptures and how the word is to be interpreted. He believed the sacred text does not have a literal historical sense; God speaks through allegories or symbols. To understand the sacred text, then, should involve interpretation of those symbols. For Clement, every text had two meanings—a literal and spiritual—however, each text must be interpreted in light of the rest of the scripture, that is, placing the text within its immediate context. This method of biblical interpretation was further developed by his student, Origen.

Clement addressed other issues, for example, the incarnation, and wrote other popular books: *Exhortations to the Heathens* and *Miscellaneous*. The latter is a follow-up to *The Heathens*, a book on how the word of God converts people.

Origen

There was yet another great Christian scholar in Alexandria. Origenes Adamantius was born in the city of Alexandria in 185. His name Origenes, "child of Horus," reflects his Egyptian heritage. Horus was the ancient falcon-god identified both with the Egyptian royal dynasty and with the sun. Origen was a student of Clement of Alexandria. In 202 Clement and other teachers of the catechetical school fled and students were martyred. In this persecution Origen's father, Leonides, was arrested and imprisoned, later suffering martyrdom. Origen himself would have been a martyr if it were not for his mother who hid his clothes from him to make it difficult for him to get out of the house. In the next year (at eighteen), Bishop Demetrius appointed him to head the catechetical school and to give regular instruction to catechumens. Origen sold his father's library of secular books so that he would be able to give instruction without fee. He had great success as a teacher and thus began a great career. Origen was an ascetic of the extreme type who took Matt. 12:19 literally; he got emasculated. This was to prove detrimental to his career, for eunuchs could not be ordained. Origen also attended lectures in philosophy from some leading teachers in Alexandria. So, for a time Origen was a teacher, student, and an ascetic. This renowned theologian and biblical scholar died in 254 as a result of torture suffered in the Decian persecution.

Origen was interested in theological and philosophical issues. He was a great writer and reports say he managed to keep six secretaries busy writing out his lectures and the thoughts he dictated. According to some sources, he wrote six thousand works.[21] Only about eight hundred of these have survived and a very small number of these exist in their original Greek.[22] Of Origen's great works are *Hexapla, Scholia*, the *Homilies, Commentaries*, and *De principiis* or *Concerning the First Principles*.

Origen was the first serious scholar of biblical criticism, and the first serious Christian Old Testament scholar. He was opposed to a literal translation of the Bible. He learned Hebrew from a tutor to investigate the text of the Old Testament. *Hexapla* was the first attempt in Christian history to establish the original text in scripture. This book was written in six columns of the Hebrew text of the Old Testament, a literal translation of that text in Greek characters, and the four Greek versions in circulation at that time (second century) among Jewish proselytes: Aquila, the Septuagint, Theodotion, and that of the Jewish-Christian, Symmachus. He added two more translations for the Psalms.

Concerning the First Principles is a work representative of Origen's theological and philosophical thinking. This work, directed against Gnostics (false teachers), was about "main" and "original things." He argued that Gnostic teaching about God and dualism was inadequate as a view of the world and a guide to conduct.

Origen's fame as a scholar went far and wide. By 214 he was known outside Egypt; he was invited to lecture in Arabia and, later, Jerusalem, Rome, and Athens. Although he was a renowned biblical scholar, he was not allowed to preach. He, did preach, however, when his friends, bishops of Jerusalem and Caesarea, invited him. The fact that Origen, an unordained person, preached made Demetrius furious, and he recalled Origen to Alexandria immediately. In 229 Origen was invited to Greece and there was ordained. Demetrius called the ordination invalid and illegal. Invalid because according to Church Canon, a eunuch could not be ordained; illegal for he alone, Demetrius, had the right to ordain Origen.

For most of his life, Origen was made to feel unwelcome in his home city of Alexandria. Notwithstanding all his personal problems, Origen contributed greatly to biblical scholarship and the destruction of Gnosticism. His book, *Contra Celsus* is one of the greatest apologies for a Church under persecution. In spite of all the contributions to the Church, this first great theologian was declared a heretic after his death.

Cyril

Cyril, was the patriarch of Alexandria from 412 to 444. He was the nephew of his predecessor Theophilus. He became popular during the Nestorian controversy, a controversy of interest to Christians even today. At the risk of oversimplifying the debate, it was about whether or not the title "bearer (mother) of God" (*theotokos* in Greek) should be applied to Mary. In Antioch, a new and upcoming center of the Church in the East, some felt that the Alexandrians had over-stretched the title of Mary in their attempt to keep the unity of divine-human natures in Jesus. These Antiocheans argued that Mary was the mother of Jesus and not the bearer of God. Anastasius, a chaplain to Nestorius, bishop of Constantinople, preached one day in Church against the idea *theotokos*, saying: "Let no one call Mary *Theotokos*: for Mary was but a human being; and it is impossible that God should be born of a human being."[23]

This made Cyril and Alexandrian theologians angry, because, since the time of Bishop Alexander (312-328), it had become a tradition in Alexandria to call Mary "the bearer of God." They asked Nestorius to excommunicate his chaplain. He refused and he himself preached a famous sermon against *theotokos*. Cyril wrote Nestorius three letters explaining how Alexandria's understanding of the nature of Jesus had led them to declare Mary "the bearer of God." Cyril said Jesus had "One nature of the Word and it made flesh . . . From two natures, One." The "One" being the dominated by the *Logos* (divine).

> The natures which were brought together to form a true unity were different; but out of both is one Christ and one son. We do not mean that the difference of the natures is annihilated by reason of this union; but rather that the Deity and manhood, by their inexpressible and inexplicable concurrence into unity, have produced for us one Lord one Son Jesus Christ. . . . Thus it is one Christ and Lord that we acknowledge, and as one and the same we worship him, not as a man with the addition of the Word . . . because the body of the Lord is not alien from the Lord; and it is with this body that he sits at the Father's right hand.[24]

From this, followers of Cyril taught that Jesus had only one nature, the divine. The human was swallowed up in the divine. Writing about how the issue of the natures of Jesus related to Mary as "the bearer of God," Cyril said the scriptures say Jesus

> became partaker of flesh and blood, like us and made our body his own, and came forth a man of a woman, not casting aside of his being God, and his being begotten of the Father, but even in assumption of flesh remaining what he was. This is the doctrine which strict orthodoxy everywhere prescribes. Thus we shall find the holy Fathers to beheld. So did they make bold to call the holy Virgin *Theotokos*. Not as though the nature of the Word or his Godhead had its beginning from the holy Virgin, but as much as his holy Body, endued with rational soul was born of her, to which Body also the Word was personally united, on this account he said to have been born after the flesh.[25]

This controversy went on for a long time. It was discussed at Synods and Council of Ephesus in 431 and Chalcedon in 451 where it was finally "settled." It is outside the scope of the present work to discuss the decisions of the various synods and councils, but suffice it to mention that Cyril is remembered by posterity as one of the main defenders of orthodoxy while Nestorius is listed as a heretic. On the other hand, many scholars consider Anastasius and Nestorius as forerunners for the Protestants on the question of Mary as "the mother of God."

Athanasius

One of the great pillars of theological thought in Alexandria was Athanasius, the defender of Nicaea. He was born in Alexandria about 295 and received a liberal education in secular learning, but he was well instructed in the scriptures (having been taught by some who suffered in the martyrdom of 311). Alexander, who had succeeded to the episcopacy of Alexandria in 312, took Athanasius into his home as a companion, secretary, and later a deacon. Athanasius had a sharp mind and at the age of twenty-one, he published a couple of serious and penetrating works in defense of Christianity against non-Christians attacking the faith.

In 319 a schism took place in the Church at Alexandria. This schism was led by Arius, one of the presbyters (elders), who propounded a thought that Jesus was neither truly God nor perfectly human; Jesus was merely a semi-god. His teaching became known as Arianism when in about 312, Arius began to teach that only God had no beginning; Jesus, his son, was not pre-existent, he had a beginning. In Arius's own words, "there was a time he [Jesus] was not." Therefore he considered it wrong to say God was eternally Father.[26] Arius maintained that although all things were made by the Son, the Son himself was made by the Father, and was therefore a creature, and not God in the strict sense of the word.[27] Arius argued that God created Jesus that he might create the world and since Jesus was the first and highest of all creation, Arius was willing to call Jesus God, but in fact, Jesus was a created being like all others. Put simply, the Son was just like any other person, not God; only that he was a better person and was thus adopted by God. Thus, "the central Arian model was that of a perfected creature whose nature remained always creaturely and whose position was always subordinate to and dependent upon the Father's will."[28] Embracing Greek views of the world, Arius contended that God, being pure spirit, could not have created the material world. Spirit and matter have nothing in common. He therefore argued that God was so far removed from the material world that it was impossible to know and have fellowship with God.

Alexander, bishop of Alexandria and Patriarch of the African Church, asked Arius to withdraw his statement and when he did not, Alexander expelled him.

Patriarch Alexander maintained that the Son, Jesus, was pre-existent with the Father and that all things were made through him; without him nothing would have been created. In other words, the Son though appearing in human form, shared the same nature and work with the Father. Therefore the Son was himself God.   Alexander's arguments were advanced by his successor, Athanasius, who argued that the Son shared equality with the Father because they had one nature. He used the Greek word *homoousian* (of the same substance) with the Father. That is to say, the Son's divinity is identical with that of the Father. Accordingly, the Son was God and Mary, therefore, was the mother or *theotokos* (bearer) of God. For Athanasius, to deny that Mary was the mother of God would be arguing that God was not born of Mary, which in effect would be a denial of the incarnation.

Arianism drew many people in the Roman empire. Emperor Constantine who had declared Christianity legal in 313, had hoped Christianity would to be the glue of his empire, but this schism threaten that vision. He therefore called a meeting of bishops at Nicaea to settle their dispute on the nature of Jesus. This first assembly of bishops is known as the Council of Nicaea, and the statement which they issued at this Council is known as the Nicaean Creed. It is part of the liturgy and is recited in Roman Catholic, Episcopalian (Anglican) and Orthodox Churches.

Athanasius, a deacon, had been prominent at the Council of Nicaea in 325, pushing the Council to declare Jesus as of the "same nature or substance" with the Father. His argument was that Jesus "was made divine, that we may become divine." In other words, without a fully divine Christ who is also fully human, there cannot be salvation. Arius did not believe either one or the other. Therefore Athanasius opposed him with all strength and mind.

In Alexandria, Athanasius had become popular and was the obvious successor to the episcopate. Bishop Alexander died in 328, but on his death bed he called for his beloved deacon who happened to be absent. In a prophetic voice the dying bishop said: "Athanasius, you think you have escaped, but you will not escape." Seven weeks later Athanasius was elected the Patriarch. Soon after his ascendancy to the episcopacy, Athanasius made pastoral visits in all his see, reaching to the Copts in the south along the Nile valley and Libyans to the west. His episcopacy was to be a troubled one. In 336, not long after he became a Patriarch, Constantine exiled him. This was to be the first of five exiles under emperors Constantine, his son Constantius, Julian, and Valens. In all his banishments, Alexandrians remained solidly behind their Patriarch. During his last exile, the popular patriarch did not go up the Nile as he had done in the previous ones; he merely moved to the outskirts of Alexandria until the authorities convinced the emperor to reconsider. Finally, Athanasius returned to his patriarchal office where he remained for a few months of relative peace until his death on May 2, 373.

Athanasius is remembered as the defender of Nicaea, and for this he is

called the "Pillar of Orthodoxy." The list of his writings opposing Arianism
show his dedication to defending Nicaea. The books are: *Discourse Against
the Arians*, *On the Incarnation against the Arians*, *Apology Against the Arians*,
History of the Arians, and the *Four Epistles to Serapion*. His earlier writings,
Against the Heathen and *On the Incarnation*, were not on Arianism.
Athanasius was a great advocate of the title "Mary the bearer of God." He
believed that because Jesus was fully God and fully human, it would be wrong
to deny Mary being the Mother of God and that, in effect, would be
tantamount to denying the incarnation.

Monasticism

Anthony

Africa's contribution to Christianity includes monasticism. The ascetic life-
style was begun in Egypt by a man named Anthony. Son of a Christian and
Coptic prosperous farmer, Anthony was born at Koma, about 200 miles up the
Nile near the city of Memphis, in 251. Unlike the scholars at Alexandria, he
never learned Greek or secular science. He and his one sister were orphaned
in 270. He put his sister in a home for virgins and started to serve the Lord.
He got his inspiration from reading the Gospel according to Matthew during
a Church service. It was the words of Jesus recorded by Matthew which
inspired Anthony's decision to lead an ascetic way of life. The words which
influenced him were: "If you be perfect, go sell what you possess and give it
to the poor and you will have treasure in heaven; come and follow me"
(Matthew 19:21). Anthony sold the three hundred acre family farm, deposited
some money for the care of his sister, and the rest he gave away. He started
living an ascetic life. He did this for fifteen years before he decided to go and
live alone in the desert, where there would be nothing to take his attention
away from religious devotion. Anthony lived there for twenty years, during
which he attracted some followers whom he instructed until his death in 356.
Like her brother, the sister of Anthony became the center for female cloisters
which spread rapidly too.
     Before he died, at age one hundred and five, he gave away his only
possessions, two sheepskins, to Serapion and to Athanasius. He told the two
disciples, who were taking care of him in his old age, not to disclose the place
of his interment. His bones were miraculously discovered in 561 during the
reign of Justinian. They were brought to Alexandria, then Constantinople,
and at last to Vienne, in South of France. They are said to have performed
great miracles in the eleventh century.
     In his entire life as a monk, Anthony left his solitude to travel to Alexandria

only in exceptional cases. The first time was in 311 during the persecution of Maximinus when he appeared in Alexandria in the hope of himself becoming a martyr. He visited confessors in the mines and prisons, encouraged them before the tribunal, and accompanied them to the scaffold; but no one laid hands on Anthony. The second time he appeared in Alexandria was in 351, at a hundred years of age. He was in the city to witness for the orthodox faith of his friend Athanasius (the Pillar of Orthodoxy) against Arianism.

Pachomius

The monastic life that Anthony introduced was primarily non-communal. The development of community life among monks as it is found in modern times was first introduced by Pachomius, a fellow Egyptian and contemporary of Anthony. Pachomius was born in 292. An ex-service man in the Roman army during emperor Maximin, Pachomius became interested in Christianity because of the Christian kindness he received while in detention in Thebais on the Nile. Soon after his discharge from the military, Pachomius converted to Christianity and then in 313 learned about monastic life-style from a local monk, Palemon. Palemon told him about the hard life of a monk. He said: "Many have come hither from disgust with the world, and no perseverance. Remember, my son, my food consists only of bread and salt; I drink no wine, take no oil, spend half the night awake, singing psalms and meditating on the Scriptures, and sometimes pass the whole night without sleep."[29] In 325 while at prayer in the desert near the village of Tabennae, an island in the Nile, upper Egypt, Pachomius was told by an angel of the Lord to "Stay here and build a monastery and many will come to you in order to be monks."[30] He built the monastery there and monks lived in community. The society of monks he had started grew very fast so that in a short time it had nine cloisters in the Thebais, with about three to seven thousand monks. He also established an order for monasteries. The leader of each monastery he called an abbot, while the person responsible for all the monasteries he named the head.

Pachomius established a cloister for nuns for his sister, whom, it is said, he never admitted to his presence when she would visit him. He would send her word that he would be content to know that she was still alive. Pachomius died in 348.

With the exception of a few people from areas of the southern regions of Africa, who lived with Anthony, monastic life never grew beyond Ethiopia. From Egypt, monasticism went east, spreading into Mesopotamia and Syria, Armenia and Paphlogonia, Pontus and Cappadocea. Most of the Greek Fathers were for a time monks. There is a close relationship between orthodoxy and monasticism, the friendship of Anthony and Athanasius being a classic example.

The Three African Popes

People are always surprised at the mention of an African being a Pope. It may not happen in contemporary times, for many reasons, but it did happen in the Early Church. In this section, we will take a quick look at the work of these African Popes, for their work had an impact well beyond their time and even into our own day.

Pope Victor I. (189-199)

The first African Pope was Victor I, sometimes referred to as St. Victor. He succeeded St. Eleutherius as bishop to the Holy See.[31] Victor was the first Pope ever to write in Latin. He is the one who popularized the use of Latin rather than Greek, in the Church. Victor is also remembered for his role in the Easter Controversy. The Churches in Asia were not celebrating Easter at the same time as the rest of the Christian Church. Asian Churches followed an old tradition which observed the fourteenth day of the lunar month as the beginning of the Paschal festival—the day on which Jews had been commanded to sacrifice the lamb. On that day, no matter which day of the week it might be, they must without fail bring the fast to an end. This custom was not followed anywhere else outside Asia. The rest of the Church, following the Gospel of John, emphasized the resurrection of Jesus on the first day of the week and therefore crucifixion of Jesus on the Friday before Easter. In order to harmonize the day,

> synods and conferences of bishops were convened, and without any dissentient voice, drew up a decree of the Church, in the form of letters addressed to Christians everywhere, that never on any day other than the Lord's Day should the mystery of the Lord's resurrection be celebrated and that on that day alone we should observe the end of the Paschal feast.[32]

Asian Churches did not agree to join the rest of the Church. They wrote letters of protest. But Victor decided to use papal authority to bring the Churches in line. "Thereupon Victor, head of the Roman Church, attempted at one stroke to cut off the common unity of all the Asian dioceses, together with the neighboring Churches, on the ground of heterodoxy."[33] Fearing excommunication from the universal Church the Churches complied, and thus the Easter controversy ended.

Lastly, Pope Victor I is remembered for ending a heresy propounded by a certain merchant, Theodotus, who refused to give the title God to Jesus. He claimed Jesus was only an ordinary person who received the Holy Spirit at his baptism.   Victor I excommunicated Theodotus saying his teaching was anathema to the Church. The feast day in honor of St. Victor I is July 28.

Pope Melchiades (311-314)

This Pope is sometimes known as Miltiades. He became Pope during the Donatist controversy. In the spring of 313 Miltiades supported Caecilian and condemned Donatists. The reader will recall that Caecilian was the bishop about whose ordination the Donatists said was invalid because a traditor, Felix Amptunga had participated.   Caecilian was supported by Emperor Constantine. The Pope alienated himself from the masses in Carthage by supporting a man endorsed by the emperor. Constantine, realizing how deep the Donatist schism was, called another Council of the bishops in the Western Roman Empire to resolve the issue, but Pope Miltiades died before the Council met. The feast day for his remembrance is December 10.

Pope Gelasius (492-496)

Pope Gelasius came to the See of Rome in 492 after St. Felix II. Pope Gelasius was the first to state that civil and sacred powers (priestly) were of divine origin and yet independent of each other. He maintained, nonetheless, that the priestly power was above the civil. Pope Gelasius is the one who introduced the principle of the power and authority of the chair of Peter. Gelasius stated that the decision announced by a Pope while sitting in the chair of Peter had no appeal. (In Church language it is stated that the Pope is infallible when he speaks *ex-cathedra*.) Pope Gelasius is also remembered for his remarkable testimony against withholding the cup from the laity during the eucharist. He termed the practice "sacrilege." Pope Gelasius wrote hundred treatises and letters addressing this issue. November 21 is set for a feast honoring Pope Gelasius.

THE DECLINE OF THE EARLY CHURCH

One of the puzzles about Early African Christianity is why it never went beyond Nubia into the southern regions of Africa although it was very strong in North Africa? Several reasons have been suggested. The first factor is the success of the Islamic holy wars, *Jihad*, in North Africa in the seventh and eight centuries. Except for the presence of Christianity in the Nile valley among the Coptic people, Christianity was completely lost in North Africa. The Coptic people have held on to Christianity despite being under islamic power and influence. When Christianity waned, two centers of theological inquiry in North Africa, the catechetical schools at Carthage and Alexandria, were also lost.

The second factor is indirectly connected to the first. It has to do with theological interpretation. The North African Church was very much divided by theological controversies, and these divisions weakened the Church. In the third century, for example, the city of Carthage had three rivals bishops: Cyprian (Catholic orthodox), Fortunatus (schismatic), and Maximum (Novatian party, those who opposed Cyprian's anti-readmission policy for the lapsed or traditors—those who surrendered the scriptures to the authorities during persecution.) In the same century we also find the controversy of the Montanists. Beginning in the third century into the next, it was the Donatist controversy, and from the fourth to sixth century, it was Arianism or the two-nature controversy, which dominated theological thinking. During this time too was the controversy concerning Mary as "the bearer of God." These controversies across the centuries gradually weakened Christian position in North Africa. Much more effort and time were taken up with theological debates than with Church growth.

Lessons From The Past

There are a few lessons that we can learn from the life and work of the Early African Church. In the early days of Christianity in Africa, the Church strongly opposed civil religion. People chose to die rather than yield to what they considered Roman paganism. The Church was uncompromising, its stand was clear: to obey God rather than people. Perhaps the words of Tertullian best expressed what early African Christians believed: "What is more foreign to us than the state?" This unbending attitude of the early Christians earned them the title of "fagot fellows." They were so called because torture was often by fire and hot irons. Persecutions had an adverse effect on the empire. It was during the times of persecutions that the Church spread. The earliest document available concerning African protest to persecution is from Scillium. The letter was dated July 17, 180, and it protests the martyrdom of the Christians of Scillium.

The attitude of the Church changed in March 313 when Christianity was legalized in the edict of Milan issued by Constantine. In this Church-State relationship, the spread of Christianity followed the expansion of the empire. In fact, emperor Justinian's belief was that imperial expansion should go hand in hand with Church extension. It is not surprising that the decline of the empire signalled the beginning of the end of Christian expansion. Once the Church feels comfortable and secure, it often loses its dynamism and vitality.

Everything was not well in this relation: the State soon began to interfere in church affairs to the extent that even questions of teaching were settled by imperial powers, as it was with the Arian and Donatist controversies. At different times the Church even seems to have enjoyed the interference of the State in Church matters. In the time of Augustine, for example, the Church had condoned and sanctioned the use of force by the State to crush its "enemies," the Donatists. Earlier, during the Arianian controversy, Arians used political power to enforce Arianism on all Christians. In 535 Justinian used his political power to force his orthodoxy on Arians. A lesson to be learned here is that the State is never a neutral partner. When the Church uses political power to silence its enemies, it cannot stand in opposition to the State.

One important observation to note is that the Early African Church, in North Africa in particular, was always a Latin Church. It drew its membership from the Latin-speaking minority. Not only did the people speak Latin and have Latin names, but they were Latinized—they sought values of "classical" society (Greco-Roman culture), which evidently the Church seemed to support. This means that the Church was a fellowship of the middle to upper class people—the bourgeois, landowners, government officials, and military officers. The Church never took seriously the culture of the Berber people. The result was that the Church never made a real impact on Berber society. It was an alien institution, and it decided to stay on the fringes of society. The only exception was the Donatist Church, which attracted the Berber and used Berber in its liturgy. The Donatist movement was in fact a protest movement of the eclipsed, marginalized, and oppressed masses in the Church and Society. Donatists protested and renounced Greco-Roman culture and Catholicism which sought to harmonize classical and Christian concepts. They protested and renounced Catholicism's association with oppressive government and extortions against the peasants. Augustine's letters and sermons indicate that Catholic priests were fully aware of the hardship experienced in the Roman provinces. Augustine depicts a clergy which had become greedy, living in ostentatious luxury and exploiting the poor.[34] The Council of Carthage, in 397, condemned bishops who acted as bailiffs on senatorial estates. In order to avoid taxes, some bishops left their lands to a landowner to administer it for them.[35] The success of Islam in North Africa in the seventh century must be seen behind this background of rejection of (1) a religion which allied itself with an oppressive system, and (2) a rejection of Greco-Roman culture. Islam only found a people who had lost faith in Catholic teaching and practice, and hope in an oppressive government. Indeed, Islam also got strength from people in rural areas who had never been reached by Christianity.

It is important to emphasize the role of culture in religion. Christianity was able to remain strong among the Copts in the Nile valley because it had incorporated some elements of culture into its monophysite liturgy. Egyptian

Christian leadership, unlike that of North Africa, respected Coptic language, art, and other values. Egyptian scholars theologized from their cultural perspective. It is in this background that the concept of "Mary the Bearer of God" was developed and strongly defended by Alexandrian theologians.

A contemporary Western theologian, Paul Tillich, says the development of *theotokos* by Athanasius should be seen in the light of traditional religion which created "the desire among Christians to have a female element in the center of religion. Egypt had such elements in the myths of Isis and Orisis, the goddess of her son, but Christianity did not."[36] Tillich does not say much beyond this, but the Isis and Orisis cult was a very important cult in the Nile valley (Egypt, Ethiopia, and Nubia) given to the Roman world. The cult was about the expectation of the resurrection of the dead. It was from this cult that Egyptians developed the concept of the resurrection of the body, which was why Egyptians embalmed the dead. Orisis, or "waters of the Nile," died yearly and was raised by the weeping Isis. Orisis was divine, a god, as well as human. People were grateful to Isis for raising the god/man, Orisis. With this religious background, it was easy for Christians in the Nile valley to understand the oneness of divine-human nature of Christ and thus their rejection of the Chalcedonian formula on the nature of Christ. The cult also prepared them for understanding Mary as the human who bore the divine-human being, Christ. Isis brought life back to Orisis, so Mary gave life to Jesus, the son of God, or God himself.

The respect for Mary is further to be understood as women are viewed in the Nile valley (and indeed for most of Africa) as sacred participants in the divine activity of giving the gift of life. A closer examination of the development of Mariology and monophysitism in the Nile valley reveals a serious attempt to Africanize Christianity by drawing from pre-Christian religious experience. This religious experience made people in Nile valley to assert their independence from Latin influence through Carthage as well as the emerging Byzantine (Greek) power.

In both the Coptic and Ethiopian Churches, the cult of Mary plays a very important role. A large collection of literature on devotion to the cult of Mary has developed in these Churches over the centuries. In the Ethiopian Church this literature reached its zenith during the reign of Zara Ya'kob (1434-1468). The Ethiopian calendar has four out of the thirty days of the month dedicated to *Igziteni-Maryam*, the rule (cult) of Mary.

Unless Christianity permeates a culture of a people, it shall always remain a foreign institution serving as the fellowship of the bourgeois and perhaps meeting their needs. When Christianity fails to ground itself in the cultural life of the people, it can never become a real force to change society and it may disappear altogether—North Africa is a good lesson. Indeed, North African Christians did try to ground their new faith in their culture, but the leadership, seeing itself as a bridge to "classical" culture, discouraged what they viewed as "pagan" practices. In Carthage, Christians adopted their ancient custom of drinking and dancing on graves as a celebration of the new life the dead had entered. In their new faith, they danced on the graves of martyrs; they danced on the grave of Cyprian, but Augustine in his sermons, deplored such a custom.[37] In fact, Augustine said there was no true Christianity in Carthage before he came.

Finally, there is the question of theological controversies. Tertullian may have over-stretched his argument when he wrote: "What indeed has Athens to do with Jerusalem? What has the Academy to do with Christians? . . . Away with all attempts to produce a Stoic, Platonic or dialectic Christianity. We want no curious disputation after possessing Christ Jesus, no inquisition after receiving the Gospel."[38] Theological issues may be interesting to the elite of the Church; the debates may produce right doctrine, but the Church should concentrate on issues and needs of the local Church in as much as it deals with the universal theological issues. It is important for a Church to maintain its particularity for it is in its identification with the particular that it can be the Church of the people, thereby a universal Church. In identifying itself with the people, the Church develops an authentic praxis, a praxis that takes into account the needs, concerns, fears, and joys of the particular people. This is a true Church, not a fellowship of the bourgeois.

The intent of this chapter was to give a short background to the beginnings of African Christianity. We have noted that during the first five hundred years of Christianity, Africa was at the cutting edge in shaping theological thought. Further, we have explored the tremendous contributions of African Christians and scholars. Their devotion, dedication, and their uncompromising faith has inspired lives of many in Africa, and elsewhere in the world, throughout the centuries. As we close the chapter, one cannot help but wonder whether this legacy of the early African Christians will be carried on. Africa is again at the cutting edge of Christianity: what will the future hold?

NOTES

1. *Migne Patrologiae Cursus Completus*, Series Graeca, vol. LII, col. 812. (Hereafter the document will be referred to as Migne P. C.).

2. Eusebius, *Church History: Life of Constantine the Great and, Oration in Praise of Constatine*, VI., 1 (New York: Scribner, 1925)

3. *Ibid.*, vol. VIII, IX section 4-5.

4. *Ibid.*

5. L. P. Kirwan, "A Contemporary Account of the Conversion of the Sudan to Christianity," *Sudan Notes and Records*, xx (1937): 289-295; U. Monneret de Villard, *Storia della Nubia cristiana* (Rome: Pontificium

Institutum Biblicum, 1938), 53-70; K. S. Latourette, *A History of the Expansion of Christianity*, Vol. 2 (Grand Rapids, Mich.: Zondervan, 1953), 194.

6. Tertullian, *Apology*, 50, 14.

7. Rendel Harris, ed., *Acta Scilitanorum*, vol. 1, sect. ii (Cambridge: Cambridge University Press, 1891).

8. Eusebius, *Church History*, VII, 11, 13, 14.

9. Quoted by John Foster, *Church History: The First Advance A.D.29-500* (London: SPCK, 1972), 75-76.

10. Eusebius, *Church History*, vol. VIII, XIII, section 7.

11. *Ibid.*, VI, 41, 11.

12. Tertullian, *De Test. amin.* 6. *The Ante-Nicene Fathers*, vol. 3 (Grand Rapids, Mich.: Eerdmans, 1973), 179. (Hereafter the document referred to as ANF).

13. Tertullian, *Apology*, 2, *ANF*, vol. 3, 18.

14. Tertullian, *De Baptismo*, 8 and 15.

15. *Ibid.*, 5 and 15.

16. Tertullian, *De Exhortatione Castitatis*, 10.

17. Cyprian, *Epistle*, xxxiii. 1.

18. *Ibid.*, lxxvi. 7.

19. Clement, *Stromateis*, 1. v. 28.

20. *Ibid.*

21. Quoted by Adolph von Harnack, *Geschichte der altchristilichen literatur* 1/1 (reprint, Leipzig: J. C. Hinrichs Verlag, 1958), 333.

22. Vinzenz Buchheit, "Rufinus von Aquileja als Falscher des Adamantiosdilogs," *Byzantinische Zeitschrift*, 51 (1958): 314-28.

23. Socrates, *Historia Eccllestica*, Imprint. (Oxford: Claredon Press), vii. 32.

24. Cyril, *Epistle* iv. J. P. Migne, ed. *Patrologia Graeca*, LXXVII. Paris: 1857-66 (hereafter the document is referred to as P. G.).

25. *Ibid.*, 44-50.

26. Athanasius, *Contra Arius oration* 1. 2. 5.

27. *Ibid.*

28. R. G. Gregg and D. E. Groth, *Early Arianism: A View of Salvation* (Philadelphia: Fortress, 1981), 24.

29. Quoted by Phillip Schaff, *History of the Christian Church*, vol. 3 (reprint, Grand Rapids, Mich.: Eerdmans, 1987), 196.

30. W. H. C. Frend, *The Early Church* (London: Hodder and Stoughton, 1971), 204.

31. Eusebius, *Church History*, V: 22.

32. *Ibid.*

33. *Ibid.*

34. Augustine. *sermons Ps* 39, 7. *Patrologia Series Latina*, xxxvi, col. 438. Edited by J. P. Migne (Paris: 1844-64); *Ps.* 48, 8; PL. xxxvi, col 516-2; and in

Ps. 38, 2 PL. xxxvi, col. 413.

35. Augustine, 24 *Epistle*, 96. 2.

36. Paul Tillich, *A History of Christian Thought: From Its Judaic and Hellenistic Origins to Existentialism*, ed. Carl E. Braaten, (New York: Simon and Schuster, 1968), 850.

37. Augustine, *Sermon* 311.

38. Frend, *The Early Church*, 93.

2

The Ethiopian Church

It has already been mentioned that Christianity existed in Ethiopia from the first century, but many historical accounts maintain that Christianity came to Ethiopia in the fourth century. Further, a claim is made that it was a foreigner who introduced Christianity to Ethiopia. In this chapter we will review the story of Ethiopian Christianity and try to put in proper perspective historical facts concerning the origin and development of the faith in Ethiopia.

THE JEWISH CONNECTION

The book of *Acts of the Apostles*, 8:26-40, tells of an Ethiopian eunuch, the minister of finance at the royal court in Ethiopia, "the treasure of Candance," as Luke describes him. The eunuch was baptized by Philip the Deacon on his way back from Jerusalem, where he had gone to worship. Luke notes that the Eunuch of Queen of Candance was reading Jewish scriptures, the book of Isaiah, when Philip caught up with his caravan. The fact that the Eunuch was reading Jewish scriptures means that he shared or was at least acquainted with the Jewish faith. The eunuch and his caravan were the first African converts to Christianity. Luke says the eunuch went home rejoicing.

Eusebius, the Church historian comments on what Luke has written.

Tradition says that he [the eunuch] who was the first of the Gentiles to receive from Philip by revelation the mysteries of the Divine word and was the first fruits of the faithful throughout the world, was also the first to return to his native land and preached the Gospel of the knowledge of God of the universe and the sojourn of our Savior which gives life to men, so that by him was actually fulfilled the prophecy which says, "Ethiopia shall stretch out her hands to God" (Ps. 68:31).[1]

The story of the Eunuch of Candance indicates two points. First, the story is another proof that Judaism preceded Christianity in Africa. The eunuch must have been familiar with Judaism, conversant enough to have taken a long journey to Jerusalem to worship. Historical evidence has established that there was a strong Jewish community in Elephantine. [2] Geddes says that it was a tradition among the ruling class of Ethiopia to go to Jerusalem to worship. "It is a constant tradition among the Habassins, that the Queen of Sheba that went to visit Solomon, [3] was emperor of their country, whose name, they say, was Maqueda; and who, within a few weeks after she returned home, was delivered of a son, beget by Solomon, whom she named Meneleber." [4]

The spread of Judaism to Ethiopia is ascribed to the Queen of Sheba and her only son, Meneleber (Menelek). [5] She sent Meneleber to Solomon where he "was to be instructed in the Law of Moses and other useful sciences."[6] Solomon received Meneleber and renamed him David. After sufficient instruction in the Law of Moses, David returned home with priests and Levites.

> David being returned home, did with the help of the priests and Levites, set immediately about introducing the Mosaic Law into his empire, and was so successful, that in few years it was embraced by the whole body of his people, and to be professed by them, until the publication of the Gospel among them. [7]

This is the story of the official introduction of Judaism in Ethiopia. It is also important to remember that another Jewish community existed in Ethiopia. The Falasha, who until the time of their repatriation to Israel in 1986 were an ethnic group in Ethiopia, are known to have embraced Jewish rituals and practices from time immemorial. According to the traditional belief in Ethiopia, the history of the Falasha dates back to the time of Jewish exodus. The belief is that "when the Israelites were returning from Egypt to the Promised Land, some of them wandered and came into Ethiopia, bearing with them five Books of Moses."[8] The same view has also been expressed by Samuel Mercer.

> It is very likely that the Falasha Jews passed from Palestine, before the time of the Babylonian captivity, to Egypt, and thence to Abyssinia, where they settled and where they have preserved their faith. . . . They know nothing of the Babylonian captivity nor of the Talmud, but they live according to the laws of Moses and they call themselves the "House of Israel. [9]

There is also another view about the origin of the Falasha. Wolf Leslau maintains that the Falasha are Hamites who were converted to Judaism either by Israelites of Elephantine in Egypt or from South Arabia. [10] In the recent years there has been a growing interest in the origin of the Falasha. One of the studies that has been published about the Falasha is by David Kessler. In chapter one, titled "Strangers in the Midst," Kessler traces the origin of the Falashas and their religion. (Falasha means foreigner in Amharic, Ethiopia's official language). He argues that the Falashas are Agaws converted to Judaism by Jews coming from Elephantine, Egypt, via Meroe. [11] We cannot settle historical problems here. Nevertheless, these studies are important for us in the present study, for they indicate the presence of Judaism long before Christianity entered Africa.

CHRISTIANITY IN ETHIOPIA

The second point gleaned from the story of the Eunuch of Candance is about the spread of Christianity in Africa. The baptism of the minister of finance of Ethiopia marked the entering of Christianity in Africa. We do not know much about the work of the Church in Africa during the first century, but prior to the fourth century, Christianity had made advances into the Askumite Empire on a limited scale (as Origen's comment suggests): "The Gospel is not said to have been preached to all the Ethiopians, especially to such as live beyond the river."[12] There were some scattered Christian communities here and there. Christianity continued to grow, and by the sixth century it had made tremendous progress, so much so that Cosmas, the medieval geographer, included the Aksumite kingdom among the countries where "there are everywhere Churches of the Christians, and bishops, martyrs, monks and recluses by whom the Gospel of Christ is proclaimed."[13] Geddes commented on the spread of Good News in the Ethiopian empire after the baptism of the Ethiopian eunuch. "It being a tradition among them, that the Eunuch that was baptized by Philip the deacon, was steward to the emperors, and who returning home after he was Christianized, converted his mistress and the whole empire to the Christian faith, in the profession whereof they have eversince continued steadfast."[14]

According to Conti Rossini, by the sixth century Christianity had spread to areas of northern Ethiopia, including much of the province of Tigre, the whole of the Eritrean plateau, and the coastal settlements. [15] Tamrat, the Ethiopian historian, comments that "such active expansion of the Church into the Askumite interior tallies very well with the strong position held by the kingdom in the sixth century as a champion of Christianity in the whole of the Red Sea area."[16]

Roman Martyrology also gives evidence of active work of evangelism in

Ethiopia beginning from the first century of the Common Era. According to this legend, Matthew, the apostle (or the writer of the Gospel According to Matthew), preached the Gospel in Ethiopia and was martyred there in the first century.[17] Also, Rufinus and Socrates claim that "when the Apostles drew lots to preach the Gospel to the pagans, Mathias drew Persia and Matthew Ethiopia."[18] The credence of this report is doubted by some Western scholars. The Synatxar of Ethiopia ignores this report. The 12th *Tigint* mentions that Matthew went to preach to the land where Apollo was being worshiped.[19] The *Tigint* says that after Matthew had converted the people of that land he went "forth from the city to the cities which were outside" where he continued to convert people. It is further claimed in the *Tigint* that Matthew was condemned to death by Justus, the local governor of the cities, because he converted people to Christianity. Other authorities suggest that the Apostle Thomas also preached the Good News in Ethiopia. The accuracy of this report is so debatable among scholars both in and outside Ethiopia that we are not going to spend our time on it.

It may be also important to mention that in about 480, Rome sent monks into Ethiopia as missionaries —Araguia (or Michael), Alef, Gavi, Afe, Adimata, Cuba, Garima, Sabam, Lebanos, Pantaleon, the patriarch Mendez. Not much is recorded about their missionary work except that they found Christianity in Ethiopia different and tried to reform it. This caused much disagreement among the people, and therefore their mission was unsuccessful.

THE STRUCTURING OF THE ETHIOPIAN CHURCH

The responsibility for structuring Christianity in Ethiopia is attributed to Frumentius. There are two versions of the life of Frumentius and the organization of the Ethiopian Church in the fourth century. The first version of the life of Frumentius is by Rufinus, while the second version comes from the Ethiopian Synaxar for 26 *Hamle*. The stories are similar but differ in important historical details. Both accounts agree that Frumentius was one of two brothers; the other was Aedesius, and that their father was a philosopher. Rufinus says the philosopher was from Tyre, while the Ethiopian *Hamle* simply says the "man was from the country of the Greeks."

Rufinus' account claims the father/philosopher was on his way home, returning from a visit to India, when he put in for water at a port of some unknown barbaric land and was attacked. In this land the inhabitants killed foreigners, especially Roman citizens, because their commercial treaty with Rome had lapsed. The philosopher was killed, but his boys were spared and were taken to the king where Aedesius was made cupbearer and Frumentius treasurer and secretary. The king died and his widow pleaded with the two men to help her raise her son and govern the land. Although the king had given them their liberty, they stayed till the regent grew. When the brothers left Aedesius went to stay with their relatives in Tyre where he later became a bishop. Frumentius went to Alexandria where he told bishop Athanasius of the excellent prospects for a Church in Ethiopia. The bishop ordained Frumentius and sent him back to Ethiopia.[20]

The Ethiopian version, as written in the Ethiopian Synaxar for 26 *Hamle*, says the father "arrived in a ship at the shore of the sea of Ethiopia, and he saw all the beautiful things which his heart desired, and wishing to return to his country, enemies rose up against him and killed him."His boys were taken captives by the men of the city, taught them war and were given to the king as a present. In the royal palace Aedesius became director of the household while his brother was the keeper of the laws and the archives of Aksum. While in the royal palace the two brothers taught the king's son Psalms and something of the Christian faith. The rest of the story agrees with the account of Rufinus except that Frumentius went to Alexandria, when Archbishop Athanasius "had been restored to his office. And he related everything which had happened unto him because of their faith in the country of Ethiopia, and *how the people believed in Christ, but had neither bishops nor priests. And then Abba appointed FEREMENATOS   bishop of Ethiopia, and sent away with great honor.*"[21]

When the two accounts are compared, one sees contradictions within Rufinus' version of the story. He does not give the name of the land where the two brothers lived. He calls it "unknown barbaric land." Yet in the same "barbaric country" lived Roman merchants who were Christians. These helped Frumentius to build a prayerhouse. If it was unknown, as Rufinus claims, how could the barbaric country have signed a treaty with Rome? Again, how could Roman merchants stay in the country if they were killed by these barbaric people? Rufinus' geographical error is corrected by Emperor Constantius in his letter to King Ezana and his brother Shaizana.[22] What we see in Rufinus' account is an attempt to create the idea that Christianity was brought in from outside Ethiopia —since Ethiopia was a barbaric land! This is to say, Christianity was brought into Ethiopia by Frumentius, and that he received help from Greek merchants calling on the ports of Ethiopian sea. If we follow Rufinus' account, then, Christianity was not preached in Ethiopia until 330. For according to Rufinus, Frumentius arrived in Alexandria, when Athanasius "had recently assumed the episcopate." Athanasius became archbishop in 328, after the death of Alexander. Frumentius spent two years in Alexandria under the feet of Athanasius, learning the teachings of the Church. To claim Christianity was not preached in Ethiopia till the return of Frumentius is to ignore the report of Origen who testified that Christianity existed in Ethiopia from the first century onwards. Origen died in 254. This means that by the third century there was something known about Ethiopian

Christianity, even in Alexandria. We again note that Rufinus ignored the Ethiopian tradition that Frumentius related to Athanasius about how people believed but had no leadership. Rufinus cited as authority for his information Aedesisus' oral report to him. A prominent Ethiopian scholar, Sellassie, is very skeptical about this claim. He says,

> it is hard to believe that Aedesius did in fact ever deliver such information to Rufinus in person. We must suppose one of the two things: either Rufinus never met Aedesius and the information was gathered from common people, or he met him, but wrote his account long afterwards when he had forgotten many details. The former alternative seems most likely and we can assume Rufinus wished to lend weight to his story by saying that he received it "not from a vulgar report, but from the mouth of Aedesius himself. "[23]

That Ethiopian Christianity was not introduced by Frumentius is attested by Archbishop Athanasius. As already indicated, Athanasius consecrated Frumentius, so his testimony is trustworthy. Athanasius says Christianity was introduced on another occasion in Ethiopia. [24] Christianity as an organized religion with its offices and hierarchy was introduced in Ethiopia by Frumentius. We note that according to the Ethiopian version of the story, it was King Ezana who sent Frumentius to Alexandria to learn about Church teachings and organization. Concerning the fact that King Ezana sent Frumentius to Alexandria, Sellassie writes that

> relations between Church and State reached a new stage. Previously, in the time of Ezana, the king took responsibility for Church affairs. Thus it was he who sent Frumentius to Alexandria to be consecrated as bishop of Aksum. He also received a letter from Constantius in which the Emperor asked to have Frumentius sent back to Alexandria to be examined on his ordination. Thus, he was not only the political leader, but he was also invested with religious authority. [25]

Soon after the return of Bishop Frumentius to Ethiopia, Christianity received the support of the king. The conversion of King Ezana estimated at approximately 330. Therefore, it was not long after organized Christianity had entered Ethiopia that it became the official religion of the empire, because of this it secured help from the government almost from its inception. The implication of the royal support was rapid growth and expansion of Christianity in Ethiopia. [26]

For bringing organized Christianity into Ethiopia, Frumentius was known as "Abba Selama" (Father of Peace). The other title was "Kesate Berham," meaning "Revealer of Light." Frumentius is canonized in the Ethiopian,

Greek Orthodox, and Catholic Churches. In the Ethiopian Church the celebration for the saint is on the 4th Tigint (October 15); it is on November 30 in the Greek Church. The Roman Martyrology places the observance of the feast on October 27.

Before we proceed, it is important to talk about the historical event from which the Ethiopian Church came to be known as orthodox. Having had his theological training in Alexandria under Athanasius, Frumentius followed the teachings of Athanasius. In 355 at the Council of Milan, Athanasius was condemned as a heretic by a group of clergy coerced by Emperor Constantius (337-361). He was an Arian, that is a believer in the teachings of a popular presbyter of Alexandria, Arius. Constantius wanted his whole empire to be converted to Arianism. He sent his envoys to all parts of the empire to convert or replace bishops who followed the teachings of patriarch Athanasius, who was known as the "Column of orthodoxy." Constantius sent Theophilus to Ethiopia and Arabia. The mission of Theophilus was not successful in Ethiopia, and that is why Constantius wrote King Ezana to send Frumentius to Alexandria to be examined by an Arian bishop who replaced Athanasius. However, the king never sent Frumentius to Alexandria; Frumentius died in Abyssinia. The Abyssinian Church itself never embraced Arianism. Having received the teachings of the Church from Athanasius, the "column of orthodoxy," through Frumentius, the Abyssinian Church remained orthodox. Thus, the name Abyssinian Orthodox or Tewhado, as it is locally called.

THE ETHIOPIAN CHURCH AND CANON LAW

Although it was King Ezana who sent Frumentius for training in Egypt, the Abyssinian Church could not be independent of Alexandria. This is explained in Canon Law which prescribes that anyone who willingly seeks guidance and training in ministry immediately comes under the authority and jurisdiction of the head of the Church which trains the priest. Furthermore, the eighth canon of the first Ecumenical Council stated that the Patriarch of Alexandria was to exercise jurisdiction over the Churches of Libya and Neopolis. Since Frumentius was consecrated by Athanasius, who was the head of the see of Alexandria, Ethiopia also came under the Patriarch of Alexandria. More legal justification of this position came when a precept was inserted in the 36th canon of the pseudo-Canon of Nicaea:

The Ethiopians have no power to create or choose a Patriarch, whose prelate must be rather under the jurisdiction of the Patriarch of Alexandria; or in case they should come at any time to have one among them in the place of the Patriarch and who should be styled Catholicus, he shall not, notwithstanding that, have a right to ordain Archbishops as other Patriarchs have, having neither the honor or authority of a Patriarch: And if it should so happen that a council should be assembled in Greece, and this prelate should be present at it, he shall have the seventh place therein, next after the bishop of Selucia: and in case he should have at any time power given him to ordain Archbishops in his province, it shall not be lawful for him to advance any of the natives to that dignity; whosoever does not yield obedience to this, is excommunicated by the synod.[27]

The Arabic version of the pseudo-Canon of Nicaea was translated into Géez (the liturgical language of the Ethiopian Church) and incorporated in the *Synodos* and also in the *Fetha Negest*, the only ecclesiastical and civil code of Ethiopia which has remained in use without substantial change.[28] There is an interesting and important historical point to be observed here. The Ecumenical Council met in Nicaea in 325, about five years before organized Christianity was established in Abyssinia. In other words, the Ethiopian Orthodox Church *a priori* acquired a canon before it was established. Could the canon have been applied arbitrarily? The Ethiopian Orthodox Church was never really happy with the council's decision. At best, we can say the Ethiopian Church has tolerated the Nicean arrangement for sixteen centuries. The fact that the bishops gathered at Nicaea included Ethiopia in their discussion and deliberations is further proof of the existence and acknowledgment of Christianity in Ethiopia before 325.

THE PROBLEMS OF THE ETHIOPIAN CHURCH

From the time the Ethiopian Orthodox Church was organized by Frumentius in the fourth century, it had two problems to confront: autonomy and isolation. Traditionally, the Ethiopian Church had connections with the Coptic Church. Because of this connection, anything that happened to Egypt in the world Christian community also affected Ethiopia. The isolation of Egypt from the world Christian community after the fourth ecumenical council at Chalcedon, in 451, was also the alienation of Ethiopian Christianity. The council met to settle the disagreement on the nature of Jesus. Egyptian bishops were monophysites, that is, they believed that through the divine mystery that overshadowed Mary, the two natures of Jesus, divine and human fused into one. Thus Jesus had only one nature, *mono* (one)-*phusis* (substance). The council at Chalcedon opposed this view arguing that Jesus was one person with two natures. Egyptian monks opposed their enemies with violence causing imperial intervention. Egypt's monophysite leader,

Bishop Dioscoros, was banished into the Nubian desert. (Centuries later, the Nubian Church became monophysite following the position maintained by the Coptic Church.) The exclusion from the world Christian community led Egypt into isolation. The only neighbors of the Coptic Church remained Ethiopians, who centuries later developed their own theological position on monophysite belief.

Ethiopia was locked in isolation with Egypt. This isolation increased when Islam overran Egypt in 640. The Coptic people along the Nile valley remained Christians, but it was difficult to maintain a close relationship with Nubia to the south—although Christianity remained in Nubia until 1276. Egyptian Muslim armies defeated Nubia and put an Egyptian Muslim on the Nobatian throne in 1276. With Muslim activities in Arabia, all Christian communities were swept out, and Ethiopia remained alone.

From 1270 through 1527, Ethiopian Christian emperors fought successfully against all Muslim invasions. Ethiopia fought Muslim states all the way to the Red Sea.[29] During the reign of Zara Ya'kob (1434-1468), the situation was so tough that Ethiopia sought help from the Pope in the struggle against "the enemies of the Church." In the following century, Ethiopia was to have more trouble from the neighboring Somali. Somali under the leadership of Imam Ahmad Ibn Ibrahim Al-Ghazi declared a holy war against Ethiopia. With the help of Turkish troops sent by the Ottoman Sultan of Turkey, Al-Ghazi launched an eleven year campaign of ruthless conquest and destruction of Ethiopia. Ethiopian emperor Lebna Dengel (1508-1540) retreated to a monastery where he died a defeated and humiliated leader. Emperor Dengel was succeeded by Emperor Galawdewos. He gathered the remnants of the Ethiopian army and prepared them to fight against Al-Ghazi. He requested help from the Portuguese in his struggle against the Muslims.[30]

The Portuguese heeded the emperor's call in 1541. After several 1543 battles, the Ethiopian army and their Christian (Portuguese) allies defeated Al-Ghazi and his nine hundred Albanian, Arab, and Turkish mercenaries. Al-Ghazi himself was killed. This success gave Ethiopians two centuries of relative peace; however, there were some conflicts between Ethiopians and their neighbors in south, especially the Galla, Sidamo, and others. During this time, missionaries from France and Spain who were mainly Jesuits wanted to win some Ethiopians to Roman Catholicism. This angered both the Church and State; in 1645 all Catholics were expelled, and no further missionaries were allowed into the country.

As Ethiopia fought against Muslim conquest, the emperors were able to forge a state with Christianity emerging as a unifying national force. The growth of the Church continued and by the thirteen century, under King Lalibela, it was strong enough to undertake a twenty year Church building project. The king (who is a saint in the Ethiopian Church) and his people built many Churches, the most outstanding being the eleven Churches in

Roha, now known as Lalibela. These Churches were curved out of gigantic multicolored rocks. These architectural beauties still stand today. Except for the Church of Saint George, which is shaped like a cross, the rest are rectangular. Murals, depicting biblical scenes and personalities, are imprinted on the walls and ceilings. The largest of these is the Redeemer of the World; it measures more than one hundred feet long, seventy feet wide, and thirty-six feet high.

With the fourteenth century revival of Christianity brought about under Tekle Haimanot, the "Saint of Ethiopia" who died in 1312, Ethiopia emerged as a great Christian center in Africa. However, the isolation of the Ethiopian Orthodox Church increased. For centuries Ethiopia had no connections with the Christian world. During this period Ethiopia developed a Christianity that is unique and indigenous, a truly African Christianity based on African spirituality and way of life. To begin with, an indigenous literature began to appear adding to the body of writings translated over the centuries from Greek, Arabic, and Egyptian. By the fourteenth century new hymns, prayers, eulogist pieces of saints and kings, and other important historical documents had already begun to appear. The greatest of the historical documents is the *Kibrä-Nägäst* (Book of Kings) which tells of the origin of the Ethiopia kingdoms and the glories of the kings from the line of the Queen of Sheba or the Solomonic kings. These writings influenced the spiritual life of the people. Along with these writings, the Church drew from the customs and traditions of its people, thus creating a liturgy which reflected the life of the people even as it was a celebration and communion with God. This spirituality remains unique to it. The Church was also involved in the cultural and economic life of the country. This period of Ethiopian Christian vitality continued to 1527.

THE ETHIOPIAN CHURCH AND EVANGELISM

The Ethiopian Orthodox Church is one of the oldest Churches in Africa, and the only one that survived Muslim attacks as well as Portuguese infiltration. But the Church is often accused of lack of "evangelical zeal;" that it never reached out to its southern neighbors. This lack of evangelical zeal can be explained. First, it is important to understand the life and work of the Ethiopian Church from an African concept of religion. Among Africans, religion is taken as a way of life in one's community. As such, there is no proselytizing in African religions. Understanding religion from this perspective, Ethiopians may have seen no reason to impose their faith on others.

There are further reasons for the lack of evangelical zeal. It has already been stated that growth of the Christian faith has come with political expansion and vice versa. Expansion of Rome, for example, led the growth of Christianity along the Mediterranean seaboard. We also know that the evangelization of the three kingdoms of Nobatia, Mukurra, and Aloa and the Island of Philae was done as part of the program of the Byzantine empire to stop the recurrent clashes on the southern frontier of Egypt.[31] The imperial expansion of Europe took Christianity into the southern African regions. Expansionism and evangelism go hand in hand. The spirit of expansion on a world scale is not found in Ethiopia. Jean-Marc Ela explains this point:

> Subjugated by Egypt and lacking the necessary material resources for its expansion, Ethiopian Christianity, by choice or resignation, held to the traditional African tolerance that lends so little encouragement to religious proselytism. More precisely, the absence of a political framework of universal pretensions account, in a sense, for the immobility of Ethiopian Christianity. The hypothesis comes to mind when we recall that the evangelization of northern Africa was the result of the colonial expansion of imperial Rome.
>
> The lack of contact between the Church of northern Africa and the Berber and Kabyle culture is an understandable outcome of the exclusive ties maintained by that Church with "Romania" which represented the combined values of Latin culture and Barbary civilization. That the mission did not extend to Africa south of the Sahara is not only because the Church of Augustine was taken up with theological controversies, but is also, perhaps indeed principally, because of the decline of the Roman Empire. As long as many kingdoms were joined together in a Roman Empire, Christian preaching could reach all peoples ruled by it. This is what Leo 1, in the sixth century thought.
>
> But the Churches of northern Africa collapsed along with the Empire. In other words, in ceasing to be Latin, Mediterranean Africa ceased to be Christian.[32]

This is a very important distinction to make for it says something about how Ethiopian rulers understood their office. They did not see themselves as conquerors but divinely appointed leaders of the people. There is no question that they fought, but it was to defend the land and the Christian faith, as we have seen in the preceding paragraphs. Mostly, they spent their time in meditation and contemplation trying to understand truth and wisdom. Ethiopian history records that King Elesbaas (Caleb) voluntarily abdicated the throne and entered monastic life in the hermitage of Abba Pentelon, where he ended his days.[33] Sellassie says King Caleb sent his crown to Jerusalem to be hung on the Holy Sepulchre.[34] In pre-Christian Ethiopia we find Queen Sheba, a good example of untiring quest for wisdom common among Ethiopian rulers. She went to King Solomon of Israel in search of wisdom.

Abu Salih, the thirteenth century Armenian writer, mentions the dual position the rulers of Ethiopia played: "All the kings of Abyssinia are priests, and celebrated the liturgy within the sanctuary, as long as they reign without slaying any man with their own hand; but after slaying they can no longer celebrate the liturgy."[35]

The second problem which the Ethiopian Church has faced over the centuries is rooted in the Canon Law passed by the first Ecumenical Council. As earlier mentioned, the Council of Nicaea put Ethiopia under the jurisdiction of the Patriarch of Alexandria. Under the Law, Ethiopians could not have their own archbishop or bishops. For centuries the life of the Church in Ethiopia was one of a continued struggle for freedom from Alexandria. Freedom is a human instinct and people will not rest until they have realized their liberation. Even people oppressed under the banner of religion seek liberation. This was the case of the Ethiopian Church for sixteen centuries. Archbishop Basilios, the first Patriarch of the Ethiopian Church, commented on the long struggle of the Ethiopian Orthodox Church: "Since the adoption in Ethiopia of the New Testament in succession to the Old Testament, the government repeatedly demanded the right of having an Ethiopian archbishop and bishops."[36] Since the fourth century, all bishops were sent from Alexandria. The head of the Church in Alexandria never consecrated an Ethiopian bishop. The problem Ethiopians had with Egyptian bishops was that each *Abune* (official title of the permanent representative of the Patriarch) ignored "the customs and the language of his flock, as well as the traditions of the Ethiopian Church and country."[37]

Ethiopians had to wait until this century before Alexandria would agree to consecrate Ethiopians to the office. For the first time in the history of their relations, Alexandria consecrated five Ethiopian bishops in 1929. The five consecrated by *Abune* John XIX, the Coptic Patriarch of Alexandria, were: *Abune* Petros, Bishop of Eastern Ethiopia, *Abune* Michael, Bishop of Southwest Ethiopia, *Abune* Abraham, Bishop of Western Ethiopia, *Abune* Isaac, Bishop of Northern Ethiopia, *and Abune* Sawiros, Bishop of Southern Ethiopia. *Abune* Petros was consecrated in Ethiopia when the Coptic Patriarch visited the country. The first two *Abune* were executed by Italians in 1936. Five bishops were an insufficient number when the size of the Church in Ethiopia is considered. Ethiopians continued to press on for independence from Alexandria. Political events in Ethiopia paved the way for the Church to get such independence. In 1937 Emperor Haile Sellassie led the Church proclamation of independence from Alexandria. The Ethiopian Church exiled the resident Egyptian *Abune*, bishop Kérlos. In place of Kérlos, bishop Abraham was elected as the new *Abune*, and he consecrated twelve Ethiopians to the office of bishop.

The political events that led to this move were precipitated by the presence of Italian soldiers in Ethiopia. Mussolini's army had invaded and occupied

Ethiopia for a period of nearly three years. The Italian army broke its links with Egypt in 1936. When Haile Sellassie defeated the Italian army in 1941, he used the break that the Italians had made with Egypt to declare independence for the Church. The Ethiopian Orthodox Church became a State Church, and some reforms were carried out. The relationship between the two Churches were obviously strained. Following Canon Law, the Ethiopian Church was excommunicated by Alexandria. It took a lot of discussions for the two Churches to reunite. It was not until 1941 that the silence between the two Churches was broken and serious talks about union were begun. These union discussions were initiated by Ethiopia, with the Emperor himself taking a leading role. In 1942 the excommunication was lifted, but there still was no reconciliation. In 1948, *Abune* Yosab 11, Coptic Patriarch of Alexandria, agreed to consecrate five Ethiopian bishops. The following bishops were consecrated in Alexandria: *Abune* Basilios, Bishop of Shewa, formerly known as Etch égé Gebre-Giorgis, and who was later elevated to the office of Patriarch of the Ethiopian Church, *Abune* Michael, bishop of Gondar Begemider and Simien, *Abune* Theophilus, bishop of Harar, *Abune* Jacob, bishop of Lakemt or Wellega, *and Abune* Timotheos, bishop of Yirgalem or Sidamo. In 1950 the healing process began; the two Churches restored their long historical relationship but at a distance. The reunion was victory for the Alexandrian Patriarch for it was he who had initiated the union talks and had taken an active role in what happened. With the restoration of relationship, came the appointment and consecration of the first archbishop for Ethiopia since the break. In addition, the Archbishop Basilos was consecrated as head of the Ethiopian Church. As sign of Alexandrian power over the Ethiopian Church, the archbishop was not consecrated among his own people in Addis Ababa but in Cairo, the seat of the Patriarch.

Until the overthrow of Emperor Haile Selassie 1, in February 1977, the Ethiopian Church was a State Church. Concerning this Church-State relationship, article 126 of the Revised Constitution of Ethiopia of 1955, states: "The Ethiopian Orthodox Church, founded in the fourth century on the doctrine of St.Mark, is the Established Church of the Empire and is as such, supported by the State. The Emperor shall always profess the Ethiopian Orthodox Faith. The name of the Emperor shall be mentioned in all religious services." Article 127 adds: "The secular administration of the Established Church shall be governed by law." The Constitution leaves the monastic and spiritual life in the hands of the Church, to be administered according to Canon Law. It is noteworthy that these two articles in the 1955 Constitution reflect most of the things carried out during the reform legislation of 1942, when the Church became the State Church. The legislation concerned regulation of management of Church property, the administration of the clergy, Church finances, and the status of the Church courts. In 1967 the government took another step in its control of the Church. An order was issued in the official government organ, the *Negarit Gazette*, defining the responsibilities of the Church Council. According to the order, the Council was to consist of the Patriarch, the chairman, and eight bishops. These bishops were to be appointed by the Emperor on the recommendation of the Patriarch. The Council was charged with the responsibility to "establish such rules and procedures as it may deem appropriate for the conduct of its affairs and generally for secular administration."

ETHIOPIA AND THE SPIRIT OF NATIONALISM

From 1935 to the 1960s, the history of the Church, and of Ethiopians as a people, raised political awareness and inspired the struggle for liberation among many people —not only in Africa but also among Africans in the diaspora, particularly those in the Caribbean and North America. St Clair Drake says that the defeat of the Italian soldiers and the assertion of the religious independence from the Coptic Church have been taken as examples of what African people can do in either politics or religion.[38] To understand Drake's point, the story of the Ethiopian success must be put in perspective of the history of the black world. This recent history has been a history of defeat by different Western powers. The victory of Haile Sellassie is taken as a symbol of "Black power."

There were some past victories too. Ethiopians led by Menelik 11, who was the King of Shoa before he became the emperor of Ethiopia in 1889, defeated an invading Italian army in the mountains at a place called Adowa, on March 1, 1896. Menelik's success was the first major victory of Africans over a European power in two thousand years.

The last African victory was that of Hanibal the Great, in 202 B.C.E. Let us not also forget that Setewayo badly defeated British warriors. The Zulu army humiliated a British regiment at Isandhlwana in January 1879. Unfortunately, this victory was not to last, for within six months the British were back and defeated the Zulu army. This explains why the victory of the Ethiopians not only "sent waves of pride coursing throughout the African world," as St. Clair Drake puts it, but also became an inspiration to the African people everywhere.

It is from this sense of victory that the term Ethiopianism, denoting African power, came into being in the African world. This was the power to be "somebody," says Drake. Ethiopia became a symbol of consciousness and pride in one's race and heritage. This symbol needed to be invoked in the formative years of political awareness and struggle for redemption in Africa and the whole African world. It was in light of the issues of self-respect and dignity that the name Ethiopia inspired some Christians to break away from

missionary Churches or those with some Western connections. These new
Churches often took the name Ethiopia, Abyssinia, or Aksum and in some
cases patterned themselves after the style of the Ethiopian Orthodox Church.
Bengt Sundkler mentions the Coptic Church, the Temple of Aksum, and the
Ethiopian Church of Abyssinia as churches in South Africa which were
inspired by the example of the Ethiopian Orthodox Church.[39] Elsewhere in
Africa, there are churches inspired by the life of the Ethiopian Orthodox
Church. In 1942 Peter Nyambo established his Ethiopian Church in Malawi,
the emphasis of which was a return to traditional culture and values. Because
of the stress on indigenous values, the Church was commonly referred to as
the Makolo Church (Church of the Ancestors). In Nigeria, the Ethiopian
Communion Church emerged in 1947, and in the following year, the Coptic
African Apostolic Church Mission came into existence.

The influence of Ethiopia among the people of the Caribbean is perhaps
best seen in the life and work of Ras Tafarians of Jamaica. (Ras Tafari was
the name of Haile Sellassie before he was enthroned emperor.) The Ras
Tafarians emphasize the power of African religion in the struggle for self-
respect and dignity. As far as they are concerned, it is only African religion
which can provide people with some sense of worth. Their argument is that
African religion has power to enable people to retrieve African culture and
history—elements needed for African identity. Ras Tafarians see Christianity
as an ideology of the Western people in their attempt to subjugate the African
race.

In the United States, the spirit of Ethiopianism was joined with the doctrine
of "Providential Design." We shall discuss the philosophy underlying this
doctrine at a later stage in this work, but for the moment, suffice it to say the
doctrine inspired many people of African descent to look back to Africa with
a kind of nostalgia, which in turn led some to return to Africa to educate and
evangelize their race. For some Africans in the United States, the doctrine
meant a return to Africa for good. The most articulate among the Africans of
the diaspora inspired by the doctrine of Providential Design included Wilmot
Blyden.[40] So it appears that after sixteen centuries of silence, Ethiopia woke
up and left a legacy of victory and self-worth among African peoples
everywhere. Ethiopia was a symbol for African awareness, power, and
redemption. This was the vision of Africa's children of the diaspora. The
anthem of the Universal Negro Improvement Association (1920) gave this
vision a voice when it said: "Advance, advance to victory, let Africa be
free."[41]

NOTES

1. Eusebius, *Ecclesiastical History*, vol. 1, trans. K. Lake, (London: Loeb Classical Library, 1927), 109-110.

2. Sergrew Hable Sellassie, *The Ancient and Medieval Ethiopian History to 1270* (Addis Ababa: United Printers, 1972), 97.

3. See 1 Kings 10:1-13 for the full story.

4. Michael Geddes, *The Church History of Ethiopia* (London: Rich Chiswell, 1825), 8.

5. E.W.H. Budge, *The Queen of Sheba and her Only Son Menyelik* (London: Oxford University Press, 1922), 42. There are several variations of the spelling of the name of the son of Queen Sheba.

6. *Ibid.*

7. *Ibid.*

8. Sellassie, *Ancient and Medieval Ethiopian History*, 96.

9. Samuel A. Mercer, "The Falashas," *Aethiops*, 3 (1930), 50-51.

10. Wolf Leslau, *Countumes et croyances des Falachas (Juifs d'Abyssinie)*, (Paris: Travaux memoires de l'Institut d'Ethnologie, n. LXI, Universit é de Paris, 1957).

11. David Kessler, *The Falashas: The Forgotten Jews of Ethiopia* (New York: Schocken Books, 1985).

12. Adolf von Harnack, *The Expansion of Christianity in the First Three Centuries*, vol. 11 (New York: G. B. Putman's Sons, 1905), 123.

13. McCrindle, trans. *The Christian Topography of Cosmas Indicopleustes*, (1897), 120. Quted by Tadeesse Tamrat, *Church and State in Ethiopia 1270-1527* (Oxford: Claredon Press, 1972), 25.

14. *Ibid.*, 9.

15. C. Conti Rossini, *La Storia d'Etiopia*, (Milan: A. Lucinni, 1928), 163.

16. Taddesse Tamrat, *Church and State in Ethiopia 1270-1527* (London: Oxford University Press, 1972), 25.

17. See *Oxford Dictionary of Church History* on Roman Martyrology.

18. Rufinus, *Historia Ecclesiastiza*, vol. XXI, col. 479, ed. J. P. Migne, Patrologiae Cursus Completus Series Latina.

19. E.W.H. Budge, *The Book of the Saints of the Ethiopian Church*, vol. 1 (Cambridge: Cambridge University Press, 1928), 139-140.

20. A. H. M. Jones and E. Monroe, trans., *A History of Ethiopia* (Oxford: Claredon Press, 1962), 26-27.

21. Budge, *Saints of Ethiopian Church*, vol. IV, 1164-1165. My emphasis.

22. Athanasius, *Apologia ad Constanitum*, ed. Migne, P.G., vol. XXV, col. 636.

23. Sellassie, *Ancient and Medieval Ethiopian History*, 100.

24. Athanasius, *Oratio de Incarnatione*, ed. Migne P. G., vol. XXV., col. 188.

25. Sellassie, *Ancient and Medieval Ethiopian History*, 143.

26. Sellassie, "State and Church in the Aksumite Period," *PICES* (Addis Ababa, 1966), chap. 1.

27. Michael Geddes, *The Church History of Ethiopia*, 20.

28. Abba Paulos Tzadua, *The Fetha Nägäst, the Law of the Kings* (Addis Ababa, 1968), 18; D. L. O'Leary, *The Ethiopian Church: Historical Notes on the Church of Abyssinia* (London: SPCK, 1936), 29.

29. Roland Oliver and J. D. Fage, *A Short History of Africa*, 5th. ed. (New York: Penguin Books, 1975), 96.

30. C. P. Groves, *Planting Christianity in Africa 1840-1954*, vol. 1 (London: Lutterworth Press, 1948), 110-111.

31. A. J. Arkell, ed., *A History of the Sudan to 1821* (London: Oxford University Press, 1961), 179-181.

32. Jean-Marc Ela, *African Cry*, Robert R. Barr, trans., (Maryknoll, N.Y.: Orbis Books, 1986), 10.

33. Martyrium Arethae, *Acta Santorium*, Oct, X, p. 758.

34. Sellassie, *Ancient and Medieval History of Ethiopia*, 143.

35. Abu Salih, *Churches and Monasteries of Egypt and the Neighboring Countries*, B. T. A. Evetts, trans., with notes by Alfred J. Butler (Oxford: Claredon Press, 1895), 286.

36. Archbishop Nicolas, *Church's Revival: Emancipation from 1600 Years' Guardianship: Free Church in Free State* (Cairo: Distributed by the Prime Minister's Library, Addis Ababa, n.d.), 24.

37. *Ibid.*, 16.

38. St. Clair Drake, *The Redemption of Africa and Black Religion* (Chicago, Ill.: Third World Press, 1970).

39. Bengt G. M. Sundkler, *Bantu Prophets in South Africa*, 2nd. ed. (London: Oxford University Press, 1961), 57-58.

40. See Drake, *The Redemption of Africa.*, 54-62; Lynch R. Hollis, *Edward Wilmot Blyden: Pan-Negro Patriot 1832-1912* (New York: Oxford University Press, 1970); see also V. Y. Mundimbe, *The Invention of Africa: Gnosis, Philosophy, and the Order of Knowledge* (Bloomington and Indianapolis: Indiana University Press; London: James Currey, 1988), chap. 4.

41. Quoted by Drake, *The Redemption of Africa*, 9.

3

Western Evangelization of Africa

Western evangelization of Africa is generally thought to have begun in the sixteenth century. In the present work we shall place its beginning in the eighteenth century, taking the period of the activities of the missionary societies as our starting point. By pushing the evangelism period into the eighteenth century, we can discuss two important periods in African Christianity: (1) beginning from the eighth to the thirteenth century, and (2) from the fourteenth to the seventeenth century.

These intervening years in the history of African Christianity are very important to discuss, because they cover the period of Islamic influence and expansion in Africa. This time was characterized by resistance and isolation of Christian communities in Egypt, Nobatia (Sudan), and Ethiopia. This separation enabled the Coptic and Ethiopian Christians to develop the distinctive characteristics of their Christianity. It is from this period in the history of African Christianity that indigenous Christianity fully developed, particularly in the Ethiopian Orthodox Church. The period covering the fourteen to the seventeenth century deserves special attention because it was a prelude to Western missionary activities in Africa. It was characterized by Portuguese trade and expansion which either accompanied or was followed by slave trade. The trade was soon to increase with the founding of European colonies in America and the Caribbean. With the increase of slave trade also came the destruction of African villages and whole societies. The inhumanity of the trade pricked the social consciousness of the Western world. Thus repulsed by the evils of slave trade and slavery itself, religious revival groups begun to seek ways to bring social injustice to an end. Evangelicals started preaching that salvation was for all, and this set in motion the idea of the evangelization of Africa. The formation of missionary societies in Europe followed by the American Board of Commissioners was, in part, a response to moral bankruptcy in the West and an attempt to stop the destruction of

African societies begun by European slave trade.

MUSLIM CONQUESTS: 640-1275

The fall of Egypt to Muslim fighters in 640 marked the end of the period of growth for the Early African Church. This date also marked the beginning of Islamic influence and expansion in Africa. By the end of the seventh century, Islam was firmly in control of the lands on the Mediterranean seaboard. Islamic control and influence in North Africa, or the *Maghrib* (the West) as the Arabic Muslims called it, effectively brought African Christianity to a period of a low ebb—lasting until the fourteenth century. Christianity was not completely wiped out by the success of Islam; some Christian communities remained on the Mediterranean seaboard. These scattered communities had to fight for their existence. In the *Maghrib*, these communities were found between Tangier and Tripoli. Muslim rulers allowed the continuation of Christian communities because they attracted lucrative trade from Europe. Since the Christian communities were valuable, the Muslims allowed them to worship and have priests, but not to evangelize.[1] Some Christians could also be found in the armies and royal courts as bodyguards. This was common among the sultans of Morocco and Tunisia, who felt more secure having bodyguards above their local rivalries.

The Coptic Church continued its struggle to survive, despite living under Islamic Egyptian rulers. The Church was protected under state law as a minority group. Under the same law, Christians were to pay tribute to their Muslim rulers and to distinguish themselves from the rest of the people by their dress. But the legal status did not permit the Church to engage in any work of evangelism or build new churches and monasteries. The most difficult time for the Coptic Church was during the two centuries following the conquest of Egypt in 640. During this period, the Fourth Crusades, orders were given to destroy churches and monasteries. (The Fourth Crusades were an attempt on the part of the Christian world, particularly Europe, to regain North Africa from the Muslims.) The Fourth Crusades increased Muslim hostility for Christians in Egypt and North Africa as a whole. Throughout this period, the Coptic Church tried as much as it could to maintain its churches and monasteries. Evidence of their efforts to maintain a Christian presence in what came to be a "Muslim world" was seen in the thirteenth century by Abu Salih the thirteenth century Armenian writer, who recorded visiting or seeing over 72 monasteries and many churches in Egypt alone.[2]

Christian persecutions under Islam were constant. Many Copts, clergy and laity, suffered. In the fourteenth century when persecutions against Copts arose under Sultan Al-Salih (1351-54), Ethiopia mobilized a large army to go and fight against Egypt. In this persecution, Patriarch Marqos of Alexandria was taken into prison. When he sent word of his imprisonment to the King in Ethiopia, the army was mobilized. Because Ethiopia had staged several successful attacks on Egypt in the past, when the news of the advancing troops reached Egypt, the Sultan was captured by the people and the Patriarch released.

There were several unsuccessful Christian attempts at missionary work in Egypt and the *Maghrib*. We have already mentioned one such failed attempt, namely, the Fourth Crusades. Other attempts were made by the Franciscan and Dominican Orders. In 1219 the Franciscans had an unsuccessful mission in Tunisia. Francis of Assis himself visited Egypt in the same year. In 1220 five Franciscans were martyred in Morocco.[3] Dominican missionaries came to Egypt in 1234. One of the successful missionaries, Raymond Lull, visited Tunisia several times in 1262, but he was stoned at Bugia.[4]

During the period under discussion, the Nubian Church in the south remained strong, although it was cut off from the Christian world. For six hundred years, the Nubian Church resisted Islam. It is remarkable that Christianity lasted a thousand years in Nubia although the country was surrounded by Islamic rulers. Could the use of the Nubian language in the liturgy and Christian literature have contributed to the viability of Christianity? It was not until the thirteenth century that Saladin, an Egyptian Muslim leader, conquered Nubia. He attacked Nubia as a revenge for European Crusades (the Fourth Crusades) against Muslims in North Africa and the Middle East. Although Nubia fell to Saladin in 1275, Christian influence continued for some time. For example, Soba did not become Muslim until 1504,[5] and according to reports of Portuguese travelers in the sixteenth century, Christians in this region were seeking help from the king of Abyssinia.

PORTUGUESE EXPANSION: 1275-1620

All in all, the period from the seventh through the thirteenth century was a difficult time for Christianity in Africa. The fifteenth century marked a turning point, with the beginning of Western evangelization of Africa. This phase came as an accident of history, especially the history of maritime Portugal and other Europeans nations. Europeans were inspired by the reports of the voyages of Marco Polo (1271-1285) and Lanzarote Malocello to the Canary Islands reached in 1312. In 1402 Spanish Franciscans began missionary work there. Several factors let to Portugal's initiating the evangelization of Africa. All these factors were related to imperial and national interest. It was trade, in the first place, which brought Portugal in touch with the islands off the west coast of Africa and onto the mainland. The crusades had made the overland route to India dangerous and more expensive; further, not much was gained by this long route. The route was to become even more dangerous and expensive with the coming of the Ottoman Turks into power in 1453. A safe and more profitable way to India had to be found. The route had to bypass the Islamic world if Portugal was to gain direct access to the treasures of Asia and Africa, namely, pepper and spices, gold, ivory, gems, jewelry, metal articles, etc. The only alternative route was by sea.

Prince Henry the Navigator of Portugal (1394-1460) initiated the search for the sea route to India. The Prince developed a maritime center for scholars and marines to study new techniques, design better ships, and to discuss exploration ventures. Henry had a personal interest in the venture. He once belonged to the Order of Knights of Christ. This Order was founded in 1319 to fight off the Muslim Moors who had weakened Christianity in Europe. Since it was believed that the sea route to India would go around Africa, Henry wanted to undertake the venture to ascertain the extent of Muslim power and undermine its influence in the southern regions of Africa by evangelizing the people in those regions. He was at Ceuta when Christians fought against the Moors in 1415. Furthermore, Henry wanted to find Prester John, the mythical Christian prince in Central Africa. He was also encouraged by the Papal Bull of 1456, issued by Pope Calixtus III. The Bull of 1456 gave the Great Prior of the Order of Christ of Portugal the responsibility for sponsoring missionaries and bishoprics in the hands of the King of Portugal. In 1493 Pope Alexander VI set three bulls (*Inter Caetera*) in which he recognized the exclusive right of the Spanish Crown to trade with lands west of the Atlantic and to "bring to Christian faith the peoples who inhabit these islands and the mainland . . . and to send to the said islands and to the mainland wise, upright, God-fearing and virtuous men who will be capable of instructing the indigenous peoples in good morals and in the Catholic faith." In other words, the Pope not only gave authority to Portugal and Spain to conquer and possess lands and their riches, but also to evangelize. The lands and wealth east of the 15th meridian belonged to Portugal; Spain had authority over the lands west of the meridian. Portugal received the land of Brazil by the agreement of 1494 which moved the line from the 15th. to 60th. meridian.

Here economic, political, religious, and intellectual needs came together to form an impetus for an African enterprise. Of these reasons, the economic factor was central. Portugal had its eyes on India and its spices, but in the process, the African gold became more important. For the purpose of safeguarding trade relations, the Portuguese offered "peace" and "friendship" and Christianity to their trading partners. However, the proclamation of the Gospel was not the primary motive in Portuguese relations with other people.

The people of the Cape Verde Islands were the first to be reached by the Portuguese in their sea expeditions. On those islands, evangelism, Portuguese style, started: the Portuguese offered trade, the cross, and the king of Portugal. Simply put, the evolution of trade, Christianity, and colonization. The Cape Verde Islands were colonized in 1402; these were to be followed by the Madeira Islands reached by the Portuguese in 1420. Christianity and trade flourished there to such an extent that Madeira and Cape Verde Islands became an Episcopal See in 1514. In 1539 these Islands were raised to an Archiepiscopal See, including the Azores, Cape Verde, and San Thome and Goa in the West Indies. These islands in the West Indies soon became suffragans.

From the islands off the coast of Africa, the Portuguese were able to make contact with the mainland. The first people to be contacted were those in the Sene-Gambia region. By the fifteenth century Christianity reached the west coast of Africa. A couple of chiefs were baptized in the area, and in 1489 the king of the Wolof in Bohemia went to Lisbon to be baptized; with him went twenty-five others. In the following year, the king was knighted by the King of Portugal. On his return home from Lisbon, the king brought with him Dominican missionaries; they were later expelled.

By the fifteenth century Portuguese missionaries had reached the area south of the Sene-Gambia. (This area was what later became known as Sierra Leone.) In 1772, partly as the result of the work of evangelicals, Lord Mansfield declared slavery illegal in England. Their cause was helped by two books written by two Africans, Ottabah Cugoano and Olaudah Equiano.[6] Cugoano was from Ghana, while Equiano was from Nigeria. These two Africans wrote about their capture and experience as slaves. Cugoano's book was published in 1787 and Equiano's book followed two years later. Both appealed for evangelization of Africa. Cugoano himself wanted to return to Africa as a missionary. A committee for the "Black Poor" in England was formed to arrange for a party of Africans to resettle in Africa. After several setbacks, a group of 411, led by Captain T. Boulden Thompson, set sail from Portsmouth, England. They landed on Frenchman's Bay on May 10, 1887. This is the beginning of the settlement that became known as Sierra Leone.

The missionaries in Sene-Gambia were Jesuits and Dominicans. When the King of Sierra Leone was baptized, it was not by missionaries from Portugal but from Spain. The Spanish priest, Father Barrerrius, named the King of Sierra Leone Philip, after Philip III of Spain. The full evangelization of the people of Sierra Leone did not begin until the nineteenth century, when the Church Missionary Society (CMS) and other similar bodies begun their work. In 1804 CMS sent Melchior Renner and Peter Hartwig, its first missionaries, to work among the Susa. Hartwig abandoned missionary work and became a slave trader. In 1806 CMS sent three more missionaries to Sierra Leone, and this was the beginning of the evangelization of the area.

Beyond the kingdom of Sierra Leone was the kingdom of Benin. The Portuguese reached Benin in 1472 through the person of Ruy de Sequira. It was not until 1480 that the Portuguese followed up the expedition of Sequira, and this time it was to capture slaves. The interest in evangelizing the area rose when Joao II became king of Portugal in 1481. He established such trade links with the Guinea coast that he was known as "Lord of Guinea." Following up the responsibility given to Portugal by Pope Alexander, Joao II planned to evangelize the Guinea coast area; his strategy was to use African kings to evangelize Africa. It was under this project that missionaries reached Benin in 1486. Around 1514 the *Oba* (king) of Benin expressed interest in Christianity. Portugal's interest was aroused by the chief's invitation of Portuguese missionaries from nearby Principe. In 1516 the *Oba* sent his son and the sons of other chiefs to be baptized. A Church was built in Benin but we hear nothing about Christianity in the area until after the death of the *Oba* in 1517.

Slowly, the Portuguese were moving southward. In 1482 Diog Cam, a Portuguese traveler, reached the mouth of the Kongo river. In 1484 Diog Cam returned home with some Africans; they converted while in Portugal and returned to Africa the following year. This was the first planting of Christianity in Kongo. In 1491 a first missionary party arrived from Portugal. In the same year King Nzinga Kuwu, along with most of his family, was baptized in the king's own town of Mbaza Kongo, where a Church was soon built. Although the missionaries had received a warm welcome, they were soon expelled because of their hostile attitude toward the people and their culture.

The situation changed favorably for missionaries when the king's son, Affonso, ascended to the throne. Under Affonso missionaries arrived in 1505, 1511, and 1521. Affonso was committed to Christianity and the material benefits it could offer his people for progress. He requested priests and technicians from King John I of Portugal. In 1513 Affonso also sent a legation to wait upon the Pope in Rome. In seeking recognition of the Kongo nation, Affonso I appointed Antonio of Nigritia as ambassador to the Vatican. (A bust of Antonio is in the Church of St. Maria Maggiore in Rome.) Affonso went further: he sent his son Henry to be educated in Lisbon where he also entered seminary and was ordained after his studies. He was appointed bishop of Utica in 1518, and thus became the first African ever to receive such a position in the Catholic Church. Pope Leo X appointed Henry vicar apostolic of Kongo, but because of ill health he never did much work. He died in 1530 in Kongo.

Although Christianity was very well established in the Kongo region, it did not last. Its failure was due to the fact that the people of Kongo found Portuguese hostility and domination unacceptable. Although the people of Kongo expelled the missionaries, evidence of a strong Christianity remained long after; long enough to be recorded by the Scottish traveler, David Livingstone who visited Kongo many years later. Livingstone recorded having found walls of big churches still standing and some people having a crucifix or just a plain cross in their homes.

The failure of the missionaries in the Kongo was compensated for by the success experienced once they got established in Angola. Jesuit missionaries arrived in Angola in 1574 and in a decade they baptized the king and many of his people. In 1584 Angola was made an episcopate by Pope Clement VIII, thus San Paulo de Luanda became the capital of Roman Catholicism south of the Sahara. Portuguese missionaries also established themselves at Sao Philip of Benguella in 1617; they attempted moving into the interior in 1685, but their work there had very little success.

Along the East coast of Africa the Portuguese contended with Arabs who had long been established in this region. Arabs, just like their European counterparts, went about spreading their culture, exploiting their trading partners, and using religion to make things easy for themselves. Arabs settled on the East coast of Africa during the period of Islamic expansion. They first established themselves on the Somali coast. Oliver and Fage say: "According to traditions retained in both Arabia and East Africa, the earliest colonialists were eight-century Shíite refugees from Oman, on the Arabian side of the Persian Gulf, who were followed in the ninth century by Orthodox Sunnis from Shiraz on the Persian side of the Gulf."[7] The Sunnis built towns in the Somali coast, developing a lucrative gold trade of the Zambezi region. They also traded in spices, ivory, and slaves. The Sunnis built settlements on the islands of Kilwa and Zanzibar from which they controlled all trans-Indian Ocean trade and commerce. Kilwa became affluent because it emerged as a very important strategic island and commercial center in the trans-Indian Ocean trade. Recording his impressions of Kilwa in 1331, Ibn Battuta, the 14th century African traveler and scholar wrote in his journal: "Kilwa is one of the most beautiful and well constructed towns in the world. The whole of it is elegantly built. The roofs are built with mangrove poles. There is very heavy rain. The people are engaged in a holy war, for their country lies beside that of pagan Zajn. The chief qualities are devotion and piety; they follow the Shaffi rite."[8] Accounts written more than a century later, in 1500, confirm the report of Ibn Battuta concerning the beauty and wealth of Kilwa: "In this land there are rich merchants, and there is much gold and silver and amber and musk and pearls. Those of the land wear clothes of fine cotton and silk and many fine things, and they are black men."[9]

When the Portuguese sought to develop their trade on the East coast, they found Arabs already well established. The Portuguese decided to build their own forts along the coast. In addition to a clash between the two exploiting civilizations, Arab versus European, it was a confrontation between two religions: Islam and Christianity. Portuguese Franciscans, under the leadership of Major D. Francisco de Almeida, plundered and occupied Kilwa on July 24, 1505. The Portuguese moved onto the mainland where they ransacked Mombasa. The following eyewitness accounts gives an insight into what the Portuguese did at Kilwa and Mombasa.

Kilwa
In Kilwa there are many strong houses several stories high. They are built of stone and mortar and plastered with various designs. As soon as the town had been taken without opposition, the Vicar-General and some of the Franciscan fathers came ashore carrying two crosses in procession and singing *Te Deum*. They went to the palace, and there the cross was put down and the Grand-Captain prayed. Then everyone started to plunder the town of its merchandise and provisions. [de Almeida set the town on fire two days after they started the plunder]

Mombasa
The Grand-Captain ordered that the town should be sacked and that each man should carry off to his ship whatever he found so that at the end there would be a division of the spoil, each man to receive a twentieth of what he found. The same rule was made for gold, silver, and pearls. Then everyone started to plunder the town and to search the houses, forcing open the doors with axes and iron bars. There was a large quantity of cotton cloth from Sofala in the town, for the whole coast gets its cotton cloth from here. So the Grand-Captain got a good share of the trade of Sofala for himself. A large quantity of rich silk and gold embroidered clothes was seized, and carpets also; one of these, which was without equal beauty, was sent to the king of Portugal together with many other valuables.[10]

From Mombasa, the Portuguese went on to Malindi which they also took. Sofala resisted Portuguese occupation. Up north in Somali, the Portuguese defeated the Arabs in 1543. In 1541 Arabs attacked Somali in order to conquer Ethiopia. This was another Muslim attempt to take over Ethiopia. The king of Ethiopia invited the Portuguese for help against the invading Muslims.[11] By 1560 Portuguese missionaries had reached inside mainland Africa. They baptized five hundred people in the Sena area (in Mozambique). Most of those baptized were workers of the Portuguese merchants in the area. In the same year King Mwene-Mutapa, of Zimbabwe, was baptized together with his wife. However, Portuguese influence in East Africa was not to last; with the weakening of their power in Europe, their influence overseas began to diminish. This was more the case in East Africa where Arab influence had not disappeared.

The people of Mombasa were the first to rebel against Portuguese control.

With the help of the Iman of Moscat, the Portuguese were driven out of Malindi and Kilwa, thus weakening their influence on Sofala. The Arabs were quick to reestablish themselves along the East coast, controlling the area north of Cape Delgado. From there northward, the Arabs escalated the trade in slaves as well as ivory. The Portuguese controlled the southern part of the coast from Cape Delgado.[12] As the Arabs regained their political and commercial influence, Islam once again became a dominant foreign religion without rivalry.

The end of Portuguese influence on the East coast started with the death of Fr. Goncalo Da Silveria, a missionary in the Sena area who is recorded to have baptized five hundred people on Christmas Day. It is alleged that he was strangled while asleep by Muslims who had conspired against him. The Muslims had told King Mwene-Mutapa that Fr. Silveria was a spy for the Indian viceroy. The Muslims further told the king that by accepting Christianity, the king had actually accepted the authority of the Indian viceroy. The death of Fr. Silveria, in 1561, marked the end of Jesuit missionary activities of the sixteenth century.

By the end of the sixteenth century the Portuguese were not the only European power along the African coastline. Prior to that Portugal had made strenuous efforts to gain monopoly rights to operations in Africa and Asia by international agreements; and Rome's recognition of Portugal's right to evangelize Africa made it all the more difficult for other European countries to enter Africa. From 1450 to 1600 Portugal was Africa's only contact with Europe. However, after the sixteenth century, other European nations had decided to disregard Portugal's monopoly. The Dutch were the first to become Portuguese rivals on the West coast; they were followed by the British, the French, and the Danes. In 1637 the Dutch took Elmina from the Portuguese and established their authority on the whole West coast. The Dutch went further south to the tip of Africa and established a settlement at the cape in 1652.

MISSIONARY ORDERS AND SOCIETIES

From the fourteenth through the seventeenth century most of the evangelism work in Africa was along the coastal areas. The work was done mostly by Portuguese missionary orders. The orders included Dominicans, Jesuits, Franciscans, and Spanish Capuchins (who worked on the southwest coast areas of Kong and Angola). These missionary orders and others were formed during the medieval period, roughly between 1098-1226. They emerged as a response to specific needs in the Church. For example, the Benedictine Order arose out of a need to strengthen, the devotional life of the

Church while the Franciscan and Dominican Orders were formed out of the need to instruct people in the faith. During the period of Portuguese and Spanish overseas ventures, members of different orders were to be found on trade ships and at commercial centers. They ministered to the crew of the ships or European traders wherever they were and also to the indigenous people in the areas where Europeans traded. These orders made serious attempts to evangelize Africa, and they built churches at the coast settlements. By the end of eighteenth century there was little visible sign of their work. With the decline of Portuguese supremacy in Europe, came the demise of evangelization efforts by missionary orders. Only ruins remained as evidence of their Christian presence. The era of the early Christian movement had come to an end and a new beginning was at hand.

The new era of African missionary activity started in the last quarter of the eighteenth century—around 1775. The old missionary enterprise had appeared before the Reformation so it had been all Catholic. The new attempts to evangelize Africa were a result of a spiritual awakening within Protestant movements in England, continental Europe, and America. This awakening brought with it a new sense of religious and moral obligation or social justice to all people. This understanding came from the remorse that arose with slavery. It can be said that Lord Mansfield's 1772 judgment to make slave trade illegal in Britain played a significant role toward the new understanding of social justice within Protestant Churches. Lord Mansfield's judgment did not set free all of the 20,000 slaves in Britain, but it did raise public awareness and discussion about the evils of slavery. This judgment, together with the work of philanthropists and evangelical revivals in Britain, gave birth to the new era of Christian movements in Africa. The eighteenth century revival movement within the Protestant tradition initiated missionary activity overseas. Other factors, apart from domestic reasons, included the reports of travelers to distant lands which stimulated interest in missionary work abroad. The reports included those of Captain James Cook, Joseph Banks, James Bruce, and later, David Livingstone. The new era of the evangelization of Africa really came in 1787 when the first settlement of Christians took place in Sierra Leone. Toward the end of the eighteenth century, Protestants were beginning to feel that the work of evangelism had been too ignored. This feeling was expressed at the inauguration of the Church Missionary Society in 1799: "there seems to be still wanting in the Established Church a society for sending missionaries to the continent of Africa, or other parts of the heathen world."

The first missionary society emerged in Britain and soon many missionary societies were formed to evangelize different parts of the world. By the time the new era dawned, some of the other societies already in operation were the Society for the Promotion of Christian Knowledge (SPCK), the Society for the Propagation of the Gospel in Foreign Parts (SPG), and the Moravian Missionary Society. SPCK was organized for the purpose of strengthening religious life of colonialists in the "New World." The organization eventually started to send its people to other parts of the world as missionaries and thereby became a missionary agent. Like the SPCK, SPG was founded by a Royal Charter in 1701 for the purpose of ministering to the spiritual needs of English settlers in the Caribbean and North America. The organization also had as its purpose evangelizing indigenous people.

The earliest of Protestant missionary Churches was the Moravian. During the period of 1732-1862, the Moravian Church boasted having sent out over two thousand missionaries. In 1732 Moravians started sending missionaries to West and South Africa (at the Cape). A long time passed before missionary societies appeared in Britain. In 1792 the Baptist Missionary Society (BMS) was founded with a primary focus on India. This was followed by the London Missionary Society (LMS), formed in 1795, which was to work in the Pacific and South Africa. The LMS, a London University venture, was ecumenical at first but it soon turned out to be mainly Congregationalist. In 1799 the Church Missionary Society (CMS) was founded; it sent its missionaries to West and East Africa, including Madagascar, as areas of its missionary work. The Foreign Bible Society (FBS) was established in 1804; also very dominant in West Africa was the Baptist Missionary Society.

Another dominant missionary society in West Africa was the Methodist Missionary Society organized in 1834. The Methodist Church in Britain had begun its overseas work earlier under the leadership of Dr. Coke and the Methodist Conference. In 1804 the London Committee was formed, but it took another 30 years for the formation of the Society. One of the outstanding missionaries sent by the Methodist Missionary Society was Thomas B. Freeman. He was of African descent—his father was from the Caribbean but his mother was English. He arrived at Cape Coast in 1838 and begun to spread Methodism in Ghana, Dahomey and Togo. Freeman died in 1890, but not until after his influence had reached the whole of West Africa.[13]

Besides the LMS, England saw the formation of another missionary society organized by universities. The universities of Cambridge and Oxford came together to form the Central Africa Mission, an enterprise which had as its sole purpose sending missionaries into the interior of South East Africa, the region around lake Malawi. The universities formed their missionary venture after David Livingstone, the Scottish traveler, had delivered lectures at the two universities. In his lectures, he had suggested and urged the universities to take a missionary venture into this part of Africa, to stop the Portuguese-Arab slave trade by introducing another form of trade, and proclaiming the Gospel. The two universities were later joined in the enterprise by two other universities, namely, Durham and Dublin. Thus the venture came to be known as Universities' Mission to Central Africa (UMCA). By 1860 the UMCA had started to penetrate into the interior of this region, as far as the southern highlands of Malawi.[14]   By 1875 the UMCA had begun to concentrate its efforts along the Indian Ocean and into the highlands of northern Tanzania, the area around Magila.

In Scotland, the counterparts of the English universities formed their own society which they named after their founding universities, Edinburgh and Glasgow. The Glasgow Missionary Society, as this missionary society was commonly known, was formed in 1796 to work mainly in South Africa; it is noted for founding an institute of higher learning for all races at Lovedale.

We have already indicated that the Church Missionary Society (CMS) established itself in most parts of the interior of Africa. From the costal areas of the Indian Ocean they went as far as the court of King Mutesa of Buganda into Sudan. From the Atlantic coast they covered most of West Africa. With the work of UMCA, CMS, White Fathers of Cardinal Lavigerie, and Holy Ghost Fathers at Bagamoyo, Christianity spread in the Southeast and eastern parts of the continent.

The spirit of missionary societies was also present in continental Europe. There, the first society to be formed was the Netherlands Missionary Society in 1797. This was followed by the Swiss Missionary Society formed in Basel in 1818. From Germany came the North German Missionary Society, or the Bremen Missionary Society so called after the city of its origin. In Germany, there were also the Berlin Missionary Society and the Neukirchner Missionsgesellshaft.   These societies were mostly found in Burundi.   In France, the Paris Evangelical Missionary Society was formed; this group worked in Lesotho.

In North America the missionary zeal was alive too. In 1840 the American Board of commissioners for Foreign Missions was organized. The Board was composed of Protestant denominations: Baptists (this was before the division into different conventions), Methodists, and Presbyterians. The Presbyterians were later influential in the evangelization of Cameroon and other parts of North Africa.

In the Catholic Church similar movements were taking place. While the earlier orders worked mostly along the coastal areas, the centers of commercial activity or Portuguese settlements, and on ships, the later missionary orders moved into the interior of Africa. Three missionary orders stand out for their activities in the interior of Africa: The Society for Divine Word, the Society of Missions, commonly known as White Fathers, and *Societas Missionum ad Afros* (Society of African Missions). Of these three, the White Fathers spread widely in the interior of Africa—covering Burkina Faso, Niger, most of the West coast, as well as East and Central Africa. Missionaries of *Societas Missionoum ad Afros* were found mostly in the southern parts of Ghana and Nigeria. The Society of Divine Word worked in the parts of Africa where the other two were not present.

MISSIONARY ADVANCE AND STRATEGY

What we see from the eighth through the fourteenth century is a stagnation of Christian growth in Africa; its advance was arrested by Islam. Muslim rulers permitted some Christian communities here and there, but it was for economic reasons. Such communities were few and too isolated to bear effective witness. Besides, they were forbidden by Islamic law to carry out any form of evangelism. Muslims used this method of isolation to weaken Christian influence and power. This strategy did not work in Ethiopia. Muslim attacks against Ethiopia drew the Church and the State even closer, making the country strong enough to repulse all Muslim invasions. The king became the defender of the faith. Christians in Nubia and Egypt looked to Ethiopia for help as the Patriarch Marqos of Alexandria did during the persecution of al-Salih, which lasted from 1315-1354. Ethiopia concentrated its efforts on defending itself against Muslim attacks, so much so that little attention was given to evangelism. From the monasteries came the translation of the Scriptures into Géez which later became the liturgical language.

Until the fourteenth century Muslims were a dominant foreign power in Africa. This changed with the Portuguese rise to power. National interests combined with Christianity so that wherever Portuguese sailors, merchants, and others went, there Christianity was also present. This alliance between Christianity and national interest was to be repeated in the succeeding centuries by other Western nations. The close association between national interests and Christianity has made Africans wonder what the real intentions of missionaries were in Africa! For some Africans, the answer is plain and clear: exploitation! Thus, Kwame Nkrumah, Ghana's first President would say:

The stage opens with the appearance of missionaries and anthropologists, traders, concessionaires and administrators. While the missionaries with "Christianity" implore the colonial subject to lay of "treasure in heaven where moth nor rust doth corrupt," the traders, concessionaires acquire his mineral and land resources, destroy his arts, crafts and home industries.[15]

Nkrumah's words have to be put into perspective to appreciate them. Take, for example, the Portuguese policy for evangelism. Portuguese missionaries entering Africa saw two enemies against their work: Muslims along the Mediterranean lands and East Africa, and the "pagan" culture which had to be replaced if success of Christianity was to be assured. Portuguese missionaries took an aggressive policy toward both enemies. They demanded that Africans not only accept the Gospel, but also the King of Portugal as the highest political and ecclesiastical authority. This is what was known as *padriado*. This policy was justified by the understanding that Portugal had a responsibility from the Pope to evangelize Africa. As mentioned above, in 1456 the Pope gave the Great Prior of the Order of Christ of Portugal putting responsibility for sponsoring missionaries and bishoprics in the hands of the King of Portugal.[16]

Along with *padriado* the Portuguese introduced the policy of *requerimiento*. This policy guided the Church's theory and practice in evangelism. People were to obey the Gospel—no one was to reject it! Any form of rejection was met with hostility. From the beginning of Western evangelization of Africa, and well into this century, the policy of *requerimiento* has influenced, if not formed, the basis of missionary doctrine. The doctrine argues that there is nothing valuable in non-Western cultures upon which the missionary can build. This doctrine of *tabula rasa* forbade traditional values to continue—everything had to be destroyed.

Portuguese demand for *padriado* and *requerimiento* resulted in little success for their evangelical efforts. People saw these as a way of expanding Portuguese power and influence. Africans would not have it, even in the places where the king had accepted Christianity. This was one of the reasons the Portuguese were driven out of some places, such as in Kongo. The hostile attitude toward other cultures is still prevalent among some missionaries in Africa, and it is one of the factors that has contributed to the formation of Indigenous (Independent) Churches. The doctrine of *tabula rasa* has made many people angry toward Christianity, and it has invoked sharp criticism of missionary work and Christianity in general. Criticism of the doctrine has been featured often in contemporary African literature.[17]

Eighteenth century missionary activities began with the emergence of a focus in evangelism, that is, to reach the interior of Africa with the Gospel. With the formation of missionary societies, it did not take long to get into the interior. Missionary zeal to preach in the interior of Africa was also characterized by yet another spirit—competition. The competition took two forms: competition among the missionaries, and Christianity versus African way of life. Competition among missionaries of various mission agencies led to what could be rightly described as a "scramble for Africa." By the nineteenth century very little of the African interior had yet to be evangelized. What was left was the competition between missionaries of various Churches to cover as much area as possible.

The spirit of competition among Churches is a subject of Munonye's first novel, *The Only Son*. In a flash-back, Fr. Smith, a character in the novel, takes the reader to his seminary days back in Ireland. There, in a lecture, Fr. Superior addresses the class, saying:

In this early phase, with so many denominations literary pouring into that pagan world, our first emphasis must be statistical success. We must bring the word of God to as many as possible as the same time. We want on our side the vast numbers who in Africa of the future will sustain the Church with their numerical strength. Call it vote of the masses if you like. In pursuit of that objective, I am afraid we've got to be impatient with the culture of the people. There just isn't the time to sort out first and label their customs as acceptable in our aim, we must ensure that all along we present to the people tangible evidence of the advantages of Christianity.[18]

A student challenges the theory on the grounds of sincerity of belief. The Fr. Superior silences the student with his dictum: "we are on virgin soil, very vast too, and we want acres and acres of it to ourselves."

Christianity was planted with the spirit of competition, and today this spirit stands in the way of a united Christian community in Africa. As long as the spirit of winning continues to dominate Christian thought and work in evangelism, all ecumenical efforts will be in vain. Africa has indeed been evangelized; the task and challenge is to uproot the spirit of competition.

NOTES

1.   Groves, *The Planting of Christianity in Africa*, vol. 1, (London: Lutterworth, 1948), 114.

2.   Abu Salih, *Churches and Monasteries of Egypt and Some Neighboring Countries*, trans. B. T. A. Evetts, with added notes by Alfred J. Bulter (Oxford: Claredon Press, 1895), 347-351.

3.   Groves, *Planting Christianity in Africa*, 116.

4.   August Neander, General *History of the Christian Religion and Church*, vol. 4, trans. Josephy Torrey, (N.Y.: Hurd and Houghton, 1871), 63.

5.   R. Cornevin and M. Cornevin, *Historie de l'Afrique des Origines a la 2é Fuerra Modialle* (Paris: Petité Bibliothéque Payot, 1964), 144.

6.   Ottobah Cugoano, *Thoughts and Sentiments on the Evil and Wicked Traffic of Slavery and Commerce of the Human specie: Humbly Submitted to the Inhabitants of Great Britain* (London: s.n., 1787); Olaudah Equiano, *Equiano's Travels* (London: Heinemann, 1967).

7.   Roland Oliver and J. D. Fage, *A Short History of Africa*. 5th. ed. (New York: Penguin Books, 1975), 99. See also an Arabic translation of Kilwa chronicles by G. S. P. Freeman-Grenville in *East African Coast, Select Documents* (London: 1962), 31-35.

8. Muhammad ibn Abdullah ibn Battuta in *East African Coast, Select Documents from the First to the Earlier Nineteenth Century*, trans. G. S. P. Freeman-Grenville, (Oxford: Claredon Press, 1962), p. 31. Ibn Battuta was born at Tangier in 1304 and he spent most of his life travelling in the Muslim world from West Africa to India and China. He dictated the accounts of his travels to Ibn Juzayy, who published them as *Tuhfat al-Nuzzar fi Ghara'ib al-Amsar wa 'Adja'ib al-Asfar*. See the English translation by H. A. R. Gibb, *Ibn Battuta, Travels in Asia and Africa* (London: Hakluyt Society, 1929).

9. Mansel Longworth Dames, trans., *The Book of Duarte Barbosa*, 2 vols. (London: Hakluyt Society, 1918).

10. *Ibid.*, 105. This eyewitness report is believed to have been written by Hans Myr, a German who travelled in de Almeida's flagship, the *Sam Rafel*. See also Barros, Da Asia, trans. G. M. Theal, *1st Decade, Records of South-Eastern Africa*, vol. 6, 1900.

11. R. Cornevin and M Cornevin, *Historie de l'Afrique des Origens a la 2e Fuerre Modialle* (Paris: Petite Bibliotheque Payot, 1964), p. 199.

12. *Ibid.*, 228.

13. See Lamin Sanneh for the influence of Freeman in West Africa, *West African Christianity: The Religious Impact* (New York: Orbis Books, 1983), 120-123.

14. I have discussed the work of UMCA in *The Legacy of Scottish Missionaries in Malawi* (New York: Edwin Mellen Press, 1992), chap. 1.

15. Kwame Nkrumah, Speech at the Conference on Independent African States. Accra, Ghana: April 15, 1958, 13.

16. Stephen Neil, *A History of Christian Missions* (Middlesex, Eng.: Penguin Books, 1973), 141.

17. Many contemporary African novelists have written on or referred to the missionary enterprise in Africa, including Chinua Achebe, *Things Fall Apart* (London: Heinemann, 1962); *Arrow of God* (London: Heinemann, 1976); T. Obinkaram Echewa, *The Land's Lord* (London: Heinemann, 1976); Mogo Beti, *The Poor Christ of Bomba* (London: Heinemann, 1971); Onoura Nzekwa, *Blade Among the Boys* (London: Heinemann, 1971); Kenjo Jumbam, *The White Man of God* (London: Heinemann, 1980); Ngugi wa Thiog'o, *The River Between* (London: Heinemann, 1965). These authors have focused on missionary insensitivity to African thought and culture.

Contemporary African poets have also written on the subject of missionaries and their work. A representative work in this field is by Christopher Okigbo, *Labyrinths* (London: Heinemann, 1971). Hugh Dinwiddy has given a survey of those novels in Anglophone Africa. See his article, "Missions and Missionaries as portrayed by English-Speaking writers of Contemporary African Literature," in *Christianity in Independent Africa*, eds. Edward Fashole-Luke, et al. (Bloomington, Ind.: Indiana University Press; Rex Collings, 1978), 426-442.

18. John Munonye, *The Only Son* (London: Heinemann, 1966), 193-194.

4

The Diaspora and the Missionary Enterprise

COLONIZATION SOCIETIES

When people speak of the evangelization of Africa, they usually do not think of the work of the Africans of the diaspora. This is because most of the books on the history of Christian missions say nothing about them. People of African descent from the Caribbean and the United States made a notable contribution to the evangelization of Africa. The philosophy of their work, self-reliance through industrial missions, distinguished their missionary enterprise from other mission agencies evangelizing Africa. This chapter highlights the missionary achievements of Africans of the diaspora on the African continent, but also examines the problems that beset their work.

The missionary activities of the descendants of Africa must be seen in light of the emancipation proclamation of slavery in England and America and the colonization efforts which followed. Prior to the declaration it was virtually impossible for diasporan Africans to undertake a missionary enterprise, but colonization societies paved the way by putting in place people who would be the nucleus and support for missionary work.

Lord Mansfield's judgment of 1772 making slavery illegal in Britain had national as well as international consequence on slave trade and slavery itself. The judgment had an impact on both religious and political thinking. The appearance of the era of missionary and colonization societies was a direct result of the judgment, because one of the issues connected with the emancipation was the resettlement of former slaves. In Britain, the Committee for the "Black Poor" was organized to address the problem. In America too, colonization societies soon were founded. As early as 1800, colonization societies in Virginia and Maryland were in contact with humanitarians in Britain. The American colonization societies, together with the Committee for the "Black Poor" in London, sponsored a settlement in

Sierra Leone for former slaves. It was not until 1817 that the American Colonization society was founded. The president of the society was General Bushrod Washington, the brother of George Washington, the first President of the United States. [1]

Colonization societies in both Britain and America got some former slaves interested in becoming settlers or in engaging in trans-Atlantic trade with the idea of improving the situation of people of African descent in Africa, Britain, and America. From 1800 on, African descendants migrated to Africa, mostly to Sierra Leone and Liberia. Some Africans of the diaspora financed other Africans' emigration. Paul Cuffee, a prosperous, ship owning Quaker, was one of the sponsors, and he himself made a trip to Sierra Leone in 1810. He wanted to go again in 1812 but the war stopped him. In 1816, he again sponsored some African emigration. "Emigrationist" ideas existed in both America, Britain, and the Caribbean. The emigration emphasis in the African American community lasted a long time, even entering into the early part of this century.

Not all who were willing to sponsor a settlement succeeded. An example of this was Albert Thorne and his settlement plan for Malawi. Thorne was a native of Barbados who grew up as a youth in Edinburgh, Scotland and studied medicine there. He was of the conviction that Africans of the diaspora were better prepared by their experience to redeem Africa. Between 1894 and 1897, Dr. Thorne worked on a plan to establish a settlement in the area around Lake Malawi. He saw the colonization of the European nations as exploitation of the African people and resources. Malawi elites, however, were suspicious of a settlement by the Africans of the diaspora. [2] Thorne's plan did not work for he failed to find supporters for the project. [3]

The idea of colonization was shared by a number of Africans of the diaspora. Sometimes encouragement to establish a colony came from some among their company who had already emigrated to Africa or were there as missionaries. A few years before Thorne started on his plan, Ousley, a missionary in Mozambique, publicly argued for establishing a colony under the Africans of the diaspora. [4] Ousley was sent to Africa as missionary by the American Board of Commissioners for Foreign Missions (ABCFM) in December 1884.

The discussion on colonization shows that the missionary enterprise of diaspora Africans was helped by the people who had settled in Africa. These Africans formed a core and support group for the missionaries among them. The evangelization of Sierra Leone, Liberia, and Benin cannot be discussed without taking into consideration the impact of the trade and commerce of the Africans of the diaspora and the influence of their settlements. [5]

THE DOCTRINE OF PROVIDENTIAL DESIGN

There is a second reason for discussing the colonization efforts of Africans of the diaspora: the Doctrine of Providential Design. Erroneous as the Doctrine was, it did capture the minds of some Africans of the diaspora to emigrate to Africa as settlers and/or missionaries. To understand the Doctrine, we must go back to the early years of the emancipation. Lord Mansfield's judgment very much helped the cause of anti-slavery groups and Quakers. These groups had been fighting for a long time for the abolition of slave trade and slavery in America. Unlike colonization societies, the Quakers and anti-slavery groups in America were not interested in colonization but wanted to send liberated Africans back to Africa as missionaries. A doctrine was elaborated to give sanction to their emigrationist plan. The Doctrine stated: "God, in his inscrutable way, had allowed Africans to be carried off into slavery so that they could be Christianized and civilized and return to uplift their kinsmen in Africa."[6]

The Doctrine of Providential Design, as it came to be known, was not accepted by all Africans in America, not even all of those who emigrated to Africa. The Doctrine actually split the African American community, basically because of its emigrationist emphasis. While some felt the return to Africa would be in accordance with Divine will, others felt they had as much right to stay in America as any other race that had come to settle. The emigrationist position must be understood in the light of the social, political, and economic experience of the African Americans. Some of those who espoused the Doctrine were particularly concerned with questions of justice and dignity. Thus, Lott Carey, a Baptist minister from Richmond, Virginia, would say: "I am an African and in this country however meritorious my conduct and respectable my character, I cannot receive the credit due either. I wish to go to a country where I shall be estimated by my merits and not by my complexion."[7] Lott Carey went to Liberia under the American Colonization Society. Eventually, the Negro Baptists formed a missionary society bearing his name because of his missionary work and efforts to organize the settlement in its early stages.[8]

The condition of Africans in America did not change. As late as 1901, seventy-six years after Lott Carey had spoken those words, Henry M. Turner, bishop of the African Methodist Episcopal Church spoke of the lack of respect for Africans in America. Writing in the *Voice of the People* Bishop Turner said:

The Negro has a much chance in the United States . . . of being a man . . . as a frog in a snake den. . . . Emigrate and gradually return to the land of the ancestors. . . . The Negro was brought in the providence of

God to learn obedience, to work, to sing, to pray, to preach, acquire
education deal with mathematical abstractions and imbibe the principles
of civilization as a whole, and then return to Africa, the land of his
fathers and bring her his millions.[9]

Bishop Turner never emigrated although he organized the Colored Emigration
and Commercial Association, an organization that had a large following in the
south.

These quoted words of Bishop Turner painted a better picture of the
condition of Africans in America. Note the sentiments of emigrationist policy,
colored with the Doctrine of Providential Design. These sentiments were to
emerge in Marcus Garvey's "Back to Africa Movement."

The more I remember the suffering of my fore fathers, the more I
remember the lynchings in the southern states of America, the more I
will fight on even though the battle seems doubtful. Tell me that I must
turn back and I laugh you to scorn. Go on! Go on! Climb ye the heights
of liberty and cease not in well doing until you have planted the banner
of the Red, the Black and the Green on the hilltops of Africa.[10]

The persistence of the emigrationist ideas has made some scholars suggest
that the desire to return to Africa was more widespread than is generally
believed.[11] African Americans joined the back-to-Africa movement, but only
a small number made it to Africa. Estimates indicate that probably not more
than 25,000 of them went to Africa between 1816-1940. The numbers were
so low that even in 1895, at the height of the back-to-Africa campaign, Turner
lamented that while 2,500 Africans had been lynched in the United States in
the past ten years, only 361 African Americans emigrated to Africa.[12] So
counting the work of the American Colonization Society from 1816-1845 to
colonize Liberia and Sierra Leone, and Marcus Garvey's efforts during the
first quarter of the twentieth century, the total number of emigrants stood at
no more than 25,000. Reasons accounting for this low number include
poverty, so unable to raise money for their families, they had no access to
shipping lines, and in addition, they were harassed by some whites for desiring
to leave.

Along with those who returned to Africa from America through the
sponsorship of the American Colonization Society and missionary groups,
other Africans returned from Britain. They too, returned either as
missionaries, settlers, or to engage in trade and commerce, particularly the
trans-Atlantic trade. They traded in many items with the Caribbean and the
Americas. Africans of the diaspora in Brazil took a leading role in the trans-
Atlantic trade, because they had more significant contacts with Africa than
those Africans in North America and the Caribbean. It is believed that this

was so because Africans of the diaspora in Brazil never completely severed their relations with Africa. Another reason mentioned is that there was a strong African presence in Brazil; and lastly, the leading role is attributed to the fact that slave trade continued to flourish there after it had become illegal elsewhere. Further, unlike their brothers and sisters in North America and the Islands, some of Brazilian Africans emigrated after their liberation. Subsequently, strong trade and commerce relations were established between Africa and Brazil. [13]

Many of those who returned from the land of their sojourn did a good job. Some of the names on the honor roll include missionaries and scholars like: Edward Jones (ordained minister of the Episcopal Church in America), Daniel Coker (cofounder of the African Methodist Episcopal Church), and William Colley. From England came Alexander Crummell and Thomas Birch Freeman; from the Caribbean came Edward W. Blyden, one of the leaders of "intellectual Ethiopianism," a teaching which sought "racial vindication." The teaching rejected the view that Africans were of an inferior race, and it drew its arguments from evidence gained from research in Biblical and classical sources. Drake has explained the origin of Ethiopianism as follows:

Black people under slavery turned to the Bible to "prove" that black people, Ethiopians, were powerful and respected when the white men in Europe were barbarians; Ethiopia came to symbolize all Africa; and throughout the 19th century, the "redemption of Africa" became one important focus of meaningful activity for leaders among the New World Negro. Ethiopianism became an energizing myth in both the New World and Africa itself for those political movements that arose while the powerless were gathering their strength for realistic and rewarding political activity. [14]

For Blyden it was not mere rhetoric that would vindicate Africa, but practical things, projects such as building schools. Blyden worked together with Alexander Crummell as teachers at Liberia College founded in August 1861. Schools did not present a complete solution to the race problems but they went a long way, thus Blyden would say

"The great problem to be solved is whether black men, under favourable circumstances, can manage their efforts . . . with efficiency." Will the efforts put forth in the Alex High School, if efficient and successful contribute to a partial solution of the problem? And, on the other hand, if these efforts fail, will the impression be deepened that the problem is insolvable, and will the gloom which has so rested upon the race increase in destiny? If so, then let me be forever discarded by the black race, and let me be condemned by the white, if I strive not with all my powers, if

I put not forth all my energies to contribute to so important a
solution. [15]

Blyden saw the vindication or "progress of the race" as part of universal
advance of human history, that is, Africans as historical beings had a role to
play toward human development: "we believe that as descendants of Ham
share . . . in the founding of cities and in the organization of government, so
members of the same family, developed under different circumstances, will
have an important part in the closing of the great drama." [16]

There were also Africans of the diaspora who returned from Brazil. [17] All
who returned felt a call to do something in the land of their ancestors.
Speaking about the call, Crummell, an ex-slave and a 1853 graduate at
Cambridge University, England, said:

There seems to me a natural call upon the children of Africa in foreign
lands, to come and participate in the opening treasures of the land of
their fathers. Though these treasures are manifest gift of God to the
Negro race, yet that race reaps but the most partial measure of their
good and advantage. It has always been thus in the past, and now as the
resources of Africa are being more and more developed, extent of our
interest therein is becoming more and more diminutive. The slave trade
is interdicted throughout Christendom; the chief powers of earth have
put a lien upon the system of slavery: interest and research in Africa
have reached a state of intensity; mystery has been banished from some
of her most secret quarters . . . and the sons of Africa in foreign lands,
insane and blinded, suffer the adventurous foreigner, with greed and glut,
to jostle him aside, and seize, with skill and effect upon their rightful
inheritance. [18]

Some of those who did great missionary work were people freed from slave
ships bound for Europe or the New World. When Britain declared slave
trade illegal, it took upon itself a mission to impound any slave ship and set
free the slaves. One of those set free by British Preventive Squadron was
Ajayi. After he and others were enfranchised, Ajayi was given to a missionary
benefactor who gave him the name Samuel Crowther. In 1826 the missionary
took him to England for a few months. When he returned he became a
teacher, and later, the Church Missionary Society (CMS) took him to be their
missionary into the interior of the West coast. Before he undertook the
missionary work, he was sent to the CMS training college in London and was
ordained a priest in 1843; he then went back to Africa to serve. In June 1864,
he was consecrated in Canterbury Cathedral as Bishop of West African
countries beyond British jurisdiction. He died in 1899 at the age of 90.

Most of those who returned had a strong sense of mission—to uplift their race. It was in the light of their achievements that Alexander Crummell spoke of slavery being within the divine plan for the salvation of Africa. Delivering a sermon commemorating the 40th anniversary of the establishment of Liberia, Crummell, said:

> the forced and cruel migration of our race from this continent, and the wondrous providence of God, by which the sons of Africa by hundreds and by thousands, trained, civilized, and enlightened, are coming hither again, bringing large gifts, for Christ and his Church, and their heathen kin. . . . The day of preparation for our race is well nigh ended, the day of duty and responsibility on our part, to suffering, benighted, Africa is at hand. In much sorrow, pain and deepest anguish, God has been preparing the race, in foreign lands, for a great work of grace on this continent. The hand of God is on the black man in all his lands of sojourn for the good of Africa.[19]

Some people among the Africans of the Diaspora criticized the teaching of the Doctrine of Providential Design arguing that it sanctioned slavery and held that the African race was inferior—the race needed slavery to civilize them. Blyden, explaining the doctrine from the position of those who espoused it, said: "When we say that Providence decreed the means of Africa's enlightenment, we do not say that He decreed the wickedness of the instruments. . . . It is not the first time that wicked hands were suffered to execute a Divine purpose."[20]

BOMBAY AFRICANS

Most of the literature on the work of former slaves in Africa is on West Africa, but there was another settlement on the East Coast, and it too had impact on evangelization. It was established by the British at Freretown; this was a settlement for the Africans who had been taken into slavery to the Middle East and Asia—such countries as Saudi Arabia, Iran, and as far as India. Those who returned were mostly children of slaves sold in India. After slavery was declared illegal, children of former slaves in India were put in mission schools. Some of the children were in a school run by Catholic Sisters of Mercy, while others were at the Church of Scotland mission at Aden, and the CMS African Asylum in Nasik, near Bombay. In these schools they were taught English, Bible, and crafts as preparation for work as missionaries.

In 1865, nine of them went to Africa with David Livingstone. In his diary notes of January 22, 1866, Livingstone referred to them as "nine Nassock boys."Writing the notes while in Zanzibar, he wrote: "I have 13 Sepoys, ten Johanna men, nine Nassock boys, two Shupanga boys."[21] One of the "Nassock boys,"Wekhamtani (spelled Wekatani by Livingstone), was fortunate enough to have found his brother and sister still alive when Livingstone's party reached the Lake Malawi area. Wekhamtani remained with his people. [22]

In 1845 the settlement in East Africa began when 150 of the liberated children anchored at Freretown, near Mombasa. The influence of the "Bombay Africans," as they were called, was great although their numbers were small compared to those settled on the Atlantic coast. The missionary activities of the Bombay Africans in Kenya, Ethiopia, and as far south as Mozambique were unique. They opened schools for freed slaves which at one time had a total enrollment of over three thousand. They had some notable people among them; the best known was William Jones. He became known in Europe and America as a writer of African geography and culture. He was an influential writer whose work had a great impact upon many Europeans.

THE INFLUENCE OF THE AFRICANS OF THE DIASPORA

The emigrationist emphasis persisted in the African community in the Americas and Caribbean until the early part of this century. As mentioned above, emigrationist ideas bloomed in the teachings of Marcus Garvey and his "Back to Africa Movement." Garvey himself returned to Africa. He was originally from Jamaica, but had spent many years in America. He started a magazine, *Black World*, which became a vehicle for his "Back to Africa Movement." He became to be known as the "Black Moses." In many respects he is thought to have revived the ideas of Turner and Blyden, but at a less sophisticated level. Emigrationist ideas of Garvey were opposed by many of the Africans in diaspora in the same way as the generations before them had rejected the ideas when they first emerged in the nineteenth century. Those who opposed the idea of moving back to Africa argued that Black people did not have to go to Africa to "redeem" and "regenerate" it. There was a belief among some of the Africans of the diaspora that they were destined to redeem Africa. This determinism may have influenced some to accept the doctrine of Providential Design. The idea of regeneration referred to a reclaiming of Africa's glorious past as seen in Biblical and historical sources. The work of reclaiming Africa's glorious past still continues. Representative works in this field include those by Chiekh Anta Diop, Maulana Karenga, and members of the Association for the Study of Classical Antiquity (ASCAC), and to a certain extent, the Afrocentric movement led by Molefi Asante. [23]

Nonemigrationists could be divided into two groups: those who emphasized sponsoring missionaries or their projects in Africa, and those who sought to "redeem" Africa by educating Africans who would return to their homes and work among their own people. In the early days, nonemigrationists supported missionary ventures or projects in Africa. Africans of the diaspora sent over two thousand missionaries to various parts of Africa from the 1800s to the early part of this century. [24] Their emphasis was on self-improvement of people, thus the emergence of "industrial missionaries." Industrial missions taught self-improvement of people through agriculture. Thus, Agbebi, an industrial missionary to West Africa, called his preaching "the gospel of coffee, cocoa, cotton and work as well as the scripture." [25] This idea was soon to be followed by Africans educated by Black schools and Colleges in America. A good example is John Chilembwe and his Providence Industrial Mission in Malawi.

It is important to mention that some of those missionaries were sponsored by the American Board of Commissioners for Foreign Missions (ABCFM) and later, the Southern white churches: Southern Presbyterians, Baptists, Seventh Day Advertists, and Methodists. Early in the planning of missionary activities in Africa, white churches in the south felt that freed Africans would be "appropriate additions to the missionary teams because they would be more resistant physically to the diseases which had plagued white missionaries and because their racial affinity give them close, sympathetic ties to the African people." [26] The participation of the Africans of the diaspora in the evangelization of Africa, and thus participation in the shaping of contemporary African history, was not well known until the 1970s when some scholars in America, Europe, and Africa started doing research and writing on the subject. [27]

The second group of nonemigrationists emphasized the necessity of educating Africans in African American schools. The chief advocate of this view was W. E. Du Bois. The idea became very acceptable among African American educators and churches. Continental Africans were educated at African American colleges. Some of them became leading statesmen, educators, and doctors. The list of those men is too long to be included in as small a work as this one. Those men came from almost all parts of Africa. From Nigeria came Nmamdi Azikiwe; James Emman Kwegyri Aggrey, and Kwame Nkrumah came from Ghana; A. B. Xuma, [28] and J. R. Rathebe were from South Africa; and from Malawi came John Chilembwe, Daniel Malekebu, and Hastings Banda.

When Tuskegee Institute in Alabama opened its doors to Azikiwe, little did people know he would become one of Africa's famous politicians. Back home he became a newspaper publisher and played a leading role in the struggle for independence in Nigeria. He continued to be active after independence as President. Nkrumah, like Azikiwe, was a statesman. A Howard graduate, he fully engaged himself in the struggle for liberation in Ghana and he became

Ghana's first President. Nkrumah became the foremost African spokesperson for the unity of Africa or Pan Africanism. The concept of Pan-Africanism sought to express the idea of freedom and solidarity of all Africa. The concept emerged toward the end of the last century to oppose British imperial policies in Africa. Although the idea of Pan-Africanism did not originate in Africa, Nkrumah used the term to raise social and political consciousness among Africans and to lay foundation for continental unity.[29] Nkrumah was not only a statesman, but also one of Africa's leading social philosophers.[30]

Pan-Africanism was a term coined outside Africa by the Africans of the diaspora.   Henry Sylvester Williams, the Trinidad lawyer, and Bishop Alexander Walter of the African Methodist Episcopal Zion (AMEZ) Church organized the first Pan-African Congress held in London in 1900. Pan-African Congress was a movement which inspired the spirit of nationalism among intellectuals all over the African world.   The gathering in London was organized as a forum of protest against the white colonizers and at the same time to make an appeal to missionaries and abolitionists among the British people to protect Africans from continued exploitation of the Western world, Britain in particular.   Two other conferences followed—in 1919 (Paris) and 1945 (Manchester).   A 1958 conference was the first to be held in Africa. Pan-Africanism became a compelling idea in the African diaspora because it was perceived as a way by which the race would vindicate itself, as Du Bois put it: "the African movement means to us what the Zionist movement to Jews, the centralization of race effort and the recognition of racial front." We get another understanding from Marcus Garvey: "all of us may not live to see the higher accomplished of an African empire so strong and powerful, as to compel the respect of mankind, but we in our life-time can so work and act as to make the dream possibility within another generation."[31]

Aggrey was born in 1875 in Ghana within the African Methodist Episcopal Zion (AMEZ) missionary field. In 1902 the bishop of the AMEZ in New York visited Ghana with the aim of seeing possibilities for establishing an Africanization process of the Church.   It was through this policy that the Church sent Aggrey to Livingstone college in North Carolina.   This was a college of the AMEZ.   After twenty years in America he returned home to Africa, where he became one of the most famous Africans.   He travelled across the continent on the Phelps-Stokes Commission.[32] This Commission was set up by the Colonial Office in Britain in conjunction with the Foreign Missions Office in America, to "make a survey of educational condition in Africa and conditions in Africa." The commission was funded by Phelps-Stokes, hence its name.   Two trips were made by the commission, and its reports were published in London and New York.

Aggrey was an orator and this gift together with others allowed him to emerge as "black world's ideal ambassador to the white, the white world's ideal ambassador to the black."[33]   The words of D. D. T. Jabavu better described Aggrey's gift of persuasion: "Without doubt," wrote Jabavu about Aggrey's brief visit to South Africa, "he has done more than any other visitor I know of, in the brief space of time, to persuade people in our circumstances of the necessities of racial co-operation between white and black."[34]

John Chilembwe came to America in 1897. He entered Lynchburg Seminary in Virginia and earned a bachelor of divinity degree. Throughout his studies at Lynchburg, Chilembwe was sponsored by black Baptists in Philadelphia. He returned home to Malawi in 1900. He built an Industrial Mission station and a school. His philosophy of education was influenced by Booker T. Washington's philosophy of self-improvement of African peoples. (Born a slave on a Virginia plantation, Washington became the founder of Tuskegee Normal and Industrial Institute in Alabama. Through personal achievements with the institute and his speeches and writings calling for African American self-improvement, he won national and international acclaim.) He outlined his philosophy in his Atlanta Exposition Address of 1895, warning African Americans that "It is at the bottom of life we must begin, and not at the top."[35]

The Negro Baptists helped Chilembwe achieve his aim by sending him teachers, Emma B. Delany and Landon N. Cheek, both of whom were good choices for the new mission. Chilembwe was troubled by the condition of his people who were oppressed by settlers and colonial administrators alike. Not long after his return home, Chilembwe found himself a spokesperson to the British administrators of the Protectorate and the settlers. He addressed issues of justice, equality, and human dignity, and he also spoke on international issues as these affected his people.

He was bold and eloquent in expressing the feelings of his people. The following letter which he wrote to a settler owned newspaper, "The Nyasaland Times" reveals those qualities.

> We understand that we have been invited to shed our innocent blood in this world's war which is now in progress throughout the wide world. . . . A number of our people have already shed their blood, while others are crippled for life. . . . Police are marching in the various villages persuading well built natives to join the war. . . . Will there be any good prospects for the natives after the war? Shall we be recognized as anybody in the best interest of civilization . . .? [Our people] have played a patriot's part in the spirit of gallantly. But in the time of peace the Government has failed the underdog. In time of peace everything is for Europeans only.[36]

Chilembwe was protesting the drafting of Malawians to fight in the First World War. He was outraged because the government had refused to compensate the surviving relatives of those who died fighting in Ashanti (in

Ghana) and Somali on the side of the British. He was further protesting the racial discrimination practiced by the government and land appropriation by the settlers. It was all this which moved him to say:

> We understand that this . . . is a war of free nations against a devilish system of imperial domination and national spoilation. . . . Let the rich men, bankers, titled men, store-keepers, and landlords go to war and get shot. Instead the poor Africans who have nothing to own in the present world, who in death leave a long line of widows and orphans in utter and dire distress are invited to die for a cause which is not theirs . . . a war whose cause they do not know.[37]

Chilembwe's protests did not produce change. Left with no alternative for social and political transformation, Chilembwe and his followers took up arms. He died on January 15, 1915 in the struggle for social justice, and his mission station was demolished.

One of the alumni of the Chilembwe's school, Daniel Malekebu, also furthered his education in the U.S.A. It was through the invitation of his teacher, Emma Delany, that Daniel Malekebu traveled to America to study, but he worked his way to America. He studied at the National Training School in Durham, North Carolina, and graduated as a medical doctor at Meharry Medical College, Tennessee. He specialized in tropical medicine at Temple University, Philadelphia, Pennsylvania, before going to study theology at Moody Bible Institute in Chicago. Malekebu returned home in 1921 with the express aim of reopening the mission station Chilembwe had started. The colonial government did not allow him to stay in the country for fear that he might organize another uprising, as Chilembwe had done in 1915.

Under the directives of his sponsors in America, the Lott Carey Convention, Malekebu and his wife, Flora Zeto,[38] were assigned to South Africa where he remained for nine months as a missionary at Shilo Baptist Church, Cape Town. From there, he was sent as a missionary to Liberia where he and his wife served as the only teachers for 150 students at Ricketts Institute, Brewerville, near Monrovia. Malekebu also "treated the sick as could be done with limited medical supplies and no hospital."[39]

While in Liberia Malekebu wrote to the Colonial Office in London through the Aborigines Protective Society, which was also based in London. Malekebu appealed the decision of the colonial administration in Malawi to deny him staying in his native country. The colonial government eventually cleared the problem, and he was allowed to return. He returned home in 1926 as a physician and a minister. Malekebu did a wonderful job in recreating a sense of self-development among the people. Describing his work in a denominational paper, *Mission Herald*, Dr. C. C. Adams, Secretary of the National Baptist Convention Foreign Mission Board, wrote:

It was not until 1926, when Dr. and Mrs. Malekebu came here that the mission experienced its great miraculous physical expansion and religious, moral and economic influenced. From 1926-1938, Dr. Malekebu baptized with his own hands 17,000persons, as often as a 300 a day. Since 1938 his ministers and evangelists have baptized many more thousands. Five years ago, Dr. Malekebu organized the National Baptist Assembly of Africa with a Woman's Auxiliary, which Mrs. Malekebu heads, and a young People's Union with a total membership of 300,000. . . . There are more than 30 buildings on the mission proper, 15 of which are beautiful, spacious and commodious, built of burnt brick. A large modern Church that would do justice to the corner of any American city sets them off as dedicated to Christ.[40]

Malekebu did more in the succeeding years. In 1974, his alma-mater, Meharry Medical College, African American Churches, the City of Nashville, Tennessee, and the State of Tennessee itself, honored him for his work as an educator, physician, minister, and theologian. He received the "FiftyYears of Service to Humanity Award" and also a presidential citation from President Lyndon B. Johnson.[41]

Dr. Banda, like Azikiwe, is another African who became a leader of a nation after some training in black schools in America. Banda studied at Wilberforce Institute in Ohio (now Ohio State University), Chicago University, and Meharry Medical College before going to Scotland and England, where he remained for over thirty years. After a short stay in Ghana, he returned home to join the struggle for independence. Dr. Banda became the first Prime Minister and President of independent Malawi.

CONCLUSION

The missionary work of the Africans of the diaspora can be divided into two periods: the period before and after 1900. These periods show two different characteristics. First, in the pre-1900 era, especially during the nineteenth century; missionary activity was very much influenced by the Doctrine of Providential Design; missionary activity also included sending settlers and missionaries to Africa. The idea of settling in Africa sought to underline the concept of "redeeming" and vindicating the African race from centuries of humiliation. It was believed that as settlers they would be models for progress. In other words, before the 1900s and a little after, Africans of the diaspora had a messianic complex about their ministry in Africa. While they continued to go to Africa as missionaries after 1900, they did not have the messianic attitude of the earlier generations. The idea of colonization had died out. When Marcus Garvey and his "Back to Africa Movement" resurrected the idea of settling in Africa, the messianic mind was not the main emphasis.

In the second phase, which started about 1900, missionary work began to include cultural exchange through the training of Africans in America. The prevailing idea was that Africans properly trained would lead their people towards redemption. Thus the cultural programs by such schools as Fisk University and Tuskegee Institute. (The Jubilee Singers from Fisk University visited South African in 1898.[42]) Tuskegee introduced its cultural exchange program in 1900.[43] Among the graduates of this cultural exchange program were Tengo Jabavu and John Dube. Tengo Jabavu distinguished himself as a leader of his people in the early part of this century. Trained as a journalist, he was a politician, churchman, and educator. As a journalist he edited *Isigidimi* while he was at Lovedale, and later he edited *Imvo Zabantusundu*. He fought hard for the establishment of the University College of Fort Hare, the highest institution of learning for black people in South Africa. His name came to be identified with Fort Hare so much so that the people knew the college as "*Koleji ka Jabavu*" (Jabavu's College).[44]

From 1900 on, vindication of the race ceased to be dominant feeling among missionaries of African descent. In their various fields, these missionaries identified with and joined the local people in their struggle for justice and dignity. For example, Rev. Thomas Branch, of the Seventh Day Adventist Church in Malawi, became involved in the people's struggle for land. White settlers used legal means and sheer brute force to appropriate land from the people, leaving them without any means of livelihood. Rev. Branch's quest for justice for the people resembled that of Rev. Sheppard who collected the data on atrocities committed by Belgians in Zaire. When the report was published it drew worldwide attention to the dehumanizing situation of Zairians.[45]

It is interesting to observe that in a period when missionary work was not generally open to women, African American Churches sent a large number of women as missionaries to various parts of Africa. In this work we have mentioned Clara Howard, who was a missionary in Zaire, Emma Delany who went to Malawi, and Mrs. Malekebu. From Walton Johnson we get names of seven other women missionaries in Africa.[46] To Zaire went Misses: Lulu Fleming, Nira Gordon, Marie Fearing, Althea Brown, Ada Jackson, and Mrs. Rochester. Miss Nancy Jones was a missionary first in Mozambique and was later sent to Zimbabwe. These women engaged mostly in teaching, with a special emphasis in home economics.

Africans of the diaspora did a lot in their missionary enterprise in Africa. It is difficult to fathom the depth and width of what they did with very minimal financial resources and sometimes limited moral support both at home and abroad.

NOTES

1. Drake, *The Redemption of Africa and Black Religion* (Chicago, Ill.: Third World Press, 1970), 42. It may be also interesting to note that Henry Washington, a former slave of George Washington, the first President of the United States, was one of the early Africans of the diaspora to return to Africa (Sanneh, *West African Christianity: The Religious Impact* (New York: Orbis Books, 1983), 79-80).

2. See *Central African Planter*, 13, no. 2, March 1897.

3. M. M. Mapuranga has a short account of Dr. Thorne's failed attempt: "Dr. Thorne's Unsuccessful Attempt at Setting a Black colony in Malawi, 1894-1923," *Malawi Journal of Social Science*, 5 (1976): 44-56.

4. Letter of Benjamin F. Ousley, December 1887, *Fisk Herald* (Nashville), vol. V, January 1888.

5. Sanneh, *West African Christianity*, 79-81.

6. Drake, *Redemption of Africa*, 41.

7. *Ibid.*, 53.

8. Sanneh, *West African Christianity*, 92-94.

9. Quoted by Drake, *Redemption of Africa*, 52.

10. Amy Jacques-Garvey, ed., *The Philosophy and Opinions of Marcus Garvey* Mclelland and Stewart, ed. (New York: Atheneum, 1986), 97.

11. See August Meir, *Negro Thought in America* (Ann Arbor, Mich.: University of Michigan Press, 1963).

12. *Voice of Missions*, August 1895.

13. An article of interest in the area of African presence in Brazil is by R. K. Kent, "Palmares: an African State in Brazil," *Journal of African History*, VI, no. 2, (1965): 161-175. For the continued presence of African culture in Brazil, see Abdias do Nascimento, "Quilombismo: The African Brazilian Road to Socialism," *African Culture: The Rhythm of Unity*, Molefi Kete Asante and Kariam Welsh Asante, eds. (Trenton, N.J.: Africa World Press, 1990), 175-191.

14. Drake, *Redemption of Africa*, 11.

15. E. W. Blyden, "A Vindication of the African Race," *Liberia's Offering* (New York: J. A. Gray, 1862), 31.

16. Blyden, *Selected Letters of Edward Wilmot Blyden*, Hollis R. Lynch, ed. (New York: KTO Press, 1978), 28.

17. See David A. Ross, "The Career of Domingo Martinez in the Bight of Benin 1833-64" *Journal of African History,* 1, (1965): 79-90. As a background to the work of the diaspora Africans from Brazil see Pierre Verger, *Bahia and the West Coast Trade (1549-1851)* (Ibadan, Nigeria: Ibadan University Press, 1964).

18.   Quoted by Joseph Harris, "Introduction to the African Diaspora," *Emerging Themes of African History*, T. O. Ranger, ed. (Nairobi, Kenya: East African Publishing House, 1968), 147. Alexander Crummell was writing from Liberia to a friend in New York in 1860. The letter was published in 1861 with the title, "The Relations and Duties of Free Colored Men in America to Africa."

19.   Drake, *Redemption of Africa*, 51.

20.   Quoted by Drake, *Ibid.*, 60.

21.   Groves, *Planting Christianity in Africa*, vol. I, 200.

22.   *Ibid.*, 334.

23.   Chiekh Anta Diop, *The African Origin of Civilization: Myth or Reality*, Mercer Cook ed. and trans. (Westport, N. Y.: Lawrence Hill and Co., 1974). The French version appeared in 1955 by Présence Africaine; Maulana Karenga and H. Carrauthers, *The proceeding of Selected of the proceeding of the First and Second conference of the Association for the Study of Classical Civilization*, 24-26 Feb. 1984 (6224 AFE), Los Angeles, and 1-3 March 1985 (6225 AFE), Chicago. *Africa Kemet and the African World View: Research Rescue and Restoration* (Los Angeles, Ca.: University of Sankore Press, 1986); Molefi Kete Asante, *Afrocentricity*, new rev. ed. (Trenton, N.J.: Africa World Press, 1988); and by the same author *The Afrocentric Idea* (Philadelphia, Pa.: Temple University Press, 1987).

24.   Jacobs et. al. have done a good job in showing the extent of the work of missionaries of the diaspora in Africa. See Sylvia M. Jacobs, ed., *Black Americans and the Missionary Movement in Africa* (Westport, Conn.: Greenwood Press, 1982). Also see Walter L. Williams, *Black Americans and the Evangelization of Africa 1877-1900* (Madison, Wis.: University of Wisconsin Press, 1982). Walton R. Johnson has a short account of the work of Africans of the diaspora in Southern Africa. He has a list of 38 names of missionaries of the diaspora in Central and Southern Africa, "The Afro-American Presence in Central and Southern Africa, 1880-1905," *Journal of African Affairs*, 4, no. 1 (January 1979): 29-44.

25.   J. B. Webster, "The Bible and the Plough," *Journal of the Historical Society of Nigeria*, 2 (December 1963): 426.

26.   Walton Johnson, "The Afro-American presence," *Mission Herald*, 81 (1885): 508.

27.   Joseph E. Harris, "Introduction to the African Diaspora," and George Shepperson, "The African Abroad or the African Diaspora" in T. O. Ranger, ed. *Emerging Themes in African History*, 147-176; also by George Shepperson, "Notes on Negro American Influences on the Emergence of African Nationalism," *Journal of African History*, 1, no. 2 (1960): 309-310; Walton Johnson, "The Afro-American Presence in Central and Southern Africa 1880-1905," *Journal of Southern African Affairs*, 4, no. 1 (1979): 28-42.

28. See Richard D. Ralston, "American Episodes in the making of an African leader: A Study Case of Alfred B. Xuma (1893-1962)," *International Journal of Historical Studies*, 6, no. 1 (1973): 72-93.

29. David Apter, *Pan-Africanism*. (New York: Praeger, 1968), 31.

30. Among his important writings in this area is *Consciencism: Philosophy and Ideology for De-colonization*, 2nd ed. (New York: Monthly Review Press, 1970).

31. Amy Jacques-Garvey, *Marcus Garvey*, 5.

32. Thomas Jesse Jones, ed., *Education in Africa: A Study of West, South and Equatorial Africa by Africa Education Commission under the Auspices of the Phelps-Stokes Fund and Foreign Mission Societies of North America and Europe* (London: Phelps Stocks Foundation,1921; New York: Oxford University Press, 1962); also Thomas Jesse Jones, ed., *Education in Africa: A Study of East Central and South Africa by the Second African Education Commission under the Auspices of Phelps-Stokes Fund, in Cooperation with the International Education Board* (London: Phelps Stocks Foundation, 1925; New York: Oxford University Pres, 1962).

33. Adrian Hastings, *Christianity in Africa* (New York: Seabury; London: Geoffrey Champman, 1976), 8.

34. He was the son of Tengo Jabavu who studied at Tuskegee Institute. D. D. T. Jabavu studied at Lovedale in South Africa. He graduated with honors in English at London University and also held a diploma of Education at Birmingham University, England. See Robert H. W. Shepherd, *Lovedale, South Africa: The Story of a Century 1841-1941* (Lovedale, South Africa: Lovedale Press, 1941).

35. Booker T. Washington, *Up From Slavery* (New York: Doubleday and Company, 1963), 159.

36. George Shepperson and Tom Price, *The Independent African: John Chilembwe and the Origins, Setting and Significance of the Nyasaland Native Rising of 1915* (Edinburgh: Edinburgh University Press, 1959), 238.

37. *Ibid.*, 234-235.

38. Flora E. Zeto, born in Zaire, was adopted by Miss Clara Howard, a missionary in Zaire. Miss Howard returned to America when Flora was about 5 and began teaching at her alma mater, Spelman College, Atlanta, Georgia. This was to be Flora's second home for many years until she married Dr. Daniel Malekebu on March 26, 1919 in the chapel at Spelman. Mrs. Malekebu was also an alumnae of Spelman.

Toward the end of the last century, entering into the twentieth, a number of Spelman graduates went to Africa as missionaries, among them Mrs. Emma Delany, of Fernadina Beach, Florida, who went to Malawi to teach at Chilembwe's school.

39. From the personal files of Dr. and Mrs Malekebu, Alumnae office, Spelman College.

40. *The Mission Herald*, November/December 1949.

41. *Mission Herald*, 1974.

42. *Christian Recorder*, June 30, 1898.

43. About this cultural exchange we refer to the reader *The Report of the Tuskegee Institute Task Force on its Visit to the Republic of South Africa*, September 25, 1874, 7-9.

44. Shepherd, *The Independent African*.

45. R. Slade, *English Speaking Missions in the Congo Independent State* (Brussels: Academie Royale Des Sciences Coloniales), 254.

46. Johnson, "The African-America Presence," 30, 31.

5

African Prophets and Evangelists

The work of Western missionaries would not have accomplished much if it were not for the interest and enthusiasm in the Gospel of the African Christians themselves. Christianity continues to grow, rolling like a bush fire since its second planting; its unprecedented growth is the direct result of dedication and hard work on the part of lay people and their clergy. It is hard to find words good enough to describe the spirit of joy, eagerness for the Gospel, and willingness to share it that lay people have in Africa. From every corner of the continent there have been people who have given themselves to the work of evangelism. A list of their names waits to be written. In this chapter we will give a brief sketch of the life and work of a few of them. The names in this chapter exclude those of early missionaries already mentioned, such as Crowther, Crummell, Chilembwe, and others.

WEST AFRICAN PROPHETS

William Wade Harris

The work of spreading the Gospel from the West Coast into the interior of the continent is associated with the name of William Wade Harris or Prophet Harris as he was widely known. Prophet Harris did not begin his ministry until he was sixty. Harris was born near Palmas and the Ivory Coast border. He first served as a teacher (1892-1909) at the American Methodist School in Liberia. He was himself a graduate of that school. Harris was a political activist and was imprisoned three times because of his political activities—in 1893, 1896 and 1910.[1] In 1909 he publicly pulled down the Liberian flag and in its place hoisted the Union Jack (the British flag).

This act put Harris in the limelight. However, he did not become popular as a politician but as a preacher. Harris was converted at the age of twenty-one but did not become involved with preaching until the angel Gabriel appeared to him in a vision while in prison. The angel commanded him to preach and heal. After his release from prison, Harris started his ministry. From 1913 to 1915 he walked and preached from Liberia, Ivory Coast, Ghana, and back to Ivory Coast. His ministry drew many people to Christ. Estimates of his converts during this period range from 60,000 to 100,000. Harris was not sponsored by anyone or Church and did not accept donations or gifts.

On his evangelistic campaigns Harris was seen with his cross, Bible, and bowl for baptism. He was a very religious man. His faith and life bore him the admiration of many. A French missionary writing about Harris said that his "faith is nourished by verses borrowed from the Scriptures. He lives in a supernatural world in which the people, ideas, the affirmations, cosmology and the eschatology of the Bible are more real than the things he sees and hears materially."[2]

Arrests were not a thing of the past for Harris when he became a preacher. After preaching for two years in Ivory Coast, French authorities sent him back to Liberia. He was arrested because he was an alien and because the French authorities had a fear of new religious movements. The French prohibited Protestant missionaries from preaching in the interior, and this was what Harris was doing.[3] It is worth noting that at the time of his arrest, he was preaching and baptizing at Port Bueto, near Abidjan, the capital of Ivory Coast. The soldier who had been sent to arrest him, together with his guide, were both baptized before they took him away.[4]

The work of Harris in West Africa had a significant influence in Liberia, Ghana, and even Ivory Coast where the authorities attempted to crush his movement once they had expelled him. Harris never established a Church bearing his name; he told his converts to build a chapel and encouraged them to join a Church of their choice. This changed after he died, when some of his Ivory Coast converts came together and founded their own Church, calling it *Eglise Harrisisté*.

Garrick Braide

As the ministry of Harris was coming to a close, another evangelist, by the name of Garrick Braide emerged in the Niger Delta. Braide was born in Abonema village, a famous traditional religious center for pilgrimage among the Kalabari people of Southern Nigeria. In 1906 he joined religious instructions, catechumen, in his own village and was baptized in 1910.[5]

Braide was confirmed two years later. Since the early times of his Christian life, Braide displayed deep spiritual qualities and powers. Braide's pastor, M. A. Kramer, observed these qualities in that early period. Writing in the official Church paper, *Niger Delta Pastorate Chronicle*, Kramer said, "there had never been any instance where Garrick consented to pray (for) any sick person in which prayers failed to be efficacious. At other times he would predict the death of someone, and the recovery of another of whom all hopes of recovery had been given up by friends and relations and it always happens."[6]

Braide soon became an evangelist, preaching in the area around his home region. He gained popularity and attracted people of all walks of life to his campaigns. The CMS Niger Mission records of 1916 attests to his influence in evangelism. According to the reports of the CMS, the Niger Mission admitted 2,916 into the Anglican Community through baptism, two-thirds of these being done in and around Braide's people.[7] In spite of the phenomenal success of his evangelistic campaigns, the Church authorities were unhappy. Bishop Johnson argued that Braide's mass conversions brought a poor quality of Christians into the Church because Braide himself had not been well trained. The situation was soon compounded by Braide when he declared himself a prophet in 1916. In February 1916 Bishop Johnson declared Braide unwelcome in the country. Mostly through the evidence given by Bishop Johnson, the colonial administrators arrested him. He spent the rest of his life in prison, dying in the influenza epidemic of 1918.

Simon Kimbangu

Another prophet emerged in Zaire, the Prophet Simon Kimbangu. Kimbangu was born in September 1889 at Nkamba in Zaire, converted in 1915, and baptized at the Baptist Church at Ngombe-Lutete in the Mbanza-Ngugu region. It was not until March 1921 that he began preaching and healing in his own village of Nkamba.[8] It was not long before the news of his success in preaching and healing miracles reached far and wide. People from different denominations came in numbers to hear Kimbangu. Others brought their sick to him to be healed. Soon a great revival emerged which was to cover the whole lower region of Zaire. His followers gave him the title *Ngunza*, translated Prophet or Messiah. He ordained twelve of his followers and authorized them to preach, heal, and to install others as local leaders.

Just as Catholic missionaries had opposed Harris in the Ivory Coast, to the Catholics and other missionaries in Zaire, Kimbangu had become a threat. Hospitals were not being well attended since most patients were going to Kimbangu. Churches, too, were being poorly attended. Through the instigation of Catholic missionaries, Belgium officials arrested Kimbangu in September 1921. He was tried of subversion and sentenced to one hundred and twenty lashes to be followed by execution. The death sentence was commuted by the King of Belgium. He was flogged and sent to Lubamba prison where he died in October 1951.

His life and work inspired many, so many that even when he was in prison his following continued to grow. Persecutions and deportations (thirty-seven thousand persons deported to different parts of Zaire) did not slow the growth of the movement. This was the beginning of the Kimbanguist Movement which is now the largest Indigenous Church in Africa. Kimbangu's ministry lasted only five months but today "the Church of Jesus Christ on earth through the Prophet Simon Kimbangu" (EJCSK) is the largest in Zaire. The Kimbanguist Church, as it is commonly known, became member of the World Council of Churches in 1968. The Kimbanguist Church is unique in its attempts toward indigenization of Christianity.[9]

AFRICAN MISSIONARIES AND EVANGELISTS

Tiyo Soga

On August 12, 1871 was a sad day for Africans in South Africa; Tiyo Soga, one of the greatest names in mission chronicles of the land had died. Soga was the first African Presbyterian minister in South Africa. Born to the family of a counselor to Chief Ngqika and of his successor Sandile, Tiyo Soga went to Lovedale Institute, a school set up by the Glasgow Missionary Society for the training of Africans and whites in South Africa for missionary work.[10] Lovedale seminary opened on July 21, 1841 with William Govan as its principal. The life of the young institute was soon disturbed by conflicts within the Church at home. In 1843 Scottish Presbyterians split into two groups: the Free Church of Scotland and the Church of Scotland. In the following year the Glasgow Missionary Society turned its work in South Africa over to the Foreign Mission Committee of the Free Church of Scotland. Continued conflicts at home forced the seminary to close in 1846. Govan returned home to Scotland because he did not know how long it would take to settle the disputes. He took with him one of the brilliant students at the school—this was Tiyo Soga.

Before taking him to Scotland, his mother was asked for permission. The faith of Nosuthu, Tiyo's mother, is noteworthy, she declared: "My son is the property of God; wherever he goes, God goes with him: he is the property of God's servants; wherever they lead he must follow. If my son is willing to go,

I make no objections, for no harm can befall him even across the sea; he is as much in God's keeping there as near to me."[11]

In Scotland Soga continued his education; he returned home in 1848 as a catechist stationed at Chumie. In 1850 war broke in South Africa, and his work was suspended. The Free Church brought him to England in 1851 where he again furthered his education: he matriculated at the University of Glasgow and got admission to the Divinity Hall of the United Presbyterian Church in Edinburgh. He was licensed to preach after his Bachelor of Divinity studies at Divinity Hall, and on December 23, 1856 he was ordained to the ministry in Glasgow, thus being the first African to be trained and ordained as a Presbyterian minister in all of Africa. Before going back home, Soga worked in Scotland for the United Presbyterian Church which had ordained him. He returned home in 1857, where he served his people until his death.

Rev. Soga was a talented man: he was a composer, writer, and translator. He wrote many superb songs and hymns, translated parts of the Bible and Pilgrims Progress into Xhosa, his language. Among his people, Soga was known as a caring pastor and loving preacher. This loving preacher continued to work on translation even as he lay dying; he managed to translate up to the end of chapter 23 of the *Acts of the Apostles* before energy failed him. After *Acts* 23 Soga just managed to scribble, "I have lost strength." He died prematurely at the age of forty-two due to exhaustion in serving his people.

The Lovedale Evangelists

North of South Africa, in Malawi, the two Scottish missions, the Church of Scotland and the Free Church of Scotland, did not lack volunteers in mission. When the first missionary party arrived in Malawi in 1875, it included four South African missionaries, namely William Koyi, Shadrach Ngunana, Mapasso Ntintili, and Isack Wauchope. These men from Lovedale (South Africa) volunteered to go to Malawi as teacher/evangelists. Shadrach Ngunana, the most educated of the four, died at Cape MacClear in 1877, the Scots' first mission settlement. William Koyi, who served the longest, left a distinguished record of service as a teacher/evangelist among the Angoni of northern Malawi. He also died in Malawi. George Williams, another African missionary from South Africa, followed the footsteps of Koyi, serving among the Angoni. He would have stayed in Malawi longer had the Scots not changed their policy toward African evangelists from South Africa.[12]

Tom Bokwito

When Henry Henderson, the Church of Scotland surveyor, was looking for a suitable site for a mission settlement, Tom Bokwito was with him as a missionary associate. Bokwito was a Malawian volunteer in mission recruited in South Africa by the Free Church first missionary party, which had also hired the four South Africans. Bokwito had been taken to South Africa by Livingstone after being freed from a slave party in the Shire Highlands. He was loaned to Henderson as an interpreter. Bokwito played a very active role in the founding of Blantyre mission, the Church of Scotland's mission station. He was an interpreter, teacher, and evangelist. Later, with six other Malawians, Bokwito belonged to a core of Africans to whom Scottish missionaries gave leadership positions at Blantyre mission.

Harry Matecheta

Perhaps the most outstanding of Malawian missionaries were Lewis Bandawe, David Kaunda, and Harry Matecheta. One of the first residents of Blantyre mission station was Kambwiri Matecheta. He had joined Henderson's search party as it passed through his village in its attempt to locate a place for mission settlement. After years of school and consideration, Kambwiri was baptized and given the name Harry. He later became a teacher and evangelist. In 1893 he was appointed head of a missionary party of two Scottish women who privately financed themselves to set up an outstation for Blantyre Mission at Nthumbi, in the central highlands of Malawi. The outstation was soon abandoned because the Portuguese had claim to the area. When it was decided to reopen the mission station in 1898, it was Harry Matecheta who was sent as the teacher-evangelist to the whole central highlands. Matecheta established schools and congregations in the region. Writing in 1931 about the influence and work of Harry Matecheta, Alexander Hetherwick, a Scottish missionary at Blantyre said:

> In the autumn of 1898, it was resolved to re-open the mission within British territory at Panthumbi—the original site of 1893, under the charge of a native evangelist-teacher—one who, in the first period of the work, had gained experience of the people and their character. . . . He had looked forward to returning to Angoniland, and resuming work there, and so he gladly responded to the call to return to Panthumbi. It was a venture, except for guidance from Blantyre he was "on his own" resources. The venture was fully justified by its results. the name of

"Father Harry," as he is lovingly and familiarly called by the people, has been a power for spiritual influence in the whole district. He is respected by all, white and black, government officials, settler, missionary, chiefs and headsmen alike. Ten years later, the Blantyre Presbytery "called" him to prepare for the office and work of the ministry, to which three years afterwards he was ordained. Today he is incharge of four native Churches, with over eight hundred members, a dozen schools . . . and with evangelists training hearers and catechumens for Church membership.[13]

Rev. Harry Matecheta was ordained April 9, 1911. His ordination was the first in Malawi. It was followed by the ordination of his classmate, Rev. Stephen Kundecha, four days later. Matecheta devoted all his life to the work of the Church in the central highlands. He served the Lord to his last days. When he died, he did not leave Malawians with only a legacy of service and devotion, but also a written account of the beginnings of Blantyre Mission.[14] Thus, Matecheta became Malawi's first Church historian.

Lewis Bandawe

In the annals of Blantyre Mission, the name of Lewis Bandawe has a special place. He was born in about 1887 in Mozambique. In 1899, at the age of twelve, Lewis Bandawe crossed the boarder into Malawi.[15] In Malawi, he enrolled in the Blantyre Mission school. At an early age, while at the mission, he became interested in the Christian faith and wanted to work for the Church. When he completed his education, he sought employment with the Church but for some reason, he was turned down. In 1913 the missionaries decided to invite him to work as one of them. This invitation came just after his wedding. Bandawe and his newly wed bride Grace gladly accepted. In the same year they "set out . . . [on foot] on an eight-day long journey from Blantyre to Meheccani in Mozambique."[16]

His assignment in Meheccani was like that of Harry Matecheta, evangelist-teacher. This means that the schoolmaster was an evangelist who preached on weekdays as well as weekends in addition to learning Portuguese. Bandawe did not just teach and learn, he also wrote. Shortly after his arrival at Meheccani, Bandawe wrote a Lomwe grammar book. Bandawe's missionary work was interrupted by the news of the Germans attack on Mozambique. After a brief break, during which he returned to Blantyre (Malawi), Bandawe went back to Meheccani to continue his work. This time he engaged in the translation of the whole of the New Testament and the Psalms; he completed his work in 1928. In the same year, he left Meheccani for good after fifteen years of missionary service in Mozambique.

David Kaunda

Scottish missionaries in northern Malawi invited David Kaunda to become a missionary. He was trained as a teacher by the Free Church of Scotland missionaries at Overtoun Institute at Livingstonia. He was sent to Chisali, in Eastern Zambia, as a temporary evangelist-teacher in 1904. He returned to Chisali in 1905, and in 1907 Kaunda wrote: "many are coming searching. . . . They do not wish me to go away, but to make Chisali as my home."[17] Kaunda did marvelous work at Chisali, the surrounding area and beyond. By 1913, through his work, schools were established in forty-five villages. There were also many converts in those villages so that when white missionaries established stations at Lumbwa and Marambo, they already had a core of Christians with whom they started their work.[18]

Kaunda left Lumbwa to train for the ordained ministry at Livingstonia in 1923. Unlike Harry Matecheta, who was ordained fourteen years after he went into the missionary field, Kaunda was not ordained till 1930, twenty-six years after he first preached at Chisali.[19] The Free Church of Scotland Missions in northern Malawi were very slow to ordain Africans into the ministry.

Kivebulaya

In his book, *The Missionary Factor in East Africa*, Roland Oliver says: "Of the African Anglican evangelists, the most rightly celebrated was the saintly Apolo Kivebulaya."[20] Indeed, Kivebulaya is remembered for his saintly life and remains the most famous African missionary in Uganda. Born of Muslim parents, Kivebulaya became connected with the Church as far back as 1894 when he accompanied a missionary expedition, perhaps as a porter, to Kasagama.[21] In the following year, Apolo Kivebulaya was baptized, became a catechist, and volunteered to go to Toro, Eastern Uganda, as an evangelist-teacher. He was ordained deacon in 1900. He was a simple man, choosing to remain a celibate, with a strong apostolic zeal spending all his life in the Western part of Uganda as a missionary. Writing about his simple life, Louise Pirouet says, "this simplicity, which was one of the marked characteristics, stands in contrast to the complexity and astuteness of many of the Ganda leaders. He was a man of endearing childlikeness . . . there was almost a Franciscan love of poverty and humility . . . by being always ready to go to some new and remote place, he found a milieu in which his spiritual genius was able to flower, and make him an inspiration to many."[22]

Apolo Kivebulaya arrived in Toro in March of 1900. He taught and visited people in their villages. Soon people started attending his catechumen classes, and by the following year the Anglican Church had a record number of baptisms, 75. In 1902 Kivebulaya was moved to Kitagwenda. Kivebulaya suffered a bitter persecution and lived on to establish a flourishing mission at Mbonga in Zaire to the west of Lake Albert.[23]

Victor Mukasa

Another Ugandan early missionary was Victor Mukasa. He was the first to be ordained in the Roman Catholic Church in Uganda. His ordination, in 1913, inspired many and not long after the Catholic Church in Baganda experienced an upsurge of many young men offering themselves for training to the priesthood. In 1939 Mukasa became the first African Bishop in Africa.[24]

CONCLUSION

We observed two types of evangelists during the Western evangelization of Africa. We see the prophetic type, such as Wade Harris and Simon Kimbangu, but we also have the mission sponsored. The prophetic evangelists were not sponsored by any Church, neither did they set out to establish one. These were the charismatic leaders who heard the call to heal body and soul. Harris, Kimbangu, and we might add Braide, were the forerunners of Indigenous Churches which seek fullness of both physical and spiritual life. The difference between these early evangelists and the latter leaders of indigenous Christianity is that the former simply proclaimed the Gospel without establishing Churches.

The second type of early evangelists worked within the various missionary societies, such as the CMS, or within Churches. Braide, Samuel Crowther, and Apolo Kivebulaya were associated with the CMS. Examples of those evangelists and missionaries who worked with Churches include: Tiyo Soga associated with Scottish Churches; the six South African evangelists to Malawi who served under the Free Church of Scotland—William Koyi, Shadrach Ngunana, Mapasso Ntintili, Isaac Wauchope, Yuraia, and George William;

Lewis Bandawe, Harry Matecheta, Joseph Bismark, and Rondau Kaferanjila who worked with the Church of Scotland. Within this type of evangelist and missionary we find a combined position of evangelist and teacher. All of these dedicated men were brought up within the particular Church they served. Their ministries generally tended to extend over the period of their life, while the prophets had their careers cut short by imprisonment. Although the authorities in West Africa imprisoned prophets, in South Africa they were tolerated.

One outstanding contribution of this second group of Africa's early missionaries is found in the field of writing. A number of these evangelist-teachers translated the scriptures into their own languages. Tiyo Soga translated the parts of the New Testament and also Bunyan's *Pilgrims Progress* into Xhosa; Maphophe translated the New Testament into Tsonga; Bandawe the whole of the New Testament and the Psalms into Lomwe. They also wrote other things, for example, Matecheta wrote a short history of Scottish missionary work at Blantyre.

There are many names of early African Christians who spread of the Gospel, but these names do not appear in mission annals. This is because mission chronicles have not been written to reflect African contributions. Things are beginning to change now with the research being done in seminaries and departments of religious studies and history in African universities.

NOTES

1. Concerning details of his imprisonment, see G. A. Gollock, *Sons of Africa* (London: Student Christian Movement, 1928); G. M. Haliburton, *The Prophet Harris* (London: Longman, 1971), originally a Ph.D. dissertation presented in 1966 to the University of London.

2. Gollock, *Sons of Africa*, 199-200.

3. Virginia Thompson and Richard Adolff, *French West Africa* (Stanford, Ca.: Stanford University Press, 1967), 581-582.

4. Harold W. Turner, "Prophets and Politics: a Nigerian Test-Case," *The Bulletin of the Society for African Church History*, 11, no. 1 (1965): 97-118.

5. G. O. M. Tassie, a Ph.D. dissertation presented to the University of Aberdeen, 1969, 351ff.

6. Reprinted in *Lagos Weekly Record*, February 24, 1917, by Rev. S. A. Coker and Garrick Braide.

7. *Proceedings of the Church Missionary Society*, 1916/1917, iv-v.

8. H. Walkin Coxill and Sir Kenneth Grub, *World Christian Handbook* (London: Lutterworth, 1968), 71.

9. William H. Crane has written some illuminating insights into the nature and life of Kimbanguist Church: "The Kimbanguist Church and the Search for Authentic Catholicity," *Christian Century*, no. LXXXVII, vol. 22, June 3, 1970: 691-695.

10. For more information about the multi-racial attempt in education at Lovedale, see R. H. W. Shepherd, *Lovedale, South Africa 1841-1941* (Lovedale, South Africa: Lovedale Press, 1941), 93-98.

11. John A. Chalmers, *Life of Tiyo Soga: A Page of South African Mission Work* (Lovedale, South Africa: Lovedale Press, 1857), 39.

12. I have discussed this change of policy in *The Legacy of Scottish Missionaries in Malawi*, 35-39.

13. Alexander Hetherwick, *The Romance of Blantyre: How Livingstone's Dream Came True* (Fife: Lassodie Press, n.d.), 111-112.

14. Harry Matecheta, *Blantyre Mission: Nkhani ya Ciyambi Cace* (Blantyre, Malawi: Hetherwick Press, 1951).

15. Lewis Bandawe, *Memoirs of a Malawian*, ed. B. Pachai (Blantyre, Malawi: Christian Literature Association of Malawi, 1971), 15.

16. *Ibid.*, 75.

17. Quoted in John McCracken, *Politics and Christianity in Malawi 1875-1940* (London: Cambridge University Press, 1977), 129.

18. *Ibid.*, 130.

19. R. D. McMinn, "A Devoted African Pastor," *Other Lands*, (July 1933): 156.

20. Roland Oliver, *The Missionary Factor in East Africa* (London: Longman, Green and Co., 1952), 193.

21. M. Louise Pirouet, *Black Evangelists: The Spread of Christianity in Uganda 1891-1914* (London: Rex Collings, 1978), 48.

22. *Ibid.*

23. About Kivebulaya's mission work in Zaire see A. B. Llyod, *Apolo of the Pygmy Forest* (Oxford: Claredon Press, 1923).

24. Hastings, *African Christianity* (New York: Seabury; London: Geoffrey Champman, 1976), 7.

II

THEOLOGY

6

Missionary Thought and Practice

In this second part of the book we will attempt to understand the life and problems of Christianity in the missionary Churches. Our investigation into the character of African Christianity will begin by examining missionary praxis during the second phase of the evangelization of African. Our aim in looking at the missionary practice is to access the impact of missionary thought and practice on the African world and life.

THE LEGACY OF THE ENLIGHTENMENT

In a report of a WCC consultation held in Ghana under the auspices of Faith and Order, the African delegates said: "The result of the encounter between Africa and the Northern Hemisphere world has been considerable frustration for many, perhaps for all Africans, at every level."[1] In studying missionary praxis it is illuminating to begin by critically examining, albeit briefly, the spiritual and intellectual background in which the missionary enterprise arose. Western evangelization of Africa started to pick up as the result of a spiritual awakening in Europe. This revival followed a period of skepticism founded in an intellectual climate in which the Christian faith had its foundations shaken. Belief in God as creator was a subject of criticism, and foundations of moral life were questioned. This skepticism or intellectual climate emerged, in part, due to the influence and the success of disciplines such as mathematics and physics or natural science. These disciplines had shown that logical thinking led to objective truth. If the same logical process were applied to other disciplines, such as religion and moral philosophy, people could arrive at objective truth about the state of things or reality. Natural science had opened a possibility for humankind to understand itself and the world more objectively. A new way of knowing or arriving at the truth emerged. This new way eliminated tradition, experience, and myth as modes of knowing. Tradition led to dogmatism or blind acceptance of authority. The problem of experience was said to be its dependence on sense perception. Since sense perception is subjective experience it can only be prejudiced, therefore not accessible for verification by another party. Feelings cannot be proven for they are not based on empirical data. In other words, prejudice rising from subjectivity, makes it impossible to separate facts or objective truth from falsity. Myth was dismissed as void of any rational knowledge for nothing mythical could be demonstrated or proven. Mathematics or natural science had demonstrated that anything could be known and proven by way of reason. If the subject under investigation could not be proven, it was either false or nonexistent. Hence the rise of rationalism or the concept of rationality.

Earlier studies in mathematics and physics or mechanics had come to the conclusion that the world was like a great machine, and that there were laws in nature which controlled movement of everything in the cosmos.[2] Arguments were made by Newton and others that since the physical world could be understood by studying the (mechanical) laws regulating the world, society and human nature could also be understood through laws of nature. Building upon the discoveries of physics, eighteenth century European minds began to take nature, or natural law, as a fundamental concept in understanding everything, including religious beliefs and practices. Everything was subject to laws of nature, including human behavior. Reason was the "key" to understanding the world. Everything was taken to the judgment seat of reason or criticism and that included religion and authority.[3] Reason was also used to understand God. The creator had to be reasonable to create nature with its rational laws, therefore reason could be used to understand the Divine mystery. This view is sometimes known as Deism. Miracles too, were also subject to reason.[4] The aim of the Enlightenment was to rid Christianity of myth and remain with truth only, and truth was that which could be discerned by pure reason.

This way of looking at the world dominated eighteenth century European minds. In fact, it was considered a sign of being truly mature or awakened to question everything. In general, this intellectual climate was believed to be the period of "awakening" in European society, hence the term Enlightenment. It was an "awakening," for society no longer took anything for granted. Europeans had come of age. European enlightened minds left a legacy of the principle of rational reason for the succeeding generations. The impact of these minds on European thinking has continued to influence many disciplines since that time.   For example, to this day, theology still struggles with the relation of faith to reason.   Another example: towards the end of the nineteenth century and into the beginning of twentieth century, New Testament studies wrestled with the place of myth in the Christian faith. These studies questioned the truth of some key issues of the Christian faith; namely, the virgin birth and resurrection.   Rudolph Bultmann's demythologization of the New Testament is a continuation of the Enlightenment project.   Bishop Robinson's book *Honest to God* is a counterargument to the demythologizing of the New Testament. [5] These studies led some New Testament commentators, such as William Barclay, to give oversimplistic interpretations of some miracles, such as the multiplication of bread. [6]

To summarize: we can say the Enlightenment believed in perfection, and in the process it introduced "nature religion." According to this religion, nature gave people all that they needed to know about God and to praise the designer of the great machine, the cosmos. This understanding was advanced by pioneers of modern science, namely, Johann Kepler (1571-1616) and Francis Bacon (1561-1626). The book of nature gave all the laws and principles for understanding deity and humankind. This was a reversal of traditional understanding that the bible was the only source of the knowledge of God. Eventually, this position led some to argue that the bible was not necessary to faith. To maintain that the book of nature was all that people needed to have faith would reduce controversies and conflicts arising from different interpretations of the scriptures.

It was argued that these laws could be empirically demonstrated, therefore there was no reason to believe myths. The Enlightenment believed it could free people from ignorance, "superstition," and tradition or unreflective life. People had to become conscious of themselves and that could be accomplished by analyzing myths and prejudices of the past (tradition). In like manner, sense perception or feelings or anything which constituted experience had to be thrown off. Experience could not provide a foundation for faith; it was by reason alone that one arrived at reality or objective truth.

When Christianity was brought to Africa, missionaries brought this baggage of the Enlightenment with them. The baggage became a stumbling block in their attempt to understand African life and world. Anything that could not be proven or was not "logical" according to their way of reasoning, was superstition and evil. Thus, the missionary emphasis on "rational reason." Africans do not understand the world by way of reason alone. Truth, in African thought, can be arrived at through speculative thought, lived experience, or mystery. It would require a whole new chapter to unpack African epistemology and I have already discussed this in another work. [7] For our present discussion, it is sufficient to say that missionaries failed to understand African thought and life.

MISSIONARY STRATEGY

What was the result of rejecting the African way of knowing?   Many
mistakes were made and the preaching of the Gospel ideolized, as Tom Colvin
has commented:

> Among the exciting discoveries of the present day are those arising from
> research in the field of history, the history of the African peoples before
> the European Colonial Era. We are now getting a picture of ancient
> African civilization with vibrant culture. . . . The idea that white men
> were bearers of light to people in total darkness may now be totally
> rejected. . . . In this re-writing of Africa's history, the work of the Church
> looks rather different from that which is presented in Mission Chronicles.
> It is wise for the Church to recognize and to admit mistakes of the past
> as well as sins of the present.   Too often it was the Church that
> obliterated old society in the mistaken belief that a completely new form
> of society must be built in order to be "Christian."Too often the missions
> were too closely associated with companies whose main object was to
> exploit African labor. Too often the Church was too closely aligned with
> imperialism. Too often missionaries have acted as though they were little
> gods.   Too often the Church has been and is on the side of color
> discrimination and colonial oppression. [8]

Tom Colvin, a Scottish missionary to Africa for over two decades, has put into
perspective the state of affairs created by European work in Africa. In this
chapter we will examine the ideas that formed missionary thought and
practice.

In his address to the senate at Cambridge University, David Livingstone
said: "I go back to Africa to open a path for Commerce and Christianity in
Africa; do you carry on the work which I have begun. I leave it with you."[9]
Later, in a letter to a friend he wrote: "If we call the actual amount of
conversions the direct result of Missions, and the wide diffusion of better
principles the indirect, I have no hesitation in asserting that the latter are of
infinitely more importance than the former."[10] Two questions arise from
these quotations: (a) why Commerce and not Christianity alone? (b) What are
these "better principles?" Answers to these questions reveal the prevailing
view about Africa and the object of European missionary enterprise in
Livingstone's time.

European understanding of Africa at that time, and as it has been in the last
400 years, was a place where ignorance, superstition, and immorality reigned
supreme; a dark continent, inhabited by uncivilized people. A long tradition

of myths, stereotypes, and characterization of Africans had drilled these beliefs into the minds of many in Europe. Reports of European travelers to Africa gave wrong impressions about Africans; for example, in his report on his travel to West Africa, Richard Burton said: "The negro is still at rude dawn of faith—fetishism—and he has barely advanced to idolatry. . . . He has never grasped the ideas of a personal Deity, a duty in life, a moral code, or a shame of lying. He rarely believes in a future state of rewards and punishments, which, whether true or not, are infallible indices of human progress."[11] In his address to the Ethnological Society of London in 1866, another British traveler, Samuel Baker, described the people of Sudan and the Nile valley in the following words: "Without any exception, they are without a belief in a Supreme Being, neither have they any form of worship or idolatry; nor is darkness of their minds enlightened by even a ray of superstition. This mind is as stagnant as the morass which forms its puny world."[12]

In the language of Burton and Baker one sees the influence of the theory of evolution as propounded by Charles R. de Brosses and Herbert Spencer in both its religious and social dimensions. According to the former's theory of religion, fetishism is the first stage of religious consciousness. In fetishism people endow natural objects such as trees or some "inanimate" things with divine power. de Brosses considered monotheism the last stage of religious development. In his human journey from fetishism to monotheism, de Brosses placed Africans at the beginning, at fetishism. This theory seems to have convincing to Europeans, for when August Comte, the French philosopher, developed his theory of (secularization of) religion, he built on and modified the theory of fetishism as advanced by de Brosses.

Herbert Spencer and the British school of anthropologists had a great impact on the ideas of human development. According to Spencer's theory of social evolution (social Darwinism, as it is sometimes called), moral improvement is the extension of biological adaptation, and social well-being is equated with the survival of the fittest. Spencer saw a relation between biological adaptation and moral progress. He maintained that socially valuable behavior, once established, constitutes moral prescription as habits; then it translates into anatomical changes that are transmitted by inheritance. [13] Simply put, the way people look and behave can be explained by studying their social evolution. On religion, Spencer said it had its origin in the worship of ancestors. Here he disagreed with Charles Tylor, a British anthropologist who maintained that religion originated in belief in souls.

From Spencer's social Darwinism and de Brosses' theory of religious development, through the work of Tylor, James Fraser, and other British anthropologists, Africa seemed in great need of help towards moral progress and monotheism. These ideas of evolution influenced the minds of those who went to Africa as missionaries and in other capacities. For them, the challenge for Europe was to bring light to Africa through Christianity and "civilization."

For Livingstone, commerce and Christianity were to give Africa "principles" of civilization. Christianity and civilization were two sides of the same coin.

The term "civilization"needs to be decoded. European understanding of civilization can be simply defined as the history and values of Western culture. The term civilization is relatively new in the English vocabulary, having first appeared in England in 1772 in Boswell's *Life of Johnson*.[14] Fifteen years earlier it had been first used in France Marquis de Maribeau in his writings. According to Emile Benveniste, who related the story of the first usage of the term civilization in England, it all happened at the writing of a dictionary.

> On Monday March 23 (1772) I found (Dr. Johnson) busy preparing a fourth edition of his foli Dictionary. . . . He would not admit *civilization*, but only *civility*. With great deference to him I thought civilization, from to *civilize*, better in the sense opposed to barbarity than civility, as it is better to have a distinct word for each sense, than one word for two senses, which civility is, in his way of using it.[15]

Whether this was the real beginning of the word or not, by the middle of the eighteenth century the word become descriptive of cultural process of England and France, as Norbert Elias notes:

> This concept [civilization] expresses the self-consciousness of the West. One could even say: the national consciousness. It sums up everything in which Western society of the last two or three centuries believes itself superior to earlier societies or "more primitive" contemporary ones. By this term Western society seeks to describe what constitutes its special character and what it is proud of: the level of its technology, the nature of its manners, the development of its scientific knowledge or view of the world and much more.[16]

The shared view in the West in the last three centuries has been that its values had in them principles of "civilization." In other words, Western societies developed because of values inherent in that culture. Seen from their sense of superiority, Africa has not developed a civilization because it lacks values such as are present in Western culture. Reports of travelers, traders, and missionaries to Africa painted a very negative picture. Lacking understanding, and not wanting to know the religious life of Africans, they concluded that Africans were superstitious and immoral. To them this was the reason Africa had not produced a civilization. Hegel claimed:

> It is manifest that want of self-control distinguishes the character of the negroes. This condition is capable of no development or culture, and as we have seen them at this day, such as they have always been. . . . At this point

we leave Africa, not to mention it again. For it is no historical part of the world; it has no movement or development to exhibit.[17]

In eighteenth century Europe, when everything was explained in terms of natural law, there were some thinkers who believed that the backwardness of Africa was due to distinctions nature had made between Africans and other races. Hume was expressing a common idea about the laws of nature and development of peoples when he explained the backwardness of Africans was due to natural law. In a footnote on the essay "Of National Character" Hume wrote:

I am apt to suspect the negroes . . . to be naturally inferior to whites. There never was a civilized nation of any other complexion than white, nor even individual eminent either in action or speculation. No ingenious manufactures amongst them, no arts, no sciences. On the other hand, the most rude and barbarous of the whites, such as the ancient Germans, the present Tartars, have still something eminent about them, in their valor, form of government, or some other particular. Such a uniform and constant difference could not happen, in so many countries and ages, if nature had not made original distinction between these breeds of men.[18]

In light of this caricature drawn to fit what was perceived to be the profile of the African, the task of Europeans in Africa, missionary or otherwise, was to teach principles of morality, a system of values and culture to bring civilization to Africa. The European venture to Africa was, to borrow from Kenneth Kaunda, "a humanist gesture —to liberate the poor benighted heathen trapped within the barbaric tribal system. At least that is what they claimed in their biographies."[19] How did they plan to achieve this? By obliterating old society and instituting new forms, as Tom Colvin has pointed out. Practices and beliefs of old society had to be rejected and destroyed. The structures and values of old society had produced nothing —no civilization, no arts, etc., instead, ignorance, superstition, and immorality had prevailed. That old society did Africans much harm was made evident by the presence of "paganism," ignorance, and polygamy. There had to be a new orientation altogether, a conversion to the Christian faith and Western values. We might call this a process of conversion by disorientation. The process of conversion by disorientation involved degrading and rejecting African values as meaningless and instilling the belief that traditional values had to be replaced by European. It cannot be denied that for missionaries, the conversion process was also a way to civilize Africans. The African condition, from the perspective of missionaries, obliged them to be involved in the civilization process. F. Eboussi Boulaga reminds his audience that to a large extent, it was and still is, "the sad state of affairs of the African condition" which inspires missionaries to Africa. He writes: "what arouses missionary enthusiasm, the exhilarating thrust of being sent, is not simply the command to go preach the gospel to all nations. It is also the distress of the retarded pagan peoples. The most striking thing about Africa is its misery, moral as well as physical. Slavery, ignorance, superstition, immorality, rage about in the most unbridled fashion."[20] In a moderate and but nonetheless critical voice, Desmond Tutu writes: "Men became missionaries from all kinds of motives, most of which were undoubtedly beyond reproach. But they would have to be persons of heroic sanctity had they not been tainted by the arrogance which was almost invariable concomitant of a dominant culture."[21]

The African condition being so wretched and pitiful, "to Christianize" meant "to humanize . . . to civilize the degraded human being." Tutu describes some aspects of the "Christian" and humanistic work.

> The missionaries were bringing the light of the Gospel to the dark continent. These poor native pagans had to be clothed in Western clothes so that they could speak to the white man's God, the only God, who was obviously unable to recognize them unless they were clad decently. These poor creatures must be made to sing the white man's hymn hopelessly badly translated, they had to worship in the white man's unemotional and individualistic way, they had to think and speak of God and all the wonderful Gospel truths in the white man's well proven terms. [22]

The task of civilizing the retarded peoples of Africa would not be easy. It would literally "mean the taming of human beings, and their progressive rearing to a normal state by education, by tutelage as if of minors."[23] And as minors, "the proper pedagogy for the African, then, will be one of firmness. It will inculcate obedience and gratitude."[24] The type of relationship that ensued from being firm with the African was explained by Albert Schweitzer, a French medical missionary to Gabon, who in 1952 was awarded the Nobel Peace Price for his service to humanity. Upon being asked about his relationship with Africans, he replied: "The negro is a child, and with children nothing can be done without authority. . . . With regard to negroes, then, I have coined a formula: I am your brother, it is true, but I am your elder brother."[25]

The first step in the civilizing and humanizing process was to take the African away from traditional society, the village, to educate him or her. Hence missionaries created "Christian villages," which became common throughout Africa. By taking the African out of the "evil space," the pagan frame of reference, he or she would discover the "truth;" for a person's actions only have meaning in light of their frame of reference. If you take the African out of the village context, superstitious actions will have no meaning, therefore the desire to do them will diminish. Furthermore, it was believed that what

Africans did in their villages had no real meaning, for those actions were carried out in ignorance and fear. Accordingly, the African's past or experience had no meaning because it did not belong to "history,"i.e. Western history. In other words, the African had no history. Africans lived, they existed, but did nothing to effect a historical process. In sum, the missionary understanding of Africans was that they had no sense of purpose or consciousness of time, therefore no goal, achievements, or meaning!

The underlying idea was that the African concept of time and space did not carry an awareness of self, which, in the West, is the basis of identity, development of culture, and history. The implication of this, from the perspective of evangelization, was the necessity for the African convert to renounce family, culture, and history if he or she were to become a true "Christian." In addition, Africans had to radically change the way they construed the world; that is, how they understood themselves and the whole creation. Africans were to cultivate Western forms of conceptualization, values, and way of life. Put simply, to become a Christian meant to cultivate Western values and to become incorporated into Western history. We also note that missionary Christianity had voluntarism as a central and constitutive element of its faith. Boulaga argues that this praxis was the foundation of the eradication of the African concept of community, persons, space, time, and culture itself.

After renouncing one's family, culture etc., could an African be treated with respect? No. The "uprooting and alienating praxis" only prepared one to be enlightened enough to become a candidate for salvation at the end of time. Baptism did not mean equality! Some missionaries held that some Africans achieved a certain level of equality, but this was equality *in the spirit*, as Donald Fraser, a missionary to northern Malawi put it.[26] Baptism was to bring the African knowledge of self and an awareness of serious moral and spiritual needs. Baptism was the power that evoked "the voice of conscience, hitherto dormant."[27] Once "the voice of conscience" was awakened, it would prompt gratitude in the African for the gift of enlightenment and saving grace received. This was all what mattered!

Baptism did not bring equality nor did ordination to the divine ministry. "Our pastors are not equal with European ministers" commented Dr. W. A. Elmslie, another longtime missionary to northern Malawi.[28] One of the reasons some African clergy chose to establish their own Churches was precisely because they would not be given equal status with their missionary counterparts.[29] This was not because the African did less than the missionary, on the contrary. Many missionaries realized and acknowledged that the growth of the African Church depended on the work of the African clergy, as Fraser later pointed out, "I mean that Africa will not be evangelized and raised by Europeans, but the African. And the efficient missionary is the one who will try to multiply himself, to restrain himself from activities which

might be more fascinating so that he may prepare Africans to do his work. "[30]
Fraser was repeating familiar words in Africa's mission history: "only let it be
said that the missionary should from the start have definitely in view, and
steadily work towards, the great and ultimate aim—to establish and consolidate
a Native Church, self-propagating and self-governing. "[31] But when the
African was prepared, the missionary would not treat him as equal. The
missionary wanted to remain in control and look down on the African clergy.

The attitude of missionaries reflected a general European mind-set seen in
all sectors of life: government, trade, and commerce. Writing to his
evangelists and pastors in 1911, Charles Domingo expressed this feeling of
"unholy alliance" among Europeans in Malawi.

Poor Resident, he thinks too much of his skin and not of his heart. What
is the difference between a white man and a black man? Are we not of
the same blood and all from Adam? This startles me much—Is Europe
still Christian or Heathen? . . . There is too much failure among all
Europeans in Nyasaland. The three combined bodies: missionaries,
government, and companies or gainers of money—do form the same rule;
to look upon the native with mockery eyes. It sometimes startles us to
see that the three combined bodies are from Europe, and along with them
is the title "CHRISTENDOM." And to compare or make a comparison
between the master of the title and his servants, it pushes any African
away from believing the master of the title. If we had power to
communicate ourselves to Europe, we would advise them not to call
themselves "CHRISTENDOM" but "EUROPEANDOM." Therefore the
life of these three bodies is altogether too cheaty, too thefty, too mockery.
Instead of GIVE they say TAKE away from. From 6 a.m. to 5 or 6 p.m.
there is too much breakage of God's law as seen in James 5 verse 4.[32]

From the beginning of Western missionary enterprise in Africa, missionary
praxis created frustrations among Africans and a conflict of cultures. Some
missionaries realized that such a conflict was bound to raise a very serious
problem down the road. Addressing a missionary conference at Zoute in
1926, Donald Fraser cautioned fellow missionaries on the danger of uprooting
the African and elevating Western values and culture. He said, "Society has
been safeguarded by many a social tie, and none of these should be cut unless
we give in their place surer bonds. . . . If our presentation of the Gospel puts
emphasis on prohibition of social practices which are not essentially evil, we
are apt to rouse antagonism of nationality when we should have made it our
greatest ally."[33] Fraser was right; it did not take long after the planting of
Christianity that criticisms on missionary practice began to be raised by
Africans. Voices of protests began to be heard such as these words from
Malawi: "We believe that the commission of the Christian Church to Africa

was to import Christ and education in such a way as to fit the manners and customs of the people, and not that it should impose on the African the unnecessary and impractical methods [customs] of European countries."[34] These Malawians further charged that the decadence of morality in African society was due to missionary praxis. Christianity, as taught and practiced by missionaries, had threatened the value system of African society. Missionary praxis had launched an onslaught on symbols which informed moral development in traditional society. Thus the protest: "We believe the immoralities now prevailing among us are as a direct result of the unnatural position into which the African has been driven coupled by the false and misleading theory [teachings] that outside one's own Church other beliefs [traditional] do no good."[35]

In another voice of protest, Levi Mumba, another Malawian, argued that missionary praxis did not only destroy society and thus its moral fiber, but also brought religious bankruptcy.

Social peace has come to Africa, but without safeguards based on local custom and law it has meant the breaking up of villages and communal organizations, with consequent deterioration in character, to the great grief of many Africans. It is the same in religious matters; many can now be said to be without a religion. One who cares to study actual facts will find rank hypocrisy in some professors of religion. They are not real believers in their acquired beliefs, and they do not follow their ancestral beliefs. This class is growing and is drifting towards religious bankruptcy. Man is a religious creature; he would do better to follow his so called superstitions. [36]

What is clear from the voices of protest is that prejudice and arrogance shaped missionary praxis and made missionaries unwilling to understand African life and world. This is why they labelled "superstition" that which was profoundly religious. Lack of understanding of African religious life led to the condemnation of all traditional practices as evil. This is what Mumba lamented when he wrote: "Our *mziro* (taboo) things have been evolved through experience for the refining and upkeep of social development. Unfortunately for us these taboos have all been scrapped as mere superstitions, with the result that our social organizations have suffered degeneration." [37]

It was with the intention of helping missionaries understand the African world that African elites like Levi Mumba wrote to explain some aspects of African life. Concerning the place of the ancestors Mumba said:

The native lives the social and religious life together; for social troubles he appeals to the living head of his family; for the spiritual he appeals through this same head to the spirits of the dead ancestors, who are the guardians in the spirit kingdom as they were on earth. One phase of their position is intermediary between him and material rulers; the other, now exalted, between him and the God-spirit. We do not confuse the issues—no living person can be a medium of intercession with the God-spirit, for he is not disentangled from material hindrances, nor can the spirit of our ancestors directly help us in our relation with the earthly chief. . . . Our regard for spirits of the ancestors does not make them gods; they are merely mediators between us and God. [38]

Mumba also asserted: "The concept of spirit alone allows the native religion to be assessed on its full worth."[39]

Some missionaries did attempt to understand the African cosmology and way of life. We must bear in mind that they sought to understand the African from their way of knowing. The motivation for wanting to know African life and practices was to find a strategy for converting the "heathen" African. Nevertheless, such missionaries discovered that Africans had well developed religious life long before missionaries came. Of course they did not speak favorably about African religiosity; they described it as "a groping for the truth." While many missionaries shared this negative view about African religious heritage, there were some who gave Africans the benefit of the doubt, and did some research to ascertain the truth for themselves. Those few who cared to know more about African religious life discovered that there was something in the African way of life to which the Gospel could appeal. This was what Alexander Hetherwick observed in his study of African spirituality.

> In his sacrificial system also, he seeks communion with the dead — communion which he feels death has not broken, for death is to him only a passage out of one state into another —and the veil between is very thin. In this world, soul spoke to soul in the mutual presentation of gifts. A gift given and received was the seal of human fellowship—and in the intercourse between living and dead gifts of sacrifice, in such form as the dead receive, are still the seals of a friendship that has not been broken.
> All this is but the foreshadowing of what great Christian truth which the Scottish Church has almost altogether forgotten, the doctrine of the Communion of Saints. All that the native craves for in his sacrifice and offerings at the grave or shrine, that longing for intercourse with the departed who he fondly believes are still alive, the Catholic Gospel can give to the African in its fullness, to add what he has found for himself. [40]

At this point Hetherwick has a footnote in which he comments:

Our creed says, "I believe in the Communion of Saints," and our Confession declares in interpretation of this faith, that we "share in each other gifts and graces." Out of this fullness of Christian teaching unfortunately, the Scottish Church has retained hardly a fragment. . . . It needed the catastrophic of the War and the demands of poignant grief for the fallen, to rouse the Church to make what is still but a faltering commemoration, . . . A yearly commemoration of the Departed which the festival of All Saints affords would do no little to keep alive in our hearts a strong faith in the communion of living and dead, which the African is seeking for, and which our Gospel in its fullness richly provides. [41]

In the main text, Hetherwick continues observation of African religious practices as follows:

We are thus able now to realize in some small measure how much there is in native belief and thought already cherished by him, to which the Gospel can at one make an appeal. The cardinal truths of belief in spirit, in a spirit world, in a Supreme Spirit in some form or another, in communion with the spirit world through prayer and sacrifice, these the messenger of the Gospel finds ready to his hand —to make the path of the preacher easier to the heart and conscience of the African tribesman. [42]

Any student of African studies, in any field, always comes across ambiguities in works of Western writers. Even among the most sympathetic missionaries like Hetherwick, one still finds a lack of understanding of African life. This limited knowledge about the African cosmology is revealed in their love-hate syndrome always present in Western scholarship on Africa. At one place they may speak romantically about African life and at another, they sound no different from those who see nothing of value in anything African. Immediately after having written romantically about African spirituality Hetherwick writes:

When I mention "conscience,"I remember that I face the strongest barrier that the Gospel has to meet in its presentation and approach to the native mind. . . . Morality does not enter into the native theosophy nor in no measure at all into his conception of God or the Spirit world, or the future. . . . Morality, therefore gives no place in native character and thought on which we can build any appeal for an acceptance of the Gospel. We find no way of approach through any sense of guilt or consciousness of sin. When any question of moral conduct is present, conscience at no time enters as a deciding factor in native life. The main determining factor in such matters is the fear of consequence which alone deters the Native from any moral misconduct and keeps him in the right.[43]

Once again, we come to another familiar stereotype of the African in Western writings. Here the stereotype emerges in the argument that there is no morality in African society and that it is fear which regulates moral conduct. This is a serious charge. One wonders what Hetherwick thought Africans truly were: creatures without a moral principle and guided by fear, could they be truly human? Hetherwick was not making new assertions about Africans. Since the Enlightenment, the lack of morality in African society had been attributed to the absence of "rational will." Such attitudes have invited Boulaga's biting criticism: "Firmness is necessary for the taming of the animal in the African. The African's obedience cannot be one that issues from human 'rational will.' These creatures are sensitive only to the subjugating values of prestige or to fear—for them literally the beginning of wisdom. The African virtue par excellence, then, will be one that flows from fear."[44]

There was no doubt in the missionary mind that the absence of "rational will" accounted for the lack of sense of sin among Africans. That the African had no sense of sin was further proven by the absence of the term "sin" in African languages which Hetherwick had "mastered." He says that Bible translators "had to build up a term for 'conscience,' in which the primary idea was that of 'digging' or 'rousing memory' in the heart. . . . For the idea of the expression of 'sin' they took a term which meant only to 'err' or to 'make a mistake' and to adapt it to ethical usage."[45] The image of the African that we get from Hetherwick is that of an underdeveloped adult or one reduced to a sub-human level. This is how Boulaga describes such a person and how he or she has to be treated:

A human being becomes a package of instincts and what is worse of depraved, unnatural instincts. Now as animality has got the upper hand, as human beings have turned into dangerous beasts in certain respects, it is evident that the only language they will understand in the beginning will be that of constraint and discipline, the language of immediate sanction by chastisement or reward.[46]

The characterization of the African such as outlined by Hetherwick reveals the extent of ignorance, among other things, that Westerners had about the real facts concerning African thought systems. This misunderstanding about African thought could be partly blamed on the development of anthropology and linguistics. From the early days of missionary work, it was not only fashionable but "necessary" to read or study anthropology and have some basics in linguistics. This was because of a common belief that knowledge of African life and mastery of their language(s) were essential to "understanding"

African thought and practice.   It was argued that mastering an African language equipped the missionary to render valuable service to Africans: to reduce African languages into script and help Africans understand themselves and their world.

The study of linguistics brought both a blessing and a curse to Africa. Indeed missionaries managed to put some African languages into writing, that's the blessing, may be! I say maybe because it is not completely true that Africa did not have scripts.   Studies have revealed that there were various types of scripts in Africa prior to introduction of European script.   These scripts had no outside influence.   In his book, *The Akan World of Gold Weights: Abstract Design Weights*, B. Niangoran-Bouah has demonstrated that at least seven African languages show affinity to ancient Egyptian writing.[47] There are a few more studies on writing in precolonial Africa beyond the familiar scripts of the Nile Valley civilization: Egyptian, Meroitic, and G éez of Aksum (Ethiopia).   Illustrations of these early scripts include the Ar ɔkɔ of the Yoruba, Mekutu al ɗé of Cameroon, and Ngombo of Angola.[48] It is also now known that every region of Africa had other forms of writing such as ideographs like the Nsibidi of the Igbo, Edo and Efik, people of Eastern and Midwestern Nigeria, or the sona or tusona used by the Cokwe, Lucazi, Mbwela and Mbunda, peoples of Angola and Zambia.[49] Nsibidi was a graphic system used to communicate philosophical knowledge; Sona, did that and more: it also transmited empirical mathematics.   There were also phonological scripts in the Central and Western parts of Africa.   So this "blessing" Africa received through European writing must be seriously questioned, or at least seen from another perspective.

At any rate, through evangelization and colonization, Africa's scripts were replaced by the European.   But in the process of getting African languages put into European writing, they also corrupted African thought.   Putting African languages into writing was part of the evangelization and civilization of Africans.   The program would enable Africans to have the scriptures in their own tongue.   Since African languages lacked corresponding words to some "key" biblical concepts, so we are told, missionaries coined words or phases to express those fundamental concepts.   This is where the curse lies. It is a curse because it eradicated or attempted to eliminate the African thought system.

What was wrong with what missionaries did? A lot and it was very serious! Words represent structures of a people's world.   They are symbols of a people's self-understanding or way of life, thus structures of life itself.   For they interpret or give meaning to the process of living and dying.   In language then, people live structures of their life, for this is the only way of verbally expressing themselves.   This is to argue that language is not just semantics. It is the whole way of seeing, hearing, feeling, thinking, and doing in the world.   To insert a concept in this structure is not just to alter the way people live (see, hear, feel, think, and do), it is to distort and even destroy life itself as they know it. For people can no longer see, hear, feel, think, and do exactly as they did before.

Concepts are crystallized deposits of how people interpret their life. To put a foreign concept into a language is to insert one people's interpretation of the world into another people's world. The result is a clash of the two worlds. This creates a conflict of meanings, a confusion in the understanding of life and the world. People get confused for no longer do words have the same structures of life that they once represented. In as much as the new concept means a lot to those who coin it, it fails to deliver the intended meaning within the framework or language structure of the people. For example, Hetherwick and his fellow missionaries translated conscience as *chikumbumtima* in the Nyanja (Malawian language) version of the Bible. *Chikumbumtima* , formed by joining together a verb *kukumba* , to dig, and a noun *mtima* , heart, is still foreign to most Malawians. It does not make much sense in Malawian thought to speak of digging into one's heart which is what *chikumbutima* means.

Creating confusion in the way people understand their world is what translators did when they coined words for the "poor Africans" whose language did not have corresponding terms for central biblical words — conscience and sin. Instead of engaging in further research to find out why these terms were absent in the local language, the translators forced Western concepts into the language. The result was a corruption of indigenous thought at a very fundamental level. But this had a very serious consequence for the Christian message. The corruption did not allow the Christian message to interact with African thought. The language they corrupted became the "Christian" vocabulary through which sermons were delivered and confessions made. There it was — a further disorientation for the African who became a Christian! Was this the cost of discipleship? In a society where religion permeates through and through, informs and orders life and whole society, to corrupt religious language is a very serious matter —a genocide. How can a people know who they are and what they are to be about when their symbols are corrupted? For it is in religion that human values and culture have their foundation.

This is not the only instance in which the so called "mastery of native" language led missionaries to some gross mistake about the African. In South Africa, Robert Moffatt concluded that Africans had no religion saying: "Satan has employed his agency with fatal success, in erasing every vestige of religious impression from the minds of the Beuchuanas, Hottentots and Bushmen; leaving them without a single ray to guide them from the dark and dread futurity, or single link to unite them with the skies."[50] Aylward Shorter has argued against the idea that mastery of language is key to understanding African thought. Speaking from his experience as a missionary, he writes: "It goes without saying that for a missionary bare knowledge of the language is not enough; it may be even misleading."[51] E. E. Evans-Pritchard, a structural anthropologist, says that

> speaking a language fluently is very different from understanding it. . . .
> Native and missionary are using the same words but the connotations are
> different, they carry different loads of meaning. . . . We need only take
> for example the use of a native word for our "God." The meaning of the
> word for the native speaker may have only the slightest coincidence, and
> in a very restricted context, with the missionary's conception of God.[52]

Geoffrey Parrinder condemns the attitude of missionaries.

> The old attitude of missionaries was usually destructive; the indigenous
> religion was not studied, it was not thought to have any divine revelations
> or inspiration, and little effort was made to use any part of it as a basis
> for fuller teaching. But it is not necessary that the old religion both
> taught some truths and produced some spiritual values and living.[53]

Many African authors have written concerning the negative missionary attitude on African culture. The most severe criticism of the missionary enterprise has come from Boulaga in his article "La démission."[54]

The idea of understanding "primitive people" was and still is, dominant in the humanities. At first, it was mainly in the field of anthropology and religion,[55] but later it became a big debate in social science.[56] Theories in anthropology and social sciences maintain that it is possible for an outsider to reach "objective" knowledge; that is, non-prejudiced and a fuller understanding about something or someone. Such knowledge is not readily available to insiders because they are not able to distance themselves from their prejudices. From this it follows that an outsider can provide explanations about certain practices insiders take for granted. It is from ideas like these that missionaries believed they understood African thought and society much better than Africans themselves.

An observation of the missionary enterprise reveals that the claim to objectivity is false. Ideas are filtered through our knowledge and experience. This means that we are always prejudiced or we have some foreknowledge about things. People are not like clean slates waiting to be written on. However, our prejudice or foreknowledge is corrected and modified as we open ourselves to facts as they are. "this openness always includes our placing the other meaning in a relation with the whole of our own meanings or ourselves in a relation to it."[57] This means "openness" does not wipe away our foreknowledge, rather transforms it, thereby transforming our attitude or feelings—ourselves! This is understanding. Gadamer has described this process as a "fusing of horizons."[58] We do not see such transformation taking place in the attitude of missionaries as they confronted African culture and life. Missionaries were convinced that they had understood Africans to such an extent that they wrote volumes about them. Parrinder rejects the claim that missionaries understood Africans. He argues that such claims were misleading for none of those missionaries "came near an adequate understanding of the complex religious system they were trying to replace."[59]

Kwesi Dickson points out that missionary attitude towards other cultures should also be understood in the light of exclusivist thinking.

Exclusivist thinking starts from the basis of one's own perspective —and ends there. The possibility of matters being viewed also from the bona fide perspective of the other person or group does not readily come into play. Exclusivist has manifested itself in many ways: in keeping at a distance the local cultural reality, either because of no serious thought is given to the possibility of the development of a form of Christianity which is not necessarily identical with the missionary's brand of it, or because the local culture is seen as a force which nullifies the missionary's dedicated efforts.[60]

Dickson has demonstrated that this attitude is deeply rooted in the Christian tradition and both Testaments of the Bible. He further argues that the Reformation, with its emphasis on *sola scriptura* and justification by faith, left no room for considering the possibility for dialogue with other religions and traditions since there can be only one true religion. Dickson contends:

Reformation theology, then, had the potential for encouraging the formulation of the kind of mission policy which would view other peoples' religious traditions as unimportant, if not dangerous. When a tradition insists that its claims have exclusive authority, the distinction between itself and other traditions is sharpened. It can hardly be doubted that Protestant theology, especially as seen in the teaching of Luther, had its effect on the Church's thinking. . . . The Reformation emphasis, echoed by Barth, implies an unbridgeable gap between Christianity and other systems of life and thought. It is clear that mission policy as it was implemented in Africa assumed this kind of thinking. It has manifested itself in the operation of Church administration systems which are modeled on the patterns developed on the European context, and in the training of clergy which often leaves the unfinished products powerless in the face of life around them and this unsuited to minister within their own cultural area.[61]

CONCLUSION

Missionary thought and practice in Africa was very much influenced by stereotypical ideas prevailing in eighteenth century Europe. Their negative images of the African had been crystallized by the stories and pictures of trans-Atlantic and European slave trade and slavery itself. From these negative pictures they developed the idea that Africans were not civilized and had no principles of morality. The task of Christian missions was to bring civilization, principles of morality, and preach salvation. Emerging out of the Enlightenment, missionaries sought to do for African society what the Enlightenment did to eighteenth century Europeans; that is, to establish rationality as way of understanding the world. Rational reason would liberate Africans! Liberation was needed much more in Africa than Europe because of the superstitious beliefs of African society.

Missionaries also brought other baggage with them; they identified Christianity with their culture, values, and history. The result of such uncritical appropriation of cultural views made Christianity an ideology of Western civilization. As an ideology, Christianity was arrogant, and quickly destroyed everything and everyone in its way. Being a cultural ideology it was used by both the colonialist and the missionary alike to promote cultural superiority.

Missionary practice leaves much to be desired. In the name of propagation of the Gospel, it destroyed African life and thought and today African Churches face many problems arising from this destruction. Many people were alienated and disoriented. As a result, Christianity is still foreign. In some missionary establishments there are mixed feelings about traditional values—the love/hate syndrome has been passed on. Traditional practices and modes of knowing are considered primitive. When changes take place in the missionary Churches, the changes are cosmetic, for example, some hymns are sung to traditional tunes and instruments once in awhile, but there have been no fundamental changes to the liturgy, or changes in the elements of the Eucharist to what people partake in their everyday (tradition) meals—their staple diet. The "Christian" vocabulary is by and large foreign. In short, Africans are unable to see, hear, feel, think, and do differently or to live an authentic African life because missionary praxis destroyed their world. There is a great need for change; a need to reconstruct the African world so that people can live and praise God in an authentic African way.

NOTES

1. "Uniting in Hope," *Report of World Council of Churches Faith and Order Consultation, Accra, 1974* (Geneva: WCC, 1975), 33.

2. Compare Sir Isaac Newton's "General Laws of Nature, by which the things themselves are form'd" in Dampier-Whetham Cecil William, *A History of Science and its Relation with Philosophy and Religion* (New York: Cambridge University Press, 1929), 183.

3. Concerning the subject of criticism see Immanuel Kant, *Prolegomena to any future Metaphysics which will be able to come forth as Science (1783)*, trans. Mahaffy-Carus, (New York: Library of Arts, H. W. Sams, 1950), 8-9.

4. For discussion on the relation between reason and faith during this intellectual climate see John Locke, *The Reasonableness of Christianity with a Discourse of Miracles and Part of A Third Letter Concerning Toleration*, ed. I. T. Ramsey (Stanford, Ca.: Stanford University Press, 1958). See also David Hume, *On Human Nature and the Understanding*, ed. Antony Flew with introduction (New York: Collier Macmillan Publishers, 1962), 115-136.

5. John A.T. Robinson, *Honest to God* (London: SCM, 1963).

6. Compare his commentary on *Mark* (Edinburgh: St. Andrews Press).

7. Harvey J. Sindima, *Africa's Agenda: An African Critique of Liberalism and a Recapture of African Values.* chap. 2 (forthcoming).

8. Tom Colvin, *Christ's Work in Free Africa* (Glasgow: Iona Community, 1964), 7-8.

9. George Seaver, *David Livingstone: His Life and Letters* (New York: Harper and Row, 1957).

10. D. Chamberlin, *Some Letter from Livingstone* (London: Oxford Universities Press, 1940), 252.

11. Richard F. Burton, *A Mission to Gelele, King of Dahome*, 2nd ed., vol. 2 (London: Tinsley Brothers, 1864), 199.

12. Samuel W. Baker, "The Races of the Nile Basin," *Transactions of the Ethnological Society of London*, v. (1867): 231.

13. Herbert Spencer, *On Social Evolution*, ed. J.D.Y. Peel, (Chicago: Chicago University Press, 1972), chap. 2.

14. Emile Benveniste, *Problems in General Linguistics*, trans. Mary Elizabeth Meek (Miami, Fl.: University Press of Miami, 1971), 289-296.

15. *Ibid.*, 293.

16. Norbert Elias, *The Civilizing Process: The Development of Manners* (New York: Urizen Books, 1977), 3-4.

17. George Hegel, *The Philosophy of History*. trans. J. Sibree, a new introduction by C.J. Friedrich (New York: Dover, 1956), 218-222.

18. David Hume, *Essay and Treatise* (1768). 152n. See also Richard H. Popkin, "Hume's Racism," *The Philosophical Forum*, IX, nos. 2-3 (1977-78): 213.

19. Kenneth Kaunda and Colin Morris, *A Humanist in Africa* (Nashville, Tenn.: Abingdon Press, 1966), 26.

20. F. Eboussi Boulaga, *Christianity Without Fetishes: An African Critique and recapture of Christianity*. trans. Robert R. Barr (Maryknoll, N. Y.: Orbis Books, 1984), 20.

21. Desmond Tutu, "Whether African Theology," ed. Edward Fashole-Luke, in *Christianity in Independent Africa* (Bloomington, Ind.: Indiana University Press; London: Rex Collings, 1978), 364.

22. *Ibid.*, 365.

23. Boulaga, *Christianity Without Fetishes*, 20.

24. *Ibid.*, 21.

25. In David Lamb, *The Africans* (New York: Random House, 1984), 142.

26. Donald Fraser, *New Africa* (London: Edinburgh House Press, 1927), 49.

27. Hetherwick, *The Gospel and the African* (Edinburgh: T. and T. Clark, 1932), 117.

28. Elmslie made this comment to the members of Chilembwe Commission of Inquiry which was investigating reasons that led to Chilembwe Rising. One of the grievances Chilembwe had mentioned in his letters to the *Nyasaland Times* was about race relations in the country. Elmslie here confirmed Chilembwe's point.

29. See J. K. Parratt, ed. "Y. Z. Mwasi and the Origins of the Blackman's Church," *Journal of Religion in Africa*, IX, (1979): fasc. 3. See also Y. Z. Mwase "My Essential and Paramount Reasons for Working Independently," *Sources for the Study of Religion in Malawi*, 2 (1979). Mwasi explains the problem of equality in the Church between the indigenous clergy and missionaries. Such cases could be found in all of Africa.

30. Donald Fraser, "The Opportunity in Pagan Africa." Address made to an ecumenical conference held in Nashville, Tennessee February 28-March 4, 1906.

31. A. G. MacAlpine, "The Missionary and the Native Church." Unpublished letter. Edinburgh University Library, Manuscripts department.

32. Charles Domingo, "To the Pastors and Evangelists," a pamphlet, Seventh Day Baptist Historical Society, 1911. Reprinted in *Sources for the Study of Religion in Malawi*, no. 9, December 1983.

33. From a collection of his letters and papers at Edinburgh University Library, manuscript department.

34. From article 1 of the *Declaration of Belief of the African National Church, 1928*.

35. *Ibid.*, art. 2.

36. Levi Mumba, "Religion of My Fathers," *International Review of Missions*, 19 (1930): 366-367.

37. *Ibid.*, 367.

38. *Ibid.*, 364, 365. See also "The Native Idea of the Divine Being," *Vyaro na Vyaro*, 15 (June 1923), Livingstonia.

39. Levi Mumba, "The Native Idea of the Divine Being," *Vyaro Na Vyaro*.

40. Hetherwick, *The Gospel and the African*, 108.

41. *Ibid.*, 108-109.

42. *Ibid.*, 109.

43. *Ibid.*, 109, 110.

44. Boulaga, *Christianity Without Fetishes*, 21.

45. Hetherwick, *The Gospel and the African*, 112-113.

46. Boulaga, *Christianity Without Fetishes*, 20.

47. B. Niangoran-Bouah, *The Akan World of Gold Weights: Abstract Design Weights* (Abidjan: Les Nouvelles Editions, 1984).

48. The following writings provide good information and illustrations on some African forms of writing: C. A. Gollmer, "On African Symbolic Messages," *Journal of the Anthropological Institute*, XIV (1985); M. Kibanda, "L'écreiture dans la civilisation Kongo: Problèmes theoriques et methodologiques," *Revue de Linguistique Theorique et Appliquee* (Janvier 1985); G. Kubik, "African Graphic Systems: A Reassessment," *Mitteilungan der Anthropologischen Gesellsscraft in Wien*, 114 and 115 (1984-1988); E. Jaritz, "Uber Bahmen auf Billardtischen-Oder: Eine Mathematische Untersuchung von Ideogrammen Angolanischer Herkunft," Mathematische-Statistiche Sektion, Research Centre A-8010, Graz, Austria, 1983.

49. Molefi Asante, *Kemet, Afrocentricity and Knowledge* (Trenton, N.J.: Africa World Press, 1990), 72-79.

50. Quoted by E.W. Smith, ed., *African Ideas of God* (London: Edinburgh Hoese Press, 1961), 83. See also Per Hassing, "Christian Theology in Africa," *Religion and Life*, XL, no. 4 (Winter 1971): 510.

51. Aylward Shorter, *African Culture and the Christian Church: An Introduction to Social and Pastoral Theology* (London: Geoffrey Chapman, 1973), 74.

52. E. E. Evans-Pritchard, *Theories of Primitive Religion* (Oxford: Claredon Press, 1965), 7.

53. Smith, *African Ideas*, 239.

54. F. B. Eboussi Boulaga, "La démission," *Spiritus*, 56, (May-August 1974).

55. Edward B. Tylor, *Religion in Primitive Culture*, with an introduction by Paul Radin (Gloucester, Mass.: Peter Smith, 1970); Lucien Levy-Bruhl, *Primitive Mentality*, trans. L. A. Clare (London: Allen and Unwin, 1923); E. E. Evans-Prictchard, *Theories of Primitive Religion* (Oxford: Claredon Press, 1965); *The Institutions of Primitive Society* (Oxford: Basil Blackwell, 1954).

56. Max Weber, *The Methodology of the Social Sciences*, trans. and ed. Edward A. Shils and Henry A. Finch, with a forward by Edward Shils (New York: The Free Press, 1949), chap. two "Objectivity" in Social Science and Policy; Peter Winch, "Understanding a Primitive People," *American Philosophical Quarterly*, 1 (1964): 307-327. The following anthologies may throw some light on the subject of understanding in human sciences: Bryan Wilson, ed., *Rationality* (London: Basil Blackwell, 1970); Fred R. Dallmayr and Thomas A. MacCarthy, eds. *Understanding and Social Inquiry* (Indiana: University of Notre Dame Press, 1977), pts. 1-3, 5; Paul Rabinow and William M. Sullivan, eds., *Interpretive Social Sciences: A Reader* (Berkeley and Los Angeles, Ca.: University of California Press, 1979).

57. Hans-Georg Gadamer, *Truth and Method* (New York: Crossroad, 1982), 238.

58. *Ibid.*, 273.

59. Geoffrey Parrinder, "Learning from Other Faiths," *Expository Times*, 1972, 234.

60. Kwesi A. Dickson, *Uncompleted Mission: Christianity and Exclusivism* (Maryknoll, N.Y.: Orbis Books, 1991), 3.

61. *Ibid.*, 82, 83.

7

Christianity and African Culture

In this chapter we shall examine African responses to the missionary enterprise. Originally, there were only two: acceptance or rejection of the foreign religion. Later, a third response emerged. This was the attempt to make Christianity authentic so that it could speak to African culture and religion, and thereby enable Africans to remain themselves and yet Christian. We will explore the factors or views which influenced these responses.

AFRICAN RESPONSES TO MISSIONARY EVANGELISM

Christianity was rejected for more reasons than can be catalogued. It could be argued that Christianity was rejected basically because it was a foreign religion and that people everywhere view the "new" with suspicion. However, such an argument would be an oversimplification of what happened. In the last chapter we saw that missionaries brought with them a lot of prejudices about Africans. Those misconceptions stood in the way of proclaiming the Gospel. Some of those who rejected Christianity did so because of missionaries's prejudice toward African life and culture. This attitude simply repulsed some Africans and turned them away from Christianity. There was a suspicious feeling among many Africans about the real intentions of missionaries; the general feeling was that missionaries had planned an onslaught on African culture. This fear was confirmed by the life of those who joined Christianity; they no longer followed African customs. In many places the converts to Christianity looked down on African life and practice just like the missionaries.

Africans converted to Christianity thought and believed they were better than their own people because by being Christians they were exposed to

European values and learned the principles of "civilization." They were therefore "civilized" by mimicking and assimilating values set before them by missionaries. It did not take long after conversion before the new converts turned their backs on their own traditions, calling them heathen practices, superstitions, and work of the devil. In his autobiography, Harry Thuku confesses to having looked down on his cultural values after his conversion. "Some people," he wrote, "when they became Christians, including myself, were no longer interested in Kikuyu things."[1] The indoctrination they received succeeded in making converts hate their past and culture, so they joined ranks with missionaries to discredit and undermine African traditional practices. After conversion the past could only be remembered with shame. For

> to present the pagan past in any light is to idealize it and consciously or unconsciously to yield all the more to anti-Christian sentiments—to a satanic hatred of the light. Any ethnology that fails in unmasking of what it means to be native fall prey to this idealist illusion, this anti-Christian conspiracy. The Christian notion of history is altogether clear and simple: a pagan past is wholly and entirely disinheritance, deprivation, and distress. The degradation of paganism goes without saying, just as does the superiority of Christianity.[2]

Boulaga highlights the internal conflicts of African converts. For some Africans, the agony or anguish of doing what the missionaries taught was at too great a price to be undertaken. Issues of concern for those Africans centered around alienation from the community and the loss of a sense of identity. In African society, identity is given by the community. Through ritual process and other everyday activities, the community "confers" identity on its members. By affirming and instructing persons through ritual and other ways, the community shows its members how to live in the world or how life and community are to be safeguarded. The question of identity makes the need to be in solidarity with one's community of vital importance to an African.

There is another dimension to the understanding of community, the concept of the dead. According to African thought systems, the dead are part of the community because they represent a past which constitutes the present. People learn from the past even as the future beckons them. To acknowledge the idea of being constituted by others is to accept one's solidarity with the community. To break away from this fellowship is to destroy the means of identity and self-realization and therefore to ruin a vision of life. This sense of community made prospective converts to Christianity wonder what their future would be. The following questions present the inner conflicts, the agony, facing prospective candidates. "If we pray with you, who is going to protect our house from all those who do not pray? And who will care for our ancestors who have not prayed with you? If I submit to this bath of yours (baptism), shall I still go home to my ancestor?" In other words, "Will your baptism give the eternal life promised by my ancestors?"[3]

Ela reminds us that this agony and anxiety of the early converts is still present and even more acute. The anxiety arises from being cut off from ones' relationships. He notes: "The entry of African communities into the Church disturbs a delicate web of social and religious relationships for many new converts. Conversions to the gospel involves sacrifice and danger."[4] Ela describes the anguish and anxiety of the African convert to Christianity as follows:

> What becomes of one's relationship to the ancestor if the baptized may only address their prayers and worship to God and to the angels, and to the saints of the Roman Church? Does not faith in Christ, lived according to the white custom, not imply an irretrievable breach with a world which, in its totality, included the living and the dead. Here we can catch the agony of the old wise men who, before they pass over into the beyond, learn that their children on being converted to Christianity, will pray to the God of the white men who brutally arrogate to themselves all the veneration which tradition had set apart for them. The renunciation of this supreme form of filial piety plunges the older inhabitants of the village into bleak prospect of total extinction: they see themselves as forever cut off from all communication with their descendants.[5]

Ela ends his description of the African struggle by raising questions which the African Church must address if it is to speak to the African heart. He asks:

> Can one then feel at peace if, it is necessary to live in a state of severance from the deceased of one's family, without possibility of contact with them, once the troubles of life are over? Have Christian rites the same potential for establishing bonds of solidarity which reach into the invisible world? Furthermore, has the Christian faith the power to forge ties of kinship which will assure mankind of peace and security in the face of death and adversity. In the final analysis, to use words of Sheikh Hamidou Kane, "is what one learns worth what one forgets?"[6]

In another book, *My Faith as An African*, Ela has carried on the question of ancestors. Here Ela asks: why should the veneration of ancestors not be part of the Christian liturgy in the African Church, since there is veneration of the saints within the Christian tradition? Drawing from the practice of ancestor veneration among the people of northern Cameroon, Ela asks:

Why should the people of northern Cameroon break their *pras* (a jar representing ancestors and the cult which is offered) only to see them replaced by Christian relics? If they find that the *pra* is a superstition that must be rejected to enter the Church, won't the mountain people make the same judgment about the use of relics? In the mountains, the *pra* of the father is respected; in the African Churches, the bones of some unknown person, placed in the alter stone, appear to be a kind of fetish. Since, traditionally, there can be no prayer to the ancestors without the object which represent them, why shouldn't African Christians be permitted to bring the *pra* to a gathering in memory of the ancestors?[7]

The anxiety over the fate of one's ancestors, the sense of loss of solidarity with the past is deep among the African "faithful." This anxiety and the agony of separation from community led Africans converts who dearly cherished their heritage to give a third response to the missionary enterprise. In their struggle to remain faithful to their heritage these converts refused to accept the missionary baggage, that is, Western culture, as part and parcel of the Christian message. These Christians wanted to embrace their past, their traditional ways of life, as well as the Christian message. They sought to address questions concerning their cultural values as these pertained to identity and solidarity with the whole community. These converts disengaged themselves from the institutions which brought the Gospel. They did this to allow the Christian message to interact with traditional way of life without the interference of missionaries. The result was a new form of Christianity—a truly African Christianity!

To recapitulate: we note three kinds of responses to the missionary enterprise in Africa. First, we find those Africans who felt their society was threatened by the missionary enterprise; these did not join the new faith. The second type of response represents those who accepted the package of Christian faith as presented by missionaries. The package of the new faith included rejecting one's past and assimilating Western values. Lastly, there were those Africans who sought to have both worlds, Christianity and a traditional way of life. From the second and third kinds of responses emerged two types of Christianity: missionary and indigenous (also called Independent Churches). Missionary Christianity takes Western thought and practice as normative for all Christians everywhere, and it raises reason above myth as the way of arriving at truth, thus rejecting myth as a mode of knowledge capable of leading to truth. Missionary Christianity rejected African cosmology and culture as ways by which divine revelation could be mediated. Enough has already been said about the influences that shaped missionary Christianity, we therefore turn to the nature and character of Indigenous Christianity or Independent Churches.

Indigenous Christianity

The two brands or movements of Christianity mentioned above are found all over Africa where Christianity is professed. Except for the Coptic Church in Egypt and the Ethiopian Orthodox Church, Indigenous Christianity appeared after the second planting of Christianity. Since missionary Christianity was the first to be established in this second phase, scholars of African Christianity refer to its Churches as historical, mainline, established, or simply as mission Churches. On the other hand, Indigenous Christianity is seen as a reaction to missionary praxis, thus the designations: native cult (nativistic movement), separatist, syncretist, or splinter groups. Nativistic movement is used by those who interpret Indigenous Christianity as a manifestation of African political resistance. Adrian Hastings has correctly observed that "Religion was the sanction for all that was most traditional in Africa; it was closely linked with all that was most colonial, and it would be seldom far from all that was most revolutionary."[8] While the political factor is indeed very important, it tends to be overemphasized. Justin Ukpong explains why people consider this Christianity as a form of political resistance.

Modern sociological and historical analysis of religious change in Africa have often tended to view the rise of Indigenous religious institutions and ideas primarily, though not exclusively, in terms of the colonialism-independence tension. Thus the socio-political factors get more emphasis than the others and are given the prime place. It appears to us that strong though the factor is, it is nevertheless not the most basic one, at least in our context. The cultural factor seems most basic for the simple reason that no cultural change can take place (apart from the case of imposition) unless there is an appropriate cultural atmosphere for it. This and the historical factor are considered to have formed the background for making the political effective. As to the theological factor it has itself been influenced by other factors, including the advance made in the social sciences.[9]

Other scholars of African Christianity refer to African Churches as sects following Max Weber's Church-Sect typology.[10] A term which has earned much usage among scholars is Independent Church. The term was first used as early as the 1930s in South Africa. It emerged at a meeting where scholars were analyzing religious movements in South Africa. They found that the African response to the missionary enterprise did not fit current typology. This unique religious phenomenon, found only in Africa, had one thing in common—the attempt to be independent from mission control or the influence of whites. It is from this characteristic that they decided to designate the

African response to the missionary enterprise as "Independent Churches."
The term has stuck, and it is the only one used to denote African Christian
initiative.

These Churches have a long history, they appeared shortly after the
planting of Christianity and are in many areas where missionary activity was
intense. Adrian Hastings says this was to be expected because

> It could be claimed indeed that the ideal locus for independency was an
> area sufficiently close to missionary activity for the seed to have been
> sown—expectations raised, new ideas unleashed—but not close enough for
> it to have been harvested, given the limitations in missionary personnel
> and the tight disciplinary requirements (lengthy probation and a heavy
> list of social prohibitions) which so often excluded from baptism those
> eager to receive it.[11]

In South Africa, where there is the largest concentration of these Churches,
they first started appearing in the 1890s. The Ethiopian movement in South
Africa, for example, started in 1892 by seceding from Wesleyan Church in
Pretoria. Elsewhere, they started to appear after the turn of the century. It
would be an over-generalization to say they are all breakaways from mission
Churches, for there are some which have emerged spontaneously even in
areas where there was less or no missionary activity.

The reasons for their emergence vary and differ; David Barrett has
identified eight factors: historical (ecclesiastical and colonial), political, social,
ethnic, theological, religious, and nonreligious. In my classification I included
translation of the scriptures, because once people had the scriptures in their
vernacular they began to see the distortions within missionary Christianity.
This, in my opinion, is one of the reasons Protestant Churches have
experienced more breakaways than the Catholic Church. Race too, I believe,
has been a strong factor toward formation of Indigenous Churches, because
some missionaries, colonialists, and traders had a low view of the African,
intellectually and otherwise. This is a strong factor in those areas with heavy
European presence, such as South Africa and Zimbabwe.

Earlier studies emphasized autonomy from mission Churches as the main
factor for secession, and ruled the theological reasons out. It is true that at
the outset theological reasons, or controversies over specific dogmas as such,
are not emphasized or mentioned at all. It has to be remembered that most
of the clergy of these churches are not theologically trained, so the way they
would express disagreement would not be in the manner of professional
theologians. The secession itself is a theological statement, and as it has
turned out, scholars are now beginning to see that the quest for autonomy is
a search for freedom and space to do theological work necessary to develop
a truly African Christianity—one which embraces African culture and religious

values. I said in my study on "The History of Independent Churches in Malawi 1900-1976," that these Churches are theological workshops striving to make Christianity African. One of the theological issues addressed in these African Churches is christology. Indeed, they do not raise the issue in the manner of the Early African Church, inquiring into the humanity or divinity of Jesus, but rather, who is Jesus to the African? What does his sonship, his power over nature, etc., mean for the African? Theological ideas now being worked on by Western-trained African theologians in the mission Churches—views like Jesus the ancestor or liberator, etc.—have for long been preached in nonmission Churches.

What are Independent Churches? Barrett defines them as

> a distinct name and membership, even as small as single congregation, which claims Jesus as Lord, and which has either separated by secession from a mission Church or an existing African Independent Church, or has been founded outside the mission Churches as a new kind of religious entity under African initiative and leadership.[12]

Bengt Sundkler and Martin West, two other scholars who have written on African Christianity, say that the term "Independent Church" fails to capture African initiatives in making Christianity meaningful and relevant. Sundkler notes, "Although conscious of the fact that 'independent' in English usage often stands as a synonym for 'congregational,' I shall here use 'Independent' in a wider sense, as referring to such religious organizations as, in their desire for independence from whites, have seceded from mission Churches."[13] Similarly, West says:

> Those Churches that are entirely under African control, and which have no links with Churches that have any white members, we call African Independent Churches.
>
> This is not an ideal term, as in some cases "independent" is taken as having a negative connotation—meaning "independent from whites" rather than stress the positive connotation, the nature of the Churches.[14]

These scholars are very right in their argument against the term "Independent Church," for the term does not say what these churches are about. The term best describes what mission Churches are attempting to do: trying to cut off their umbilical cord and become "independent" from control of former Mission Boards or Councils and their agencies in Europe and America. Control comes through "aid" or "block grants" from the founding Churches. Mission Churches are also seeking ways to free themselves from forms of organization, values, and spirituality of their founding Churches.

It is important to point out that terms such as Independent Church, separatist, native cults, etc., are classifications used by scholars. Members of these churches do not refer to themselves as members of an "Independent Church." Mostly, they identify themselves as members of an African Church. Sometimes they name their Church after their founder: Kimbanguist Church after the prophet Kimbangu; *Eglise Harristé* after prophet Wade Harris, and so forth. At other times they will use designations which best describe what they are about or what their founder(s) sought to achieve by establishing the particular church. For example, when Yesaya Zerenje Mwasi, a Malawian Presbyterian, named his Church the *Mpingo wa Afipa mu Africa* (Blackman's Church in Africa), he wanted to emphasize the initiative and ability of Africans to organize and manage a church on their own, outside the influence and power of Scottish missionaries. Charles Chinula, another Malawian Presbyterian, named his Church *Eklesia la Wanagwa* (Freedom or Liberty Church) to emphasize freedom from the control of Scottish missionaries and freedom to explore and integrate traditional customs and practice in Christianity—indigenization.

By whatever name these members choose to call themselves, these Churches must be taken seriously because they present a different way of understanding Christianity, and try to address issues arising from the encounter between African Western values. Even more important, they try to separate the gospel from Western values which missionaries paraded as Christianity. These churches try to bridge the gap between the past and the present; between African culture, religion, and Christianity. The gap was created by missionary Christianity which tended to devalue traditional African culture and to dismiss its religion as heathen or pagan. As can be noticed, this practice left no room for appreciation for all that was good in traditional society, nor for the assimilation of traditional ideas and rituals in Christianity. This problem has been well expressed by Fashole-Luke, one of Africa's leading theologians. "Western missionaries stressed aspects of discontinuity between Christianity and african cultures and traditional religion to such an extent that they excluded aspects of continuity between Christianity and African cultures and religion. They condemned without proper evaluation African religious beliefs and practices and substituted Western cultural and religious practices."[15]

We see, therefore, that the task these particular African Churches undertake represents both a rejection and a reconstruction: rejection of missionary praxis, and at the same time, an attempt to recapture the Christian message as well as African way of life. The quest is for an authentic African Christian faith: to be African and truly Christian. Authentic is here used to denote total satisfaction of human needs. This is what makes them unique as Kofi Appiah-kubi has observed: "The most significant and unique aspect of these Churches is that they seek to fulfill that which is lacking in the Euro-

American missionary Churches, that is, to provide forms of worship that satisfy both spiritually and emotionally and to enable Christianity to cover area of human life and fulfill all human needs."[16]   Appiah-kubi asserts "that spiritual hunger is the main cause of the emergence of Indigenous African Christian Churches. . . . In these Churches the religious needs of healing, divining, prophesying and visioning are fulfilled by Christian means."[17] African theologians at the Faith and Order consultation in Accra explained why missionary Christianity has not been satisfying to most Africans. They said this was "because of the cultural form in which it is clothed, the Christianity of the missionaries cannot be assimilated, nor can it help people to face up to difficult situations."[18]

In the light of the work undertaken by these African Churches, I have decided to designate them as Indigenous Churches so as to emphasize what they are about, to indigenize Christianity. I am fully aware that not all of them seek to indigenize and that the multiplicity of precipitating factors prohibits generalizations, but all studies agree that integration of the Gospel into African life seems common. Indigenous Churches attempt to provide a satisfying Christianity. The task of finding satisfaction in the Christian faith involves deconstructing "idolized" Christianity of the missionary enterprise and retrieving traditional African way of life. So far, the project has met with limited success because those engaged in the work get side-tracked easily. Secondly, they begin copying ways of mission Christians thereby undermining their original intent.

Notwithstanding its limited success, Indigenous Christianity, has set in motion a theological movement seeking a new paradigm for understanding Christianity in Africa. Unfortunately, the task of Indigenous Churches has not been fully acknowledged. Prejudice on the part of those in the "mainline" Churches has created a general lack of understanding of what Indigenous Churches are about. The result has been complete ignorance concerning the spirituality informing these Churches. Gabriel Setiloane says that people often see Indigenous Churches as the arena for venting out political frustration for the politically oppressed, and thus perceived as interesting sociological phenomena. Various reasons are given for their rise: they are viewed as Zionist, Pentecostal movements or some other heretical sect from the West, to Ethiopianism and African nationalism, says Setiloane. He argues that rarely are these churches seen for what they are, namely, "attempts, however crude and untutored, of the African genius to hold its own, a preserving of the African Indigenous understanding of the workings of divinity (or shall we straight away say 'GOD'?)."[19] Through this unsophisticated way, Indigenous Churches form the vanguard of African resistance to the corrosion caused by Western theological teachings on the "ways" of religious thinking and practice (the ritual, the dance, etc.) which takes place in "mission controlled" Churches.

Setiloane points out that the spirituality which informs and sustains

Indigenous Churches is to be found in the African concept of "*UMUNTU* (person). Setiloane says it is important to understand that "*UBUNTU* (Zulu), *BOTHO* (Sotho-Tswana) or *UBUNTUNGUSHI* (Bemba) is a concept much deeper than the European word for Person or Personality can translate, meaning the very essence of being, the equivalent of 'the soul' in Western Christian language."[20] This fact shows that in Indigenous Churches we are dealing with deeper things, "a theology of Man," as he calls it. This is a theology not learned from a classroom, but from one's mother's knees and from life's experience. This is a theology about one's humanity denied Africans in the mission Churches.

Commenting on the legacy of evangelization Ela, like Setiloane, also says that the missionary enterprise failed to recognize African humanity.

> Missionary endeavor touched only the aspects of African humanity which seemed worthwhile, leaving as unproductive a no-man's land disfigured by tangles of questions, doubts, hopes and unfulfilled expectations of every kind. If it were possible to begin the mission over again—something which must be done in many regions where those already in receipt of the sacraments must be evangelized afresh—one thing which would have to be taken very seriously is the whole sphere of the African as a human being who was belittled and cheated under the old system of traditional evangelism.[21]

What we see in Indigenous Churches is an attempt to recognize African humanity, *umunthu*. It is a new understanding of the theological task. The new approach emerges from the way Africans construe the world. The task before African Churches is not to reinterpret certain aspects of the doctrines of the Church, rather to seek a new paradigm for understanding Christianity in Africa. This is a paradigm based on or arising from African epistemology for only such a framework can enable people to be truly African and Christian or to live an authentic African Christian life. It cannot be over-emphasized that only a paradigm rooted in the African cosmos and experience can make Christianity authentic in Africa, for what is at stake is the way people understand the Gospel in light of their world. This is not only a problem over interpretation of doctrine but questioning the very paradigm, the epistemology in which the doctrines arise. What Indigenous Churches are attempting to do is a matter of crucial importance to the future of Christianity in Africa. The significance of understanding African way of life was noted by delegates to the WCC Faith and Order Consultation in Accra, Ghana in July-August 1974. Under the title "A Statement of African Challenge," the Consultation noted:

> for all Africans, even after many years of Christianity, and standing fully within the Christian Revelation, spirituality and world-view of their

fathers is still very present. We feel, therefore, that all the expressions of the Christian Faith up to now, from whatever area which makes up the Christian Church (Orthodox, Roman, Catholic and Protestant) do not speak to us at the depth of our situation, past, present or future. However, when we come to the Crucified One straight out of our cultural and historical situation, it is then that He has meaning, and becomes not only *our* Savior, but also the Savior of Mankind. He then helps us to see God as the One and Only, the Inscrutable and incomprehensible. For from our unique heritage, we bring the view that God is *UVELINGQAKI*, One whose beginning or end no man can know or describe, *UNKULUNKULU*, a Power greater than all powers; *MODIMO*, that which permeates all and gives life and *LESA*, the ground of being of all that is.[22]

African theologians meeting at Ibadan in 1966 expressed the need for a continuation from African heritage to Christianity.

We believe that God the Father of our Lord Jesus Christ, Creator of Heaven and earth, Lord of History, has been dealing with [hu]mankind at all times and in all parts of the world. It is with this conviction that we study the rich heritage of our African peoples, and we have evidenced that they know Him and worship Him.

We recognize the radical quality of God's self-revelation in Jesus Christ, and yet it is because of this revelation we can discern what is truly of God in our pre-Christian heritage: this knowledge of God is not totally discontinuous with our people's previous traditional knowledge of Him.[23]

Finding new forms of worshipping and expressing the Gospel at the depth of the African situation, past, present, and future is the challenge the African Church is called to do. For it is in exploring new ways of talking about human experience of Deity or doing these new things, moving into new depths, that the Church testifies that there are many ways of divine disclosure. As Ela says, there is more than one way of being Christians.

There is a way of believing, of reading the bible, of celebrating the mystery of salvation and of structuring religious communities which no one can do in our stead. Instead of always referring to what our teachers have thought and to the ways which they have signalled for others, let us set out instead from where we are, from the social and historical situation in which we find ourselves here and now. Let us make a deliberate choice; let us run the risk of being ourselves instead of reiterating ready made formulas and becoming part of hidebound institutions; let us opt for the adventure of confronting the word unuttered today in a specific context, and of breaking completely new ground.[24]

Indigenous Churches attempt to find new ways of expressing the Christian faith in Africa. At the 1976 meeting of the Ecumenical Association of Third World Theologians, African participants called for a shift in methodology to meet the challenge of the African situation. They said:

The African situation requires a new theological methodology that is different from the approaches of the dominant theologies in the West. African theology must reject, therefore, the prefabricated ideas of the North Atlantic theology by defining itself according to the struggles in their resistance against the structures of domination. Our task as theologians is to create a theology that arises from and accountable to the African people.[25]

AFRICAN COSMOLOGY

The greatest contribution Indigenous Churches have made to the theological task in Africa is the importance of beginning with the African way of life or cosmos when doing theology. Traditional Western theology puts emphasis on transcendence, but Indigenous Churches say theology is a human attempt to understand divinity, so it ought to begin with understanding human life and the basic symbols which inform the manner of living or totality of life, thus their emphasis on healing or the battle with the world, evil spirits, ritual process, power of the word, personhood, and community. John Martin, in his study of Zionists Churches in South Africa, has observed that healing is holistic in these Churches: "The operative understanding of health now emerging is that it is dynamic state of well-being of the individual and of society; of physical, mental, spiritual, economic political, and social well-being; of being in harmony with the each other, with the material environment and with God."[26]

Although the ideas stressed upon in Indigenous Churches are from African culture, they find resonance in both the Old and New Testaments. Take the concept of community, for instance, or evil spirits, these are concerns which run through the bible. Their theological relevance is enormous: the concept of community in the Old Testament implies solidarity of the people of *Yahweh*; in the New Testament it is the unity of the body of Christ, the Church. Since community in African thought system includes the dead, or ancestors, this paves way for Africans to understand the concept of communion of saints. Ancestors have interest in the activities of the living, so do the saints. All ancestors trace their descendence to the founding ancestor, the proto-ancestor; in Indigenous Christianity Jesus is that proto-ancestor, the first in the line of ancestors, therefore concerned with the activities of all the living and the dead.

In the preceding paragraphs I have sketched some of the concepts emphasized in Indigenous Christianity. In the following pages I will elaborate and thereby demonstrate the significance of some of the ideas and practices in Indigenous Christianity for theology in Africa.

Community

We have already started on the concepts of community, but let us explore it a little further. Indigenous Churches see themselves as extensions of traditional communities. Thus there is a deep feeling for the welfare of all members. This is not responsibility for spiritual welfare alone but for all that concerns basic human needs. In other words, Indigenous Churches are not places people go for worship and then go their separate ways. They are places where people come to affirm and be affirmed by listening and telling each other stories of their life; stories of joy and of pain. It is a place one comes to feel at home, a family, or a "commune," where one's identity is acknowledged and recognized. "It is possible," Marthinius Daneel has commented, "that precisely such a need for personal identity, for a label by which men and women can recognize themselves it terms of those whom they know face to face is the fundamental (if not largely unconscious) motive in the formation of independent Churches)."[27] So prayers include things that pertain to material and spiritual well-being. Indigenous Churches are concerned with all things which make life worth living, so as it is in traditional society, it is the responsibility of each and everyone to make life worthwhile in Indigenous Churches. It is this sense of belonging to a concerned and caring community which, in many ways, has been one of the attractions to Indigenous Churches.

The concept of community includes ancestors, who in African thought stand for human destiny, the fulfillment of life, as Englebert Mveng comments: "Human beings are beings with a destiny insofar as they are the battleground for the struggle between life and death, the combatants who take sides with or against life, and the initiates in whom the victory of life over death (or its defeat by death) is verified. The fact is that the vocation of human beings on earth is to ensure the victory of life over death."[28] Boulaga as Mveng writes.

Human beings receive their fullness from others, in the form of a sense of and meaning for life. Destiny is human life perceived and accomplished. Those who die in the very act of doing what is meaningful pass, by virtue of the mediation of the living, into the sphere of forces that structure the community and give it its orientation—the sphere of the presences that animate the community and make existence an adventure worth living.[29]

Africans have a very strong sense of the dynamic presence of ancestors in their life. Ancestors are guardians of ways of living which mediate life; they represent an exemplary past. As people bound in time and space, Africans seek to understand their life within a temporally historical context. That is, they try to understand their present in light of the past. Why look back? People are not thrown into a present without a past; pastness is part of their present. 'Zulu Sofala expresses this idea as follows: "The present is the meeting point between the past and the future, the past is transmuted into the present, and the present is in the passage to the future. Thus those already born are the ancestors, and the living are the unborn in a passage of transition. There is a strong cohesiveness that binds all aspects of existence."[30]

Upon death, one enters a new "realm beyond psychological illusion, for he or she has reintegrated the origin, and been reintegrated into it. Now the exemplar is one with the Spirit, who is all in all, everything in everyone."[31] This explains why Africans are very much concerned about communion with ancestors. Ancestors therefore are not just people's memory of the immediate or distant dead. Ancestors are alive and as exemplars they have an interest in the well-being of the living. People invoke them for guidance, thus Boulaga can say "the personality of dead is so intimately linked to theirs [the living] that they can themselves pronounce words their absent exemplar could have spoken."[32]

The question of ancestors is a very important one to African Christians for salvation is not complete for Africans unless it includes the ancestors. Africans seek to be reconciled not only with the living but also with those who constitute them. Real happiness or the foundation of authentic faith for Africans is in making this reconciliation a present possibility. Ela explains:

the quest for real happiness which respects the claims of the ancestors and at the same time is lived in the light of the Gospel must become the task of the Church in an African milieu. From such a quest would emerge the possibility of a true grasp of the essentials of the faith. From now on, African Christian communities must have the courage to lay aside the security of missionary work organized according to the requirements of worship in favor of a practical response to deep-rooted human needs. For it is the whole person which is at stake here, what takes place when someone's entire existence is reorganized in the light of something which gives direction and meaning, while leaving it rooted within a given culture. In the last analysis the question facing the Church every day is the question of the relevance of faith at the heart of a vast network of primary symbols arising out of the world view peculiar to Africans.[33]

Closely connected with the concept of community is the understanding of life. Traditional society has a holistic approach to life. Life is understood in several ways in Africa: cosmological, biological, spiritual, and relational. I will use the Malawian term *moyo*, which I have used in other writings, to explain the African concept of life. In "Bondedness, *Moyo* and *Umunthu*. . ." I state that in the first place

> *moyo* refers to cosmological order since it inhabits life. This means creation is understood as life. Life begins and "end," biologically, yet on the other hand, life continues to transcend itself in different ways. In other words, *moyo* as the foundation of creation has no end. *Moyo* is both material and yet mystery or spiritual. Humankind participates on both levels of *moyo*. [On the biological level] *moyo* means being alive or the act of living connected with activities of biological existence. . . . *Moyo* refers to physical well-being, simply health. In everyday speech *moyo* refers to health, physical well-being as well as the state of an individual or community. In light of these interpretations the term is used as a word for salutation, announcing good health, well-being and peace.[34]

Moyo also means right relations between people, sharing, openness, and spiritual well-being. These are nonmaterial things but nonetheless necessary to support biological life. To exclude the socio-religious dimension of *moyo* would be to neglect the fact that *moyo* is constitutive in the meaning of persons, central to which is respect. People are to be respected for what they are—persons! On the social level, *moyo* means the art of living together by affirming and acknowledging one another as persons and establishing genuine communication. One begins to learn this art of living together, as a community, in a ritual process. Note that Africans maintain that life is not only given, biologically speaking, it is also learned or received from others through ritual. This means the community owes the individual life.

This holistic understanding of life moves Indigenous Churches to take the ministry of healing as one of their important ministries. This healing is not only physical, although that is a larger part of it, but also social, that is, between persons who may have psychologically hurt each other. But the healing could also be spiritual. It is not uncommon in Indigenous Churches to have someone come forward asking for prayer for spiritual wholeness. Healing as wholeness of the individual and community is the totality or fullness of life, the feeling of socio-psychological, physical, and spiritual fulfillment. But restoration to health is the beginning of this fulfillment. Various studies on Indigenous Churches all agree that healing is one of the primary reasons for joining Indigenous Churches. Appiah-Kubi explains why people go to these Churches with their sick.

> In dealing with psychosomatic problems these Churches are very successful through the powers, techniques, and willingness of the spiritually endowed leaders and members. They are also successful with chronic diseases considered incurable by Western technological medicine. . . . In the established Churches, medical practice has become so specialized that the ordinary pastor has been radically excluded from service for the sick; thus healing and worship have become separate. In the Indigenous African Churches there is a reintegration of healing and worship. This corresponds with the Akan understanding, for religion in the Akan concept must be concerned with health and fertility of human beings, animals and land.[35]

These views have also been noted by Ukpong who writes:

> Traditionally, for the African, religion is not merely a matter of going to Church or observing a set of principles; it is a way of life that permeates all spheres and levels of living. One seeks material well-being, like *healing*, as well as spiritual well-being, like forgiveness of sin, within the religious context. But the missionary presentation of Christianity, coming as it did from a background that knew much of secularism in society, tended to separate Christianity from life-concerns and to present it as a set of principles, thus ignoring the African's view point. Healing for example, is entrusted to a secular institution, the hospital. But one brought up in the African thought system will almost always be seen seeking healing in a religious context. In other words, while the African readily accepts Christianity and is committed to it, he/she soon finds out that it does not respond to his/her needs as did the traditional religion, and hence he/she reverts to the latter occasionally as a supplement.[36]

Here we have shown that community means a lot to Africans. Community does not refer to a loose association of individuals, but to an organic union, a solidarity among the living and with the dead—a fellowship in which everyone cares and feels responsible for the other.

NARRATIVE: METAPHOR, SYMBOL, MYTH, AND RITUAL

Narrative

In discussing ancestors it was stated that pastness is part of people's present. This means that in temporality, pastness takes on narrative structure. People keep describing their past as they seek to understand the present. Narrative structure is used in Indigenous Churches to recapture identity or "African humanity belittled and cheated under the old system of evangelism" as Ela has said. Narrative is used in preaching to recapture the essence of the Gospel and to allow it to be alive and speak to the African condition. It is a preaching that uses biblical and people's stories to express theological truth. In the following pages I will expound narrative theology by exploring its various dimensions.

Narrative is description of life event(s) told in form of a story. (In African society stories take different structures, poetry, song, or narrative.) This is to say narrative is a description of lived experience. This description is guided by certain images, metaphors, and symbols which control the flow, rhythm, or the tensions of events within the story. Let us clarify this by drawing an example from one of the New Testament narratives—the passion narrative. This is the story about the sufferings of Jesus. It is a story about physical agony and mental anguish; it is about trial, flogging, and crucifixion. What has just been said constitutes the rhythm of the narrative. The flow of the narrative is controlled by the symbol of the cross, for it is here where suffering leads. The cross is the identifier, for it points people to the *who* and *what* of the story, that is, the subject matter, who suffered and for what? Or what was the suffering all about? Unlike songs, symbols point beyond themselves, that is, to infinite possibilities. The cross points beyond suffering, it opens a whole new vision of life. In a word, symbols have a surplus of meaning.

What make symbols inexhaustible in meaning is their double intentionality; they have literal (manifest) and latent meanings, and the latter is reached only through participation in the former. By participating in what is manifest, one is assimilated in that which is symbolized and is led by it beyond itself. This does not mean that through symbols one is able to see or to understand fully, because symbols reveal even as they conceal. Symbols are integral to narrative because of their ability to communicate or express that which is beyond concept. Symbols, along with images and metaphors are part and parcel of the description of lived experience; they form part of communicative action of a discourse or narrative structure.

Narrative does not use speculative thought or abstract concepts and arguments. This is because it emerges from lived experience—what really happened! Although narrative does not use argument to defend its position, it is not an uncritical or unreliable description of events. Narrative is the only form of communication that challenges the mind's creativity to pass on profound truths of life without being caught in empty words. This creative process of handing down truth involves being analytical. Words, metaphors, and symbols are carefully selected to embellish and yet communicate profound truth. Distortions are sifted to enable the audience to relive the experience or participate in the event. Since narrative arises out of lived experience, it is also "common" or "shared" knowledge. Being "common knowledge," it can be verified or the gaps can be filled, and distortions corrected by or from the experience (knowledge) of others who share that knowledge. Once again, let us turn to the passion narrative to illustrate the reliability of narrative. The passion story is told in all the synoptic Gospels. They do not tell it exactly the same way. The flow and the rhythm differ from writer to writer, but the controlling symbol is the same. The narrators compliment each other, thereby giving the reader a full blown picture of the *what* and *who* of the narrative. Without using argument, narrative transmits truth in a reliable way. Thanks to narrative structure!

Metaphors

Metaphors and symbols are used in narrative not only to deliver a message but to make the message alive and down to earth. Use of symbols in the telling of stories or in delivering a message comes natural to Africans. In African society symbols play a crucial role in understanding everyday experience. In traditional society everything is expressed in metaphors by way of symbols, be it joy or sorrow. Nothing is outside or beyond the sphere of symbols and metaphors. The centrality of symbols in the African society lies in the fact that they have a capacity to arouse imagination or creativity and mobilize people. In this way, symbols give people directionality or make a vision clearer.

Metaphors are important in the telling of a story because of their power to bring new meaning out of two familiar yet unrelated and sometimes contradicting words, ideas, or images. Metaphor is a way of knowing generated by bringing into tension two terms, images and words or contexts to create a third and new meaning. Metaphor does not collapse the familiar terms, images, etc. into each other. Rather, by drawing similarity and difference between two (sometimes opposing) words, ideas, or images, metaphor releases the potential within the familiar to bring about a completely new meaning. Through metaphor, the familiar is transformed, thereby bringing new knowledge and understanding. In short, metaphor allows people to express certain ideas or profound truth more clearly where normal lexical meaning and grammatical structures cannot.

Metaphors and symbols are very close. Metaphors develop from similes. Similes use "*like*" or "*as*" to create new meaning: "The kingdom of God is *as* if a man should scatter seed;" "The kingdom of God is *like* a grain of a mustard seed;" "*like* the eye of a needle." When a simile gains acceptance in everyday speech, it drops the terms "like" and "as." At this stage, a simile is transformed into metaphor and a continued use of metaphor transforms it into a symbol. We might therefore define symbol as sedimentation of metaphor. A person who is as powerful *as* a lion may eventually be called a "lion," lion symbolizing strength. While metaphors may become symbols, the reverse is not true. Symbols do not become metaphors but part of lexical meaning or everyday speech.

When similes drop "as" and "like," when they have been transformed into metaphors, their meaning may not be readily available to someone with a limited vocabulary or sense of imagination. For example, my youngest sister in-law when she was three, cried whenever one of her sisters complimented her looks with the metaphor "*chimphadzuwa*." The literal meaning of *chimphadzuwa* is "sun-blotter" or "sun-killer"! The implication is that the face of a beautiful girl or woman outshines the sun. To say a girl's face outshines the sun is to metaphorically express perfect beauty which makes the girl the center or focus of attention and affection. My sister in-law cried because she did not realize that her sisters were expressing admiration; they were complimenting her as a perfect beauty or as a gem in their midst! Metaphors or metaphoric expressions challenge the mind's imagination to create meaning or make "sense" from what is said.

When used in narrative, metaphors open up a new horizon or new meaning in life by transforming everyday reality. The power of metaphors to bring new meaning from the familiar make them crucial when talking about the relation between people and the sacred. By the use of metaphors, people are able to speak of divine mysteries in ordinary language; or to see the transcendent in ordinary life. In other words, metaphors show people that the transcendent and ordinary life cannot be separated. This is to say, "religious" metaphors call people to live an ordinary life but in a new way. The new way is revealed by the new meaning generated by the metaphor. This is what Jesus does when he points his audience to the ordinary in life, mustard seed, and calls them to see God's work through it. Along with symbols, metaphors are able to empower people as they struggle to fulfill their dreams or order their future accordingly. Metaphors have the potential to transform and recreate our world or the way we think about ourselves and others. This is to say, narrative awakens self and social consciousness, thereby giving people a new vision, a new understanding of reality, life, and the future.

The use of narratives has allowed Africans to examine the encounter between African culture (way of life) and Western values. Many sermons in Indigenous Churches are based on biblical narratives particularly those on God's mighty acts of redemption. Accordingly, theology and preaching have taken narrative form. The concept of a Christian community in Indigenous Churches is that of a story telling community; a community which finds strength in the exchange of faith experience and those experiences take a narrative form.

Story telling is not absent in mission Churches. Most lay preachers in these Churches also employ narrative in preaching. Narrative is very important in preaching because it brings biblical stories to life so that they "speak" to the people as if the stories or events narrated happened in their own lives. Story deals with bringing to life original experience—the event—for people to participate in it and make it their own. To say this in religious language, is to claim that stories have a "sacred" dimension to them that transforms them into "sacraments" which in turn transforms their listeners. In addition, stories have a moral character. By this we mean that stories are told for their practical relevance. People's lives are influenced by stories they hear, stories which intertwine with their own experience. In this way, stories cease to be "mere" stories but stories of their own life and experience. In short, identity is formed by the stories in which people find themselves to be participants.

Narrative is the basic mode of expressing fundamental truths people hold or of handing down understanding of divine as well as human life. Africans realize this practical ethical potential in the art of story telling. This accounts for the universality of narrative in African preaching, more so in Indigenous Churches than their counterparts. Unfortunately, those with theological training in the Mission Churches look down on narrative. From their homiletics classes and the whole theological studies, they are taught to appeal to reason and not "tell stories" for stories are uncritical by their very nature. In theological seminary students learn that narrative is the infantile stage of reasoning, employed by those who cannot comprehend abstract concepts and truth. For people with unsophisticated reasoning abilities, use of images and stories to express basic ideas is certainly proper but not for a theologically trained person. Here we see the vestiges of the Enlightenment. The result of such negative attitudes toward narrative is dry sermons, unrelated to the life of the people, the African reality, or the biblical situation itself from which the Gospel arose. Part of the success of the preaching ministry of Jesus was due to the fact that he did not follow the ways of the educated Jews of his time who adopted Greek culture and ways of thinking. Jesus, like all ordinary people, used a narrative approach in preaching; in fact all his theology was narrative. Jesus used narrative, invoked images and things used or known in the everyday life of his audience. Through narrative he was able to speak about the deep mysteries of God.

African preachers use narrative to transmit profound religious thought and build character. The Gospel story is one with practical demands. It demands people to make the Gospel story their own. This is precisely what the African preacher seeks to achieve with her/his sermon as he/she employs symbols and metaphors in narrative. In his studies of African sermons, Horst Buerkle has observed that for the African preacher "the persons and events of both Testaments are always near to the preacher and his congregation, as if they were part of their own time . . . the attempt to reproduce biblical history through illustrations drawn from local African scenes is a common practice . . . the African preacher confronts us with the relevance of the symbol."[37]

Ritual

Along with narrative and symbolism there has appeared a renewed emphasis on ritual. In Indigenous Churches they have all sorts of rituals concerned with all circumstances of life: birth, health, death, etc. It is only natural that a people whose life is marked by ritual from birth to death should find religious meaning and satisfaction in life through performance of ritual. Being close to nature Africans pattern their lives in accordance with the rhythms (rituals) of creation. It may be helpful to show what Africans think about nature. In African thought, nature is never *only* or *just* nature; something that can be objectified and carelessly spent. Nature is not to be manipulated. Nature, as the cosmos, is real, alive, and sacred! Modalities of life are revealed by nature. Likewise, nature reveals knowledge of the sacred. This patterning of life to cosmic rhythms is based on the understanding that these rhythms stand for order, harmony, and permanence of creation, and there is unity between different forms of life. African theologians meeting at the Pan African Conference of Third World Theologies underscored this understanding of the unity of life when they said: "There is unity and continuity between the destiny of the cosmos. The victory of life in the human person is also the victory of life in the cosmos."[38]

What is ritual? Ritual can be defined as a way of expressing communion or solidarity with the living, the dead, the origin of life, deity, through word, action, or material means. People participate in this communion to find fullness of life. Ritual may also be understood as people's attempt to explain the mystery of life or the unexplainable. Ritual is about human life and cosmic origin and destiny. This "explanation" of the incomprehensible does not exhaust nor completely reveal the mystery it seeks to "explain." There is always a dimension that is not fully comprehended, but the "explanation" given by ritual suffices for the time. Ritual is always "part" disclosure for the "whole" for the full view is never realized.

Ritual has two dimensions; it points to divinity, ancestors or that which constitutes the original event, the *event* upon which the present act is based or sanctioned. But ritual also concerns human community. When ritual points to the Creator, participants may have two things in mind: (a) to express gratitude to the Creator and ancestors for blessings and care of successive generations; or (b) to entreat the Creator and ancestors to avert imminent danger, that is, divine intervention. Whatever the case may be, expressing gratitude or imploring the Creator and ancestors for help, ritual shows its centrality in human community.

The second dimension of ritual concerns people—strengthening community. Ritual as a process draws people together to celebrate their unity as a community and at the same time to express their willingness to stand and suffer together. Ritual is a seal of willingness to suffer and celebrate life together as people who belong to one another, one community of the living and the dead and Deity. Ancestors hear and suffer with the living and together they implore the Great Spirit to intervene. In other words, ritual process symbolizes the unity of people with the cosmos and their common destiny since what happens to people also affects the destiny of the cosmos. "The struggle between life and death," says Mveng, "does not take place solely in the heart of human beings; it fills the entire cosmos. All that exists—spirits, cosmic forces, natural elements, living and dead human beings—are mobilized to struggle."[39]

Closely integrated in ritual is myth. All rituals have a myth which set them into being: no myth, no ritual. The general view about myths is that they are fake stories or tales without any significance or with vague reference to what might have happened. I take myth as a form of narrative which describes people's pastness, which constitutes them. Myth is concerned with foundational events and situations which explain who we are. This is to argue that myth is not fiction imposed on our world; rather, a way of apprehending truth. Myth is a mode of knowing, dealing with foundations of life and creation. The knowledge delivered in myths is not self-evident or self-intelligible. This is because myth mediates knowledge through ritual and symbols. To understand myth, one has to decode it or engage in ritual process. Ritual process reproduces the original context in which a particular myth arose. Thus through ritual, people decode meaning or trace the origin of life as it is embodied in a myth. We see the role of myth as bringing awareness of origin and one's relation to the sacred.

To illustrate: Malawian creation myths speak of a Deity whose original intent was to dwell with people forever. These myths say people forced the Deity to climb to the heavens above. One of the creation myths states that, at the dawn of time, when ravens and all the other birds laid their eggs on the ground (a metaphorical way of expressing serenity and peace), *Mulungu* lived on earth.[40] Driven by their great appetite for wild game, people burnt all the grass and forests to clear it for easy hunting. The fire caused destruction of life. It burned all birds, insects, animals, and all crawling creatures. Even worse, the fire burned *Mulungu*'s abode.[41]

What is the concept of the world or creation involved here? Without giving an elaborate commentary on the myth, we will make a brief overview of its theological implications. The myth focuses on relationship between people and creation and also between people and their creator. *Mulungu*'s intention for people and all creation was to be in perpetual communion. People broke the relationship through greed. Appetite (or uncontrollable acquisitiveness) is given as the primary motive for disregarding the welfare of other creatures. The world was meant to be shared by all including the Creator. It was to be a place of fellowship and communion of life, a human fellowship, but also a harmonious relationship between people, nature, and Mulungu. Self-interest broke that fellowship thus destroying the original order and bringing suffering to all creatures and *Mulungu*. The immediate result was separation from *Mulungu*. Self-interest led to the violent act of disinheriting other creatures or nature which was meant to be common property. Self-interest brings disorder is the central theme of this creation myth.

The second dimension of ritual focuses on people. Ritual is a seal of bondedness to one another and to the cosmos. The second dimension of ritual also concerns people as co-creators of the human species. To develop this further, we consider ritual as a process of transformation to personhood. In African society community confers on persons, "personhood," *umunthu* as we say in Malawi, that state of realizing fullness of life or one's humanity and dignity. The process involves awareness that life is sacred and that human life is the microcosm of creation. This is to say that in the order of creation, human life stands at the center. The centrality of human life in creation makes it special and worthy of respect. Therefore the orientation process points to those things which enhance or demean life. It is the task of the community to make one aware of things that make for life. The orientation process takes place through ritual. The initiate is drawn into a new understanding of life and creation in general through ritual process.

Ritual process raises consciousness of one's identity, one's humanity which would otherwise not be known. The point is that through symbolic action, words, narrative, or story, people define one's personhood and at the same time open possibilities to a richer and fuller meaning of life. The process of incorporation of ritual is necessary for it shows one's role in organizing the self in relation to the total community. Through the ritual process, initiates learn about their new roles and responsibilities in society. This "new" knowledge opens possibilities for self-understanding and a new vision of life. In other words, the incorporation event becomes a transforming moment—a moment when one's identity is disclosed. The transforming moment, a moment of self-awareness, is brought by ritual process. Disclosure of a new identity comes with new possibilities and challenges in life.

The new identity is understood as social. This means that the self is understood as social and self-understanding as that which one receives from others through ritual and at other times. In African society, a person is defined in relation to community as Mbiti's dictum states: "I am because we are, and since we are, therefore I am."[42] Mbiti says:

> In traditional life the individual does not exist and cannot exist alone except corporately. He owes his existence to other people, including those of past generations and his contemporaries. He is simply part of the whole. The community must therefore make, create or produce the individual; for the individual depends on the corporate group. Physical birth is not enough: the child must go through rites of incorporation so that it becomes fully integrated into the entire society. These rites continue throughout the physical life of the person, during which the individual passes from one stage of corporate existence to another. The final stage is reached when he dies and even then he is ritually incorporated into the wider family of both the dead and the living . . . Only in terms of other people does the individual become conscious of his own being, his duties, privileges and responsibilities toward himself and toward other people.[43]

Mbiti's point is that one becomes a person or realizes personhood only in light of a framework of togetherness. African wisdom is emphatic concerning being bonded to each other and the necessity for living in a framework of togetherness, community. For example, Malawians say, *Kali kokha mkanyama* (the lone person is a prey) meaning, one can only survive in the company of others, or without community one falls prey to the ills and dangers of the world. The purpose of life is realized only in a framework of togetherness. This concept of person very much stands in contrast to the Enlightenment tradition according to which persons are defined in relation to will, as with Nietzsche, or rationality and memory, as with Descartes. Descartes' dictum: *ego cogito sum* (I think, therefore I am) is based on memory and rationality. In formulating this dictum, Descartes argued that he could doubt the existence of everything else but the one thing he could be certain of was that he *existed* or that he *was*! The argument was based on human capacity to think rationally and remember. I do not want to dwell on this issue but let me make a few observations. I maintain that *cogito* is empty of meaning for "thinking" or reflection is always mediated by something that objectifies it! That could be ideas, action, work, or movement. In other words, things objectify the self, or Ego. This is another way of saying that the Ego loses and finds itself in things that are external to it. From this it follows that reflection, "therefore I am," is a second level act.

Tradition

Ritual process must be understood within the concept of tradition, that sum total of collective experience of a people. In Africa, tradition constitutes the totality of the experience of successive generations accumulated since the dawn of time. Therefore, tradition represents tested wisdom of the ancestors. It is both the medium and the message of practical wisdom gathered throughout generations. In ritual, these words of wisdom are again heard. Through spoken word and/or symbolic action of ritual, the wisdom of the ancestors is again proclaimed. The initiate, in pain and suffering shared by the whole community, meditates on the wisdom of the ancestors. The words of the ancestors engage the mind of the initiate thus orienting the mind toward transformation of character. To summarize: ritual sharpens the sensitivity of the mind giving it greater freedom to orient itself into things that point to the fullness of life, i.e. personhood.

CONCLUSION

Indigenous Christianity is anchored in the African cosmos where everything has a sacred dimension. Order and harmony characterize the African cosmos. In everyday life, order and harmony translate into continuity and fellowship. This is the continuity of life and community, thus the emphasis on respect and preservation of life or persons and community. Life must be allowed to break all barriers to reach its fullness, for people to realize *umunthu*, that actuality or experience of living to the fullest of one's potential and abilities. That which is life, or life in the African cosmos, does not end with death, it is eternal. Life, in its essence, or *moyo*, as we say in Malawi, is not limited to the world of physical appearances or matter. It breaks forth all limitations including death, and thereby draws the ancestors in the realm of the living. Community consists of the living and the dead. Communion with those who have departed physical life is sought through memorials or other rituals. The dead have entered the spiritual world, they are near the Great Spirit, the origin of *moyo* itself.

This, in short, is a summation of African cosmos and way of life. Basic symbols of life, persons, and community constitute and control the tempo of things. Indigenous Christianity has appropriated these basic symbols to ground the faith in people's life. This has been done in an attempt to enable people to find meaning and identity in Christ. Narrative, ritual, and myth form the spirituality of Indigenous Christianity. Noting the influence of African spirituality on African Christianity, Bengt Sundkler observes that unlike Western Protestantism with its individualism, African spirituality seems to be grounded in the strong corporate nature of the Christian life, that is, in community and fellowship. Sundkler comments that "This characteristic pattern of corporate worship shows through most vividly and dramatically in the life of Independent African Churches, with their roots both in genuine African experience and in an archetypal inspiration of Biblical teaching."[44]

Before we close, let us briefly summarize the theological message from the tom-tom beat of the drums from Indigenous Churches. The beat is calling Africans to make Christianity authentic, that is, to take the African context as part of divine revelation. This is to say, the ways by which God disclosed divine nature to the ancestors should be included in the new way, namely revelation through Jesus. In this way Jesus joins African ancestors and is integrated into the African community as a proto-ancestor. This is important for people to whom ancestors play a critical role in their life. Through this integration, African spirituality is allowed to organize the way of life in this "new" order, thereby preventing the African from being a religious schizophrenic. In short, the tom-tom beat is calling Africans to make a new interpretation of revelation and christology.

The third doctrine Indigenous Churches are redefining is ecclesiology. By rejecting the image and meaning of being a church as given by the Mission Churches, Indigenous Churches are saying that although the Church has a divine origin, the knowledge of its self-understanding, ecclesiology, is shaped by historical and cultural circumstances. Indeed, when the Church left Palestine, it left an understanding of the world unique to Jews and it took on Greek metaphysics. In other words, when the Church came to Europe, it became part of European culture and the changes continue for each historical period and culture.

From Indigenous Churches we learn that to hold on to one particular image of the Church, and to maintain that that image should transcend time and space, is to imprison the Church and idealize the image as the Church. The image, from the past and elsewhere, cannot provide a genuine praxis to deal with the concrete. It can only provide an imaginary praxis because it is a relic. As a relic, its liturgy, music, and practice only drowns the people with the power of its spell. Imaginary praxis fails to provide censure for conditions of the present. This praxis neglects the *distance* that separates the people from the bygone days and culture.

The image is not the church. What the church is, transcends time and space; the form follows the historical circumstances of the called of God—*ekklesia*. Hans Küng says the real church not only has history, it exists by having a history. There is no "doctrine" of the Church in the sense of unalterable metaphysical and ontological system, but only one which is historically conditioned, within the framework of the history of the Church, its dogmas, and theology.[45]

I have listed above some of the main theological issues Indigenous Churches are redefining. In the body of the chapter, other aspects of the Christian faith and practice were discussed. There is no dimension of the faith which is not being quietly analyzed and redefined in Indigenous Churches. Mission Churches are just beginning to engage in this very important task of grounding Christianity in Africa. The vitality of any faith depends so much on how far deep it is rooted in the life of those practicing it. A faith that is not rooted in the life of its practitioners will always remain alien. An authentic faith takes control of the whole person in thought and deed. This is what Indigenous Christianity is seeking to achieve. The tom-tom beat from the drums of Indigenous Churches is calling people to make Christianity authentic. For it is in being truly African and truly Christian that people shall experience redemption in Jesus Christ.

NOTES

1. Harry Thuku, *An Autobiography* (Nairobi: Oxford University Press, 1970), 6.

2. Boulaga, *Christianity Without Fetishes*. trans. Robert Barr (Maryknoll, N.Y.: Orbis Books, 1984), 25.

3. Sanon, quoted by Jean-Marc Ela, *From Charity to Liberation* (London: Catholic Institute for International Relations), 6.

4. *Ibid.*, 5.

5. *Ibid.*

6. *Ibid.*, 5-6.

7. Ela, *My Faith as an African*, trans. John P. Brown and Susan Perry (Maryknoll, N.Y.: Orbis, 1988; London: Geoffrey Chapman, 1989), 26-27.

8. Adrian Hastings, *A History of African Christianity 1950-75* (Cambridge: Cambridge University Press, 1979), 17.

9. Justin S. Ukpong, "African Theologies Now: A Profile," *Spearhead*, 80 (February 1984): 6.

10. Max Weber, *The Sociology of Religion*, trans. Ephraim Fischoff, introduction by Talcott Parsons (Boston: Beacon Press, 1964).

11. Hastings, *A History of African Christianity 1950-1975*, 69.

12. David Barrett, *Schism and Renewal in Africa* (Nairobi: Oxford University Press, 1968), 50.

13. Sundkler, *Bantu Prophets*, 18.

14. Martin West, *Bishops and Prophets in a Black City* (Cape Town: David Philip, 1965), 3.

15. Fashole-Luke, *Christianity in Independent Africa* (Bloomington, Ind.: Indiana University Press; London, Rex Collings, 1978), 357.

16. Kofi Appiah-kubi, "Indigenous African Christian Churches: Signs of Authenticity" eds. Kofi Appiah-kubi and Sergio Torres, in *African Theology en route* (Maryknoll, N.Y.: Orbis Books, 1979), 118.

17. *Ibid.*, 117-118.

18. WCC: Faith and Order Commission: "Giving Account of the Hope in us," *Report of the Yaoundé Faith and Order Seminar*, 51.

19. Gabriel Setiloane, "How the Traditional world-view persists in the Christianity of the Sotho-Tswana," ed. Fashole-Luke, in *Christianity in Independent Africa*, 408.

20. *Ibid.*, 409. Quotation from a speech delivered at a "Consultation on Indigenous Churches" at Mindolo Ecumenical Institute, Zambia, 1962.

21. Ela, *From Charity to Liberation*, 6-7.

22. WCC Faith and Order Commission: "Uniting in Hope," 34.

23. Dickson and Ellingworth, eds., *Biblical Revelation and African Beliefs* (London: Lutterworth, 1969), 16.

24. Ela, *From Charity to Liberation*, 9.

25. In Appiah-kubi and Torres, *African Theology en Route*, 193.

26. John Martin, "They Have Grown-And On Their Own," *International Review of Mission*, 72 (October, 1983): 588.

27. Marthinius Daneel, "Charismatic healing in African Independent Churches," *Theologica Evangelica*, 16, no. 2 (August 1983): 29.

28. Englebert Mveng, "Black African Art as Cosmic Liturgy and Religious Language," ed. Appiah-kubi and Torres, in *African Theology*, 138.

29. Boulaga, *Christianity Without Fetishes*, 149.

30. 'Zulu Sofala, "The Theater in the Search for African Authenticity," ed. Appiah-kubi and Torres, in *African Theology*, 127-128.

31. Boulaga, *Christianity Without Fetishes*, 150.

32. *Ibid.*, 149-150.

33. Ela, *From Charity to Liberation*, 8-9.

34. Sindima, "Bondedness, *Moyo* and *Umunthu* as the Elements of Achewa Spirituality: Organizing Logic and Principle of Life," *Ultimate Reality and Meaning: Interdisciplinary Studies in the Philosophy of Understanding*, 14, no. 1 (1991): 12.

35. Appiah-kubi, "Indigenous African Christian Churches," ed. Appiah-kubi and Torres, in *African Theology*, 121, 122.

36. Ukpong, "African Theologies Now," 11.

37. Horst Buerkle, "Patterns of Sermons From Various Parts of Africa," in David B. Barrett, *African Initiatives in Religion* (Nairobi: East Africa Publishing House, 1971), 222-231.

38. *Pan African Conference of Third World Theologians Communique.*

39. Mveng, "Black African Art," 140.

40. Mulungu is one of the common Chewa designations for divinity. Among Malawians, divinity is known by modes of revelation. The Great Spirit is identified by the various manifestations of its power in creation. Here Mulungu means creator. There is controversy among scholars as to the original meaning of Mulungu, but there is no disagreement that the term refers to the Creator Spirit (cf. Smith, ed. *African Ideas of God*, 59; J. M. Schoffeleers, "Symbolic and Social Aspects of Spirit Worship among the Mang'anja," a Ph.D. dissertation presented to Oxford University, 1968, 191). Namalenga is also used to refer to this mode of revelation. Other modes of revelation are Chiuta, meaning the Mighty One, the one who pulls everything together (Chiuta literally means a large bow associated with the rainbow); Makewana, mother of all creation. Leza and Mphambe designate the patient Sustainer and Provider, the Powerful One, whose might is compared to lightening.

41. There are different variations of this myth among Malawians of the central and southern parts. For more creation myths from Malawi, see also Nthara, *Mbiri ya Achewa* (Zomba and Lusaka, Northern Rhodesia: Nyasaland Literature Bureau, 1949), 13. Also J. M. Schoffeleers and A. A. Roscoe, *The Land of Fire: Oral Literature from Malawi* (Limbe: Popular Publications; Lilongwe: Likuni Press and Publishing House, 1985), 17-38; Schoffeleers, "The Beginnings of Life," *Vision of Malawi*, 3, (Dec. 1972): 13-17.

42. John Samuel Mbiti, *African Religions and Philosophy* (New York: Doubleday, 1970), 141.

43. *Ibid.*

44. Bengt Sundkler, "Worship and Spirituality" ed. Fashole-Luke, Gray, et al. in *Christianity in Independent Africa*, 545.

45. Hans Küng, *The Church* (New York: Doubleday, 1976).

8

African Theology

THE ORIGIN OF AFRICAN THEOLOGY

The challenge that Indigenous Christianity has taken very seriously is to make Christianity authentically African. The process involves deep theological reflection. Indigenous Churches have not only done this, but they have also put into practice the changes called forth by their theological reflection. Though unsophisticated in their approach, these Churches have posed a challenge to mission Churches to engage in the kind of theological thinking which will help to produce an authentic African Church. Scholars in the mission Churches have responded to the challenge by seeking a theology capable of producing a truly African Church. Their search has produced a number of theological approaches. This chapter will explore and analyze the various theological trends in the mission Churches.

Literature in African theology is currently written in European languages, mainly English and French, although there is some literature in Portuguese. These languages reflect the colonial divisions in Africa. There are very few Africans who are fluent enough in more than one of these languages to write in any of them without much difficulty. This linguistic problem makes it difficult for most African scholars to know what research has been done in one part of Africa or literature available on the subject of their inquiry. In most cases all they know is what is available in the European language they use as a medium of communication. This problem is common among all African scholars irrespective of their field. It is much more acute in the study of African theology because in other disciplines research findings are readily translated and shared by the world academic community. African theology is not yet of interest to most non-African theologians. The language problem therefore leaves most African theologians with limited knowledge of the literature available. Thus, some of the books which claim to deal with "African Theology" only refer to the body literature on the subject available in one language in which the author is fluent.[1]

Our study of African theology will be a general survey of the views and some of the literature in the field. The literature is enormous; over five thousand articles (published in various journals), monographs, and books! A study by Mbiye Lumbala on the literature of African theology covering the period 1976-1980 listed 320 entries ranging from articles, books, to dissertations.[2] An earlier list in *Revue Africain du clerge* covering 1925-1975 gave 4,077 entries. The figure is much higher now. This chapter will mention just a few of the articles and books which have shaped the African theological discourse.

We begin our study by creating a working definition of theology. I perceive theology as interpretation of life as understood and experienced by a particular people vis à vis Divinity. Interpretation is what people do as they relate the story of their life, their experience, and vision. Theology emerges in telling stories of lived experience—*what is*—and expectations of the future or transcendence of life. I agree with Setiloane who defines theology as "a verbalization of human experience of/with Divinity. An aggregation of this experience from all facets of the community becomes the theology of that community."[3] In his introduction to African theology, Setiloane has expanded on the meaning of theology.

> African theology is an attempt to verbalize African reflection about Divinity (do theology) from the perspective of African grassroots background and culture. This background and culture is seen and judged not only as an ingredient but as a determinant to the ultimate answers this theology gives to questions regarding the nature of Divinity and humanity; imperatives arising therefrom regarding human relationships, single and in communities; and questions about death and thereafter.[4]

To speak of the transcendence of life is to make reference to Divinity. Human life cannot mediate itself; the future of life lies with Divinity, who is source of life and therefore *LIFE* itself. This notion of life makes theology a narrative of people's life experience. Special religious experiences or moments of divine disclosure and workings of Divinity are not the only concern of theology for Africans. Theology is about the whole of human experience seen within the entirety of life and its transcendence. This approach to theology is based on the fact that for Africans, there is no part of life which is not within the domain of Divinity.

From this we can say every person is a theologian, for at one time or the other, everybody deals with questions of life and destiny (faith) amidst contradictions of life. This theology generally takes an oral (narrative) form.

Commenting on oral theology Mbiti has said: "Oral theology is produced in the fields, by the masses, through song, sermons, teaching, prayer, conversation, etc. It is theology in the open air, often unrecorded, often heard only by small groups and generally lost to libraries and seminaries."[5] Oral theology provides a very important source for written theology, which will be our focus in this chapter. By concentrating on written theology we do not seek to give the impression that this theology is superior to oral theology. No! Our aim is simply to study the origin and development of a discipline.

Early Influences

A discipline that is now known as African theology emerged in the 1950s. Many people consider the publication of Placid Temples' *La Philosophie Bantoue* (Elizabethville, 1945) as a precursor to African theology. Tempels, then a Flemish missionary to Belgium Congo (Zaire), studied and analyzed African culture and thought system to arrive at its basic conceptual framework. His purpose in undertaking the project was threefold: (1) to prove that Africans had a philosophical system, albeit different from European; (2) that in having a grasp of the African conceptual scheme, Europeans (colonialists, missionaries, and traders) would be better prepared to work among Africans—they would understand how the African mind operates; and (3) to "save" Africans from Western materialist philosophy entering Africa. Tempels' work revealed that Africans had a well structured and defined philosophical framework, as well as an elaborate religious system based on what he called "life-force." Taking "life-force" as African basic ontology, he concluded that for Africans "to be" is "to have life-force."

Inaccurate as Tempels' "life-force" theory was, it inspired his students to do advanced research into the philosophical thought of their people.[6] It was from Tempels' group of students that the first African theologian emerged—Vincent Mulago, a Catholic priest. Mulago received his doctorate from Urban University in Rome in 1955. His dissertation: "Life Unity among the Bashi, Banyarwanda and Barundi," was published in part in 1956.[7] Another inspiration for African theology came from the work of Alex Kagame, a Rwandese priest, also a student of Tempels. Kagame's doctoral dissertation on "Rwandese philosophy of Being" published in 1956, along with Mulago's book, prepared the way for the emergence of a discipline which came to be known as African theology.[8]

The publication of these two works also came at a time when there was a growing concern among many of the African elite to be truly African and authentically Christian. There was a deepening sense of alienation and loss of identity, especially among Christians. Something had to be done to recover the sense of identity, but caution was to be exercised in undertaking the task of recovering identity to ensure that people would not lose the Christian faith which had now become part of their new self-understanding. African clergy decided to disengage themselves from missionary theology and to start thinking about the Christian faith in their own terms.   New ways of understanding Christian teachings were explored and experimented.

The birth of African theology must also be seen as part of a general consciousness-raising initiative inspired by the Negritude movement, a cultural movement seeking the values and spirit of African civilization. The movement was started in Paris in the 1930s by black students and political activists mainly from the Caribbean and Africa. It did not gather momentum until after the second World War.[9] In 1947 leaders of the movement launched *Présence Africaine*, a journal which became the vehicle of expression for the people of African descent.   Through its editor, Alioune Diop, *Présence Africaine* sponsored the African Culture Society to organize meetings which would promote efforts in African religious thought and theological research.

There was also another factor which led African priests to start thinking of an indigenous theology: politics.   Since the Second World War, African political movements started gathering momentum. With the rising political awareness, came also the desire and quest to be authentic in all aspects of life, including religion. African politicians, writers, artists and historians were far ahead of clerics in finding authentic forms of expression. With the emergence of African theology, African clerics joined the rest of the African elite in the struggle for a new identity for Africa.

In 1956 priests influenced by the new thinking advanced by negritude, put together a document, which has now become one of historical significance, *Des prêtres noirs s'interrogent* (African Priests Wonder or Ask). In the forward to the document, the authors stated why they had decided to produce their own theology and to stop importing ideas: "The African priest must say what he thinks about the Church in his own country in order to advance the kingdom of God. We do not claim that the African priest has never gotten a hearing, but amid the tumult of voices talking about missions his voice has often been tiny and easily muted even though he would seem to be the most qualified to speak."[10]

The development of African theology itself came in stages and with initiatives from various groups and organization. The first initiative came from the African Culture Society, which in 1959 organized a meeting of African philosophers and theologians during the Second Congress of Black Writers and Artists held in Rome. The Society also organized a study poll of African Christian intellectuals in 1962 while Vatican II was in session. The main points from the reflections were published in 1963 as *Personalité africaine et catholicisme*. In 1961 the Society organized a colloquium in Abidjan, Ivory Coast, and in 1970 called another colloquium in Contonou.

The Abidjan gathering dealt with African religions in general, while the second forum discussed African religions as source of "civilized" values. African theologians and scholars in traditional religion gathered again in Abidjan in September 1971, this time under the auspices of African Culture Society and UNESCO.

In 1969, a year before the meeting in Contonou, African theology got another push from the All Africa Conference of Churches, which organized a meeting of African theologians at the University of Ibadan, Nigeria.

The African Theology Project

The term "African theology" did not become popular until the 1960s, and even then it was not clear what it really meant and what methods were to be used in the discipline.[11] The debate was initiated by teachers and students at the Catholic Faculty, University of Lovanium in Kinshasa, Zaire. The debate started in a seminar on January 29, 1960 when Alfred Vanneste (Dean of the Faculty) and Tshishiku Tshibangu, who later became auxiliary bishop of Kinshasa, presented papers on theology in Africa. Other participants were Vincent Mulago (teacher),[12] and students Ngindu Mushete[13] and M. F. Lufuabulo.[14] The proceedings of the debate were published in the *Revue du Clergé*.[15]

The opening papers of the debate are interesting and worth reviewing. In his presentation titled *"Vers une théologie de couleur africaine"* (Towards a theology with an African slant; note here that "African Theology" was not yet being used), Tshibangu argued that Africanization was not simply a matter of having African bishops and lay leaders, nor reforming parish and pastoral structures and adapting the liturgy.[16] He maintained that Africa must have an African Church arising from an African theology.[17] Tshibangu proposed that African studies and African theology go hand in hand towards creating a theology for an African Church. His idea was to look for "seeds" for the gospel in religious life of the people. He maintained that African religious life contained many elements which could be considered "latent theological seeds." Once purified, these "seeds" could be used as "religious analogues" to illuminate theological problems and serve as the foundations of a theological discourse.[18]

D'abord une Vraie Théologie (First, a True Theology) was the title of Vanneste's response to Tshibangu's paper. In his presentation, Vanneste argued that since Christianity is a universal religion, theology must be valid for all cultures and races.[19] He further contended that since theology is a science, it must, like all sciences, pursue its vocation for truth with all seriousness.[20] His point was that theological research should follow scientific objectivity, that is, disinterested research. The implication of this for African theology was that there was no use in trying to appropriate primitive concepts which were magical in inspiration.[21] (Note here how the missionary reproduced Enlightenment arguments). Adaptation was therefore descending to lower academic levels, not rising, and that with adaptation African theologians would only succeed in shutting themselves up in a world of their own and thus risk being considered second class theologians by the rest of the world.[22] In the debate which followed, most people sided with Tshibangu.

Tshibangu's approach, namely, looking for "latent theological seeds" in African religious life, was advanced by O. Bimwenyi-kweshi in his voluminous doctoral dissertation which addressed the problem of African theology.[23] Many other theologians from both Franco and Anglophone Africa follow this approach. Bénézét Bujo, a Zairean priest who is currently the Chair of Moral Theology at the University of Friebourg, Switzerland, argues that in this approach "no effort is made to work up this 'raw material' into a genuine, even if tentative, theological synthesis," which would lead to an incarnated Christianity in Africa.[24]

An important meeting in the development of African theology was held in Kinshasa July 22-27 1968, under the title *Colloque sur le théologie africaine*. This was the Fourth Theological seminar, again organized by the Theological Faculty of Kinshasa. This meeting crystallized the idea of the possibility of an indigenous African theology. Several papers were presented; noteworthy were presentations on the problem of African theology in the light of Vatican II, world theology, and African theology. At this colloquium, Vanneste spoke more carefully, but without changing his original and basic position that theology must be universal; no one supported his position. Papers from the conference were published as *Renouveau de l'Eglise et nouvelles églises* (Mayidi, 1969).

The Catholic Faculty at Kinshasa took a leading role in developing African theology. By 1967 the Faculty had established the Center for the Study of African Religions. The Center publishes a biannual journal *Cahiers des religions africaines*, and since 1977 it also publishes *Revue africaines de théologie*.

Debate on the Name

The 1968 meeting in Kinshasa concluded and crystallized the idea that, yes indeed, there can be such a discipline as African theology, but the seminar did not produce a definitive name for the new discipline. The question of the name produced yet another debate: was the discipline to be called African theology or African *Christian* theology. This time the debate was not confined to Zaire alone—West and East Africa became involved too. Some people, V.Y. Mundimbe, for example, wondered whether it was necessary to talk about African theology when it did not even exist as a discipline. He wrote, "some fellow priests believe in the possibility of an African Theology road. . . . Among them, thought precedes action. It is as if Plato, before beginning his work, had announced that he was going to create Greek Philosophy."[25] Others proposed that the term be changed to "African *Christian* Theology." Among the advocates of this term are John Agbeti[26] and Fashole-luke.[27] Other names in this debate included: Kwesi Dickson,[28] E. Bolaji Idowu,[29] Byang Kato,[30] John Pobee,[31] Harry Sawyer,[32] and Gabriel Setiloane.[33]

In 1963 Mbiti introduced another term, *Theologia Africana*.[34] The term did not gain popularity; Mbiti himself does not use it. Kwesi Dickson used it once as a title of his article: "Toward a Theologia Africana." Sawyer and Pobee have each employed the term only once. In 1972 John Agbeti argued for the term *African Christian Theology*.[35] Agbeti's concern was over the content of the theological enterprise. He had observed that anything passed for African Theology. He wanted people to be clear about what could and could not be included in the enterprise. According to Agbeti, African Theology refers to theology of *traditional* religion which is based on general revelation. On the other hand, African *Christian* Theology is founded on Jesus Christ. This term too, has not been widely used. Fashole-Luke is very constant in his use of African *Christian* Theology.

Byang Kato took issue with Agbeti's distinction.[36] In this book, *Theological Pitfalls in Africa*, Kato warned African theologians against universalism for "the stage was well set for" it. He attacked Mbiti and Idowu. Kato also attacked ecumenism for its role in preparing a stage for universalism. Evidently, Kato had misunderstood the point Agbeti was trying to make. Kato understood him advocating a return to African traditional religions. Kato accused "many theologians [of] spend[ing] their time defending African traditional religious practices that are incompatible with Biblical teaching."[37] S. Erivwo in his review of Kato's *Theological Pitfalls in Africa* argued that Kato had misrepresented the position of Agbeti. Erivwo reminded Kato that Agbeti was not "advocating a return to African traditional religions rather than expressing Christianity more meaningfully to the African."[38]

THEMES IN AFRICAN THEOLOGY

Having traced the beginnings of African theology, we will now turn to the themes in the discipline: adaptation, inculturation, indigenization, Black and liberation. Some scholars put the first three together as indigenization. That is fine, if one does not care to know about the historical development of theological thought in Africa, but to follow the evolution of the discipline, we will treat the first three as different stages or moments within a single discourse, namely, cultural retrieval in African theology. I will not give a full analysis of Black and liberation theologies because I have done that in *Voices From the Margin: Introduction to Liberation Theologies*.

Adaptation

In the early period of African theology, the focus was on adaptation, a study of themes in African culture which transmit the Christian message. In explaining what the task was all about Mulago said, "The word 'adapt' may shock certain ears. We need only to point out that it means presenting dogma in a form that is accessible to the people."[39] Methodologically, those working on adaptation sought to remain within the Western theological tradition, specifically the classical format. After the manner of "classical theology," the theology of adaptation made the doctrine of revelation the central focus. Adaptation was also informed by the insights drawn from African philosophy, a discipline which appeared with Tempels' *Philosophie Bantoue* and the seminal works of Kagame. This overdependence on philosophy produced theological works not grounded on good biblical foundations. Adaptation was and still is followed mostly by Catholic theologians, with Vincent Mulago and Charles Nyamiti leading the way. Both of them are very serious scholars; they draw on ethnological materials, but Nyamiti draws from scholastic philosophy and neo-scholastic thought as well.[40] What comes from this kind of approach is an African theology patterned after the (European) speculative thought. Nyamiti seems to be bent on restating the Catholic dogmatic position but in terms of African tradition. Nyamiti is so serious about this project that in his latest work, "Some Items on African Christian Theism," he has given a method for teaching this approach in African seminaries.[41]

Adaptation theology made some significant contributions to African Christianity especially in the areas of liturgy and "Africanization" of the sacred offices. The main weakness of adaptation theology is that it does not move out of the Western paradigm. It repeats Western concepts or matches them with ideas from African tradition. Advocates of this theology even talk of a systematic African theology. These theologians seem to be caught in Western epistemological scheme into which they try to fit select African concepts. It is to this effect that Ngindu Mushete makes the following criticism of adaptation:

The major defect of this theology of adaptation has been its *concordism*.

It tends to equate Christian revelation with the systems of thought in which it has found historical expression. How deeply can we really penetrate into religious truth if we set up a comparison between certain elements of African culture isolated from their overall context on the one hand and Christianity viewed as a closed system of absolute truths on the other hand?[42]

Mushete calls adaptation theology "stepping-stone" because the theology looks for "certain beliefs, rites, symbols, gestures, and institutions of traditional that seem compatible with the data of Christian faith."[43]

Inculturation

Mushete represent another movement in the debate of African theology. Theologians in this movement have "two major preoccupations. First they seek to establish closer contact with the major sources of revelation: the Bible and tradition. Second, they want to open up wholly to the African milieu and its problems. . . . The desire to return to the sources naturally has led to a passionate debate on 'African Theology'."[44] This approach to theology has been identified as inculturation because of its emphasis on culture. This movement does not make a clean break with Western methodology but it opens itself to other theological approaches. Unlike adaptation theology, which looks to philosophy for help, this movement looks to the Bible and traditional religion. This is to say, the project of inculturation is not interested in philosophical arguments and achieving a systematic theology. Inculturation, following traditional religion, seeks to be life-oriented or interested in examining all that affects the human condition.

The second approach looks at the members of the African community who have heard and accepted the Christian message and who are now trying to proclaim and live it in their own cultural milieu. Gradually this milieu is purified and superseded through a life of faith exercised with full freedom. This paves the way for a new and perhaps unforeseen incarnation of the Gospel.[45]

The difference between adaptation and inculturation lies in the method which controls the final product. Briefly stated, adaptation does not succeed in breaking from missionary or Western theology. It looks to dogmatics and philosophy for guidance. On the other hand, cultural retrieval is bible centered and draws from traditional religion.

Indigenization

The issue of the content and method in African theology has been argued in many theological meetings, major Church councils, as well as assemblies. The question centers around whether or not traditional culture can be appropriated by African theologians. When the issue was first raised, the first assembly of All Africa Conference of Churches (AACC) meeting in Kampala, Uganda (April 20-30, 1963) gave a non-committal and non-directive statement, it simply said: "traditional African culture was not all bad; neither was everything good." The second assembly of the AACC meeting in Abidjan, Ivory Coast, six years later (September 2-12, 1969), was a little bit more directive. It said African theology "is a theology based on the Biblical faith of Africans, and which speaks to the African soul. It is expressed in categories of thought which arise out of the philosophy of the African people, This does not mean it is narrow (syncretistic). To speak of African theology involves formulating clearly a Christian attitude to other religions."[46]

According to the definition of the second AACC assembly, African theology attempts to understand the scriptures as they speak to the African context. This theology uses African categories to reach the African. Idowu argues that dialogue between theology and African categories is fundamental, therefore a priority for the African theologian because he or she must first "apprehend African spiritual values with African mind while, at the same time, they possess the requisite knowledge of fundamental facts of the faith which they are seeking to express and disseminate in indigenous idiom."[47] Pobee too says, "African theology is concerned to interpret essential Christian faith in authentic African language in the flux and turmoil of our time so that there may be genuine dialogue between the Christian faith and African cultures."[48]

Sinde Sempore argues that it is necessary to look at Africa's religious past so as to comprehend better the present with its all naunces and direct the future. He says what religion is for the African today, and what forms it took in the past to express the vision of the people, "constitute for the theologian a vast field of investigation and a fertile soil for a meeting ground between the Gospel and the African desire for a God of joy."[49] He insists that the theologian should focus on the contribution of African cultures because "the Christian message only takes form and strength from its encounter and critical dialogue with a given culture. It aims to become the thread of the human fabric which unfolds within a whole culture and it is very important for any theological project that this human fabric be evaluated."[50]

From Idowu, Pobee, and Sempore, we see that African theology has focused on the dialogue between African culture and the Gospel. It is the interaction between the Gospel and African culture which will produce an authentic African faith and theology. It is to this effect that John Kurewa has written,

"An African theologian should be a person who participates in African culture
. . . African culture becomes a crucial factor in doing theology with and for
the African Christian community."[51]   Culture is not an end in itself for
African theologians, but it is appropriated as a hermeneutical key for
discovering possibilities for understanding the Gospel as Africans and
communicating it in African categories to the African Christian. This task has
generally been called contextualization, inculturation, or indigenization. This
is a critical task in developing African identity and faith practice.   Mbiti
explains:

> Culture is the human pattern of life in response to mankind's
> environment; . . . the only lasting form of Christianity in this continent is
> that which results from a serious encounter of the gospel with indigenous
> African culture when people voluntarily accept by faith the Gospel of
> Jesus Christ. A Christianity that is heavily intertwined with an imported
> culture may indeed be very impressive, but it cannot be a substitute for
> this kind of Christianity, that should grow out if the spontaneous free
> impregnation of the gospel in the fertile womb of culture. . . . What is
> the message of the Gospel to our culture in the areas of human problem
> and needs, such as oppression, exploitation, poverty, starvation, injustice,
> destruction of human life, extravagant spoilation of nature, pollution and
> dangers to human survival (such as armaments, wars, domination, even
> science and technology)? How can the Gospel raise an alarm through our
> culture in the areas of urgent concerns.[52]

According to Mbiti, culture is about the meaning of being a temporal and
historical people. In other words, culture taken as a framework of
interpretation provides an understanding of the meaning of the human
encounter with Divinity in a particular space and time. Temporality is about
embodiment of space as a particular space; culture defines that space. This
is the space in which things of significance happen or have happened to a
people. These events are what we call historical. For an African theologian,
culture defines the space where divine disclosure has been encountered by
Africans in a concrete historical situation. The task of African theology is to
grasp and interpret people's experience of divine disclosure in those temporal
(cultural milieu) and historical contexts.

The result of taking culture as a locator of temporal and historical
experience of the people has been a new understanding of the Christian
responsibility as evidenced by (a) liturgical adaptations—prayers and music;
and (b) a new approach to biblical studies.[53]   K. Mgojo describes the new
approach as follows:

> This approach realizes that much of the Western tradition has been

generated by Western categories (European or Americanization) rather than a fidelity to the scriptures. This approach tries to return to the scriptures to find a framework for a local theology. This approach is aided by the recognition of the similarity between cultural situations in the Bible and local cultural situations in many cases. The obvious strength of this approach is its fidelity to the scriptural witness. A genuine Christian identity, often surpassing that found in the older Churches in the West, seems assured—it also seems to provide a way out of Western cultural hegemony. Let us be reminded that the Bible is a cultural document representing the response in faith by a variety of communities. An ideal type of New Testament Church is a cultural creation of a given era.

The Gospel does not fall from the sky. Our faith is *fide ex audito*. The presence of the Gospel is tied up with the mystery of the incarnation. The Gospel is only a living reality when it is incarnated in a concrete context and partakes of the ambiguities and limitations of history. Only then is the Lord truly present in his community.[54]

Another result of the hermeneutics of culture has been a broader understanding of the concept of salvation. Gabriel Setiloane notes that there are two meanings of salvation in African thought. He stresses the point that salvation among Africans takes place in what Westerners call the "secular" for

in reality there is no such thing as "secular" being separate apart from the "sacred." Divinity through the participation of the *Badimo* (ancestors) is shot through with the totality of existence. Even at its best Christian ethics of society do not in my view reach this depth of insight. . . . The African position, I believe, is much more incisive. It says all aspects of life (its totality) are spheres of Divine activity in all its intensity—and one ignores this at one's risk.[55]

Setiloane says the secular-sacred divisions do not exist in African thought systems and this is because Divinity participates in the life of the community. In other words, the "holy" permeates the whole of life.

Divinity (*Bo-Modimo*), comprising *Modimo* and *Badimo* is not detached or outside the entity of the community; instead it is present, manifesting itself in the energy dynamism that generates the very life of the community and maintains its morality and wholeness through the *Badimo*- the ancestors, as they participate in it imparting to everybody, every moment, and every day the *mysterium tremendum et fascinans*: holiness. There is no "sacred" apart from the "secular." The ideal for all is harmony, peace—*lotsididi* where the unity of all the elements are maintained with the totality, each carrying on with its functions of justice, fairness, fully conscious of inter-dependence and that no part is greater than the whole. For life is a totality and salvation is when it is kept so.[56]

Setiloane explains the second meaning of salvation as follows:

Salvation, therefore, is when peace, order and happiness are maintained in the community. This way all live and let others live. A disturbance of this harmony in life is a threat to the well-being of the whole, and therefore calls for the punitive intervention of Divinity. . . . We need to admit here that the concept of salvation, in as far as it implies a prior situation of a falleness or built-in depravity (original sin), is foreign to African thought and worldview. If ever the term salvation were to come to mind as we are using it here, it would be expressed by an understanding of harmony within and between the elements that make up the community, and that would mean people, animals, vegetation and nature generally.[57]

For a long time, the concept of culture as a hermeneutical key was not accepted by all African theologians. In South Africa, many theologians who identify themselves as Black theologians question the validity of culture for African theology, given the present social, economic, and political problems of Africa in general, and the race problem in South Africa in particular. Among the many theologians who have voiced disenchantment with indigenization are Allan Boesak, bishop Manas Buthelezi, and archbishop Desmond Tutu. Black theologians in South Africa maintain that the indigenization process is uncritical or that it is partial and not total criticism of the Western paradigm. It is with this in mind that Boesak calls indigenization a "cultural theology" or a "religion of culture."[58] Buthelezi was more critical of the indigenization process. He described it as "ethnographic" because it starts from the African way of life or the African cosmos. Since it proceeds from the African world, "it becomes a mechanical program in which objectively identifiable motifs of the African world view are used to indigenize an already existing Church which is un-indigenized."[59] Buthelezi found indigenization unsatisfactory for two reasons, namely, its method and appeal to the past. We may summarize his arguments as follows: (1) indigenization is a superficial exercise because it gives legitimation to Western theology. This is done by marching African thought with Western theology in an already culturally-colored Christian teaching; (2) the project invokes the African past, but this past does not have the necessary power to deal with the present socio-economic and political realities of contemporary Africa.

Setiloane has observed a shift or rather a change in the bishop Buthelezi's early attitude towards the idea of culture in African theological enterprise.

Setiloane recalls that

in 1973 in Uppsala Manas Buthelezi (now bishop Buthelezi) would hear
nothing about seeing Divinity at work in the so called "heathen" and
archaic past of the African experience, as expressed, not necessarily
correctly, by Social Anthropological study. He was nervous about
reference to the African traditional past in doing theology, and likened it
to the study of fossils. I understood this as a fear of taking skeletons out
of the Black cupboard and using them to diminish the Black man's claim
to credibility. But in 1975 in Tanzania in a symposium of Black
Theologians, African and United States, Buthelezi opened up and
accepted the Black man's past could be helpful in his self-
understanding.[60]

Archbishop Tutu has also spoken about the weakness of indigenization,
contending that

African theology has failed to produce a sufficiently sharp cutting edge.
. . . It has seemed to advocate disengagement from hectic business of life
because very little has been offered that it is pertinent, say, about the
theology of power in the face of coups and military rule, about
development, about poverty and disease and other equally urgent present
day issues. I believe this is where the abrasive theology may have a few
lessons for African theology.[61]

Tutu, like all Black theologians in South Africa, advocates a critical and
prophetic theology, a theology which will turn the African condition upside
down—liberate Africans. They believe that Black Theology has the power and
tools for bettering the African condition. It is important to mention that
although Tutu is critical of the indigenization process, he does not consider
this theology to be different from black theology because they are both
concerned with the same issue.

African and black theology must be concerned—and vitally concerned—with
liberation because . . .   liberation is a serious preoccupation at the
present time and it is not seen as being an alternative to personal
salvation in Jesus Christ. No, it is seen in Africa as the inescapable
consequence of taking the gospel of Jesus Christ seriously. Only a
spiritually, politically, economically free Africa, where Christianity is today
expanding faster than anywhere else in the world, can make a distinctive
contribution to the life of the body of Jesus Christ and to the world
community as a whole.[62]

In another work, Tutu has shown the relation between African and Black theologies:

> I myself believe I am an exponent of black theology, coming as I do from South Africa. I also believe I am an exponent of African theology, coming as I do from Africa. I contend that black theology is like the inner and smaller circle in a series of concentric circles . . . I and others from South Africa do black theology, which is for us, at this point, African theology.[63]

The accusation that Tutu (and other black theologians) has leveled against indigenization theologians has not gone unaddressed. Setiloane says the accusation is unwarranted and it is due to a confusion. He says:

> the advocates of black theology keep taunting us with being politically docile (e.g. Desmond Tutu's article "Black Theology/African Theology: Soul Mates or Antagonists?"), is that of the application of the Gospel to the problems of people in the community. I believe that Desmond Tutu, like most of us South Africans, is confused as to which call he feels most deeply—African theology or black theology. Therefore he lays at the wrong door the charge of having been brainwashed to think that Western value systems and categories are of universal validity. I maintain that his summons that African theology recover its "prophetic calling" is a Western Christian cliché. Black theology, which he professes to embrace, has far too easily employed Western Christian norms and terms like "prophetic" without examining their presupposition."[64]

In another work Setiloane has said that the criticism of African theology made by black theologians "is understandable, coming from the quarter of Black Theology, and must be conceded." While conceding, he argues that what a Church does or says has to be seen within the socio-political context which it exists. The Church is not of the world, but still in the world, therefore not completely free of the evils of society. Setiloane says,

> it must also be accepted that the Church in any situation is never free of the evils of the society in which it finds itself. And therefore it often finds it difficult to be prophetic (although I do hold that a prophet can only be a prophet in his native situation and country). Also there is a difference between witnessing against a political system Christians experience as their own, and to the formations of which they have been party, and witnessing against one which they feel as having been imposed upon them and is foreign; like the South African Black man in South African political system. Also, witness by rejection is much easier than witness by

conversion.[65]

Setiloane, however, agrees with Tutu that the process of indigenization must take seriously political issues.

When African theology ventures into the political area, and I agree with Desmond Tutu that it is high time it did, it will need to clarify not only its theological views regarding the all-pervasive, all-powerful, tremendous, inscrutable Divinity, but also its position toward the one dynamically related community if being—human, animal, and vegetable—and its theology of humankind as a participant in Divinity.[66]

Setiloane and Mgojo are not the only South African theologians who support the indigenization process, Goba is another. He is a Black theologian but in his article on theological education in Africa, he said it is necessary for theological education to pay attention to "the black/African worldview as well as the existential fact of oppression and therefore our quest for authentic liberation. . . . as a Church in the process of liberation, we need to retrieve the African worldview which blacks commonly share in South Africa."[67] Goba has attempted this in his book, *An Agenda for Black Theology*. Under the heading, "The Quest for a Theological Revolution," he reminds Black Theologians

that culture as an ideological system cannot be separated from the structure of our everyday experience. . . . Culture legitimates who we are and at the same time is the medium through which our faith expresses itself. . . . Black theological reflection as a cultural revolutionary praxis is the call to rediscover the true meaning of Christian tradition as mediated in God's liberating activity in Jesus Christ. What this means is that the black Christian community participating in the process of liberation must redefine the essence of Christianity on the basis of our black socio-cultural experience in search of new liberating paradigms for human existence.[68]

Lately, the process of indigenization has also been supported by Benjamin Witbooi, another South African theologian. His argument for the project emerges out of a practical concern.

There are many transitional rites still (observed) and often the Church turns a blind-eye. Black Christians are often forced to engage in secret or midnight escapades in order to avoid discovery by Church leaders. The result half-baked Christians and half-baked Africans. Cultural observance should not be ignored, but should be integrated in the life of the Church in order for people to be fully integrated.[69]

It is not only the South African black theologians who have expressed dissatisfaction with retrieving cultural practices. Indigenization is questioned by a number of African scholars and the feeling is not limited to South Africa—it is universal in Africa. Kwesi Dickson argues that the failure to appreciate African culture in South Africa and elsewhere is indicative of a major and deeper problem, namely, a cultural dislocation:

> there has been a cultural dislocation, the result of the contact with European world, and this dislocation has not perhaps been recognized for what it is—certainly not by the Church in Africa which continues to function in blissful ignorance, by and large, of the serious cultural handicap under which it labors. While the feeling that African culture cannot be relevant in the present situation may rise from a misunderstanding about, or even ignorance of, what the cultural reality is, there is also the possibility that the thought of giving recognition to this reality is a source of uneasiness arising from the feeling— unarticulated, and perhaps unrecognized—that in the order of things African culture is inferior to Western culture, aspects of which are to be encountered in the urban areas in Africa, in the educational institutions, in the governmental systems and in the Church.[70]

Black Theology

The complaint of South African theologians against the project of indigenization is that it does not address the socio-political and economic reality of contemporary Africa. South African theologians call for a prophetic theology, a theology that struggles with the socio-political and economic realities, and in their case, problems arising from the system of *apartheid*. To restate a well known fact, *apartheid* is based on racial superiority. The suffering of the majority of South Africans is all because they are black. Manas Buthelezi explains: "Blackness is a life category that embraces the totality of my daily existence. It determined the circumstances of my growth as a child and the life possibilities open to me. It now determines where I live, worship, minister, and the range of my closest associates. Can you think of a more decisive factor in life?"[71]

South African theologians focus on their socio-political situation for "a theology that does not take into account this situation will never be able to interpret the Gospel or to say what the Spirit has to say to the people in this situation."[72] Archbishop Tutu puts it this way:

Black theology rises in a context of Black suffering at the hands of
rampant white racism. And consequently black theology is much more
concerned to make sense theologically of the black experience whose main
ingredient is the black suffering in light of God's revelation of himself in
the Man, Jesus Christ. It is concerned with significance of black
existence, liberation, with the meaning of reconciliation, with
humanization, with forgiveness.[73]

The Archbishop describes black theology as assertive and he explains why.

It is much more aggressive and abrasive in its assertions, because of a
burning and evangelistic zeal, as it must convert the black man out of his
subservience and obsequiousness, to the acceptance of the thrilling and
demanding responsibility of full personhood, to make him reach out to the
glorious liberty of the sons of God. It burns to awaken the white man to
the degrading into which he has fallen by dehumanizing the black man,
and so it is concerned with the liberation of the oppressor equally as with
that of the oppressed. It is not so naive as to think that only economic or
political oppression are what matter. But liberation must be understood
in a total sense as removal of all that keeps us in bondage, all that which
makes us less than what God intended us to be.[74]

South African theologians seek to decode the myth of *apartheid* by
demythologizing the concept of superiority of the white race; race is their
hermeneutical key.

The starting point for theological reflection is the existential situation in
which the Gospel finds man. . . . If the Gospel means anything at all, it
must save the Black man from his own blackness; it must answer his basic
existential question "Why did god create me black?" Black theology
challenges established Christianity to engage in a dialogue with the Black
people who feel that somehow theology has not taken them into
consideration.[75]

While there is a general agreement that race is a hermeneutical key for
decoding the myth of *apartheid*, questions have been raised concerning what
constitutes blackness: is blackness a physical reality or an attitude towards
suffering of the victims of injustice. For Buthelezi, blackness is a condition,
"an anthropological reality that embraces totality of . . . existence." Boesak
universalizes blackness: "Blackness does not in the first place designate skin
color. It is a discovery of a state of mind, a conversion, an affirmation of
being (which is power). It is an insight that has to do with wisdom."[76]
Boesak maintains that one may not be black but have a mind that identifies

with the sufferings of the lowly and downtrodden. For this reason, he insists that people should not be excluded from the struggle for justice because they are not physically black.

> The growth of black consciousness is, because of this particular political and ecclesiastical situation in South Africa, of a special significance. What does this mean for the black South African? In the first place, it means a black solidarity that encompasses not only African, but all the different groups in the black community. It means that blacks no more speak of "colored" (what does it mean any way?) or of any particular group designated as "non-white" by the white government. We are black people, and we share a black community that cuts across all the artificial barriers of separateness, apartheid, of being-closer-to-white-peopleness that up to now have divided us. It seeks a community of blackness, a community in which reconciliation with our black selves and with our black brothers and sisters is of prime importance.[77]

Under the system of *Apartheid*, the lighter the skin, the more privilege one gets. Boesak wants to liberate those caught up in the idea of "being-close-to-white," because they have a lighter skin complexion. He is appealing to them to come to themselves and realize that their privileged position is itself bondage for it stands in the way for discovering true (African or black) identity and the meaning of community. In a community people rejoice and suffer to together. Boesak therefore appeals to these people to be reconciled with their African heritage. On the other hand, Boesak is speaking to those with an exclusive idea of blackness, to liberate them, by raising their consciousness of being bonded with all people into one humanity, with various shades of skin color. He does not minimize the fact that the skin color of the oppressor is white, but he wants people to concentrate on the struggle for a community beyond *apartheid*.

While appreciating the sensitivity of the problem of blackness and the need for reconciliation, some black theologians, mostly those in the Black Consciousness movement, feel uncomfortable with universalizing blackness. These theologians do not seek to perpetuate the race classifications under *apartheid*, but their problem is with the idea that "conversion" or "solidarity" with the oppressed makes one black. They feel that when blackness is considered as a mental attitude, it abstracts the reality or the experience mediated by being black. These theologians agree that universalizing blackness broadens the power base, but they feel that to take blackness as an attitude, minimizes the pain suffered for being black in South Africa. Boesak is fully aware of the pain endured by those who are black. As early as 1977 Boesak said: "Black people in South Africa are not being oppressed because they are Muslims, or because they are Methodists, or because they are wayward Presbyterians or Dutch Reformed; they are oppressed because they are black, because they are not born white."[78]

Black theology started in the United States; it is a product of African American culture and tradition. It seeks to understand the scriptures in the light of the black condition. To this end, black theology draws from the experience of black people and Church. It seeks a black Christian perspective in dealing with present socio-economic and political reality of black people. In order to avoid narrowness, black theology identified itself with the cause for social justice elsewhere but basically, its roots are in the African American community.

Racial discrimination in South Africa made South African theologians much more inclined towards black theology. Of course the circumstances are not the same: in South Africa black people are a majority, over 27 million of them being oppressed by about 4 million whites. The term black theology was borrowed by South African theologians to express their struggle for a full humanity. Black theology in South Africa, as in the United States, seeks to articulate African humanity and experience. Mgojo describes black theology as "an attempt by black Christians to grasp and think through central claims of the Christian faith in the light of Black experience."[79] Likewise Boesak says black theology "is the black people's attempt to come to terms theologically with their situation. It seeks to interpret the gospel in such a way that the situation of blacks will begin to make sense."[80] We get the same idea from Archbishop Tutu.

> The Church of God must produce a relevant theology which speaks to the hopelessness and despondency. The Church of God must declare the Lordship of God and Christ—that God is the Lord of history and of this world despite all appearances to the contrary, that He is God of justice and cares about oppression and exploitation, about deaths in detention, about front-end loaders, squatter's shacks, about unemployment and power.[81]

The emergence of black theology in South Africa is connected with the rise of the Black Consciousness Movement which emerged with the South African Student Organization (SASO).[82] Black consciousness is an attempt to create a spirit of self-appreciation among black people, of their blackness and traditional values. This exercise is undertaken to retrieve identity, distorted and beaten out of shape by the ideology of whiteness. The most articulate of the Black Consciousness Movement was Steve Biko, who died on September 12, 1977 at the age of 31, of head and brain damage sustained during beating and torture in a prison cell. Biko saw in Black Consciousness the possibility of mobilizing black people in the struggle towards true humanity and freedom. The first task was to conscientize the people, who for a long time had been led to believe they were nothing and their values did not matter simply because they were black. It was in light of the task of conscientization that Biko wrote:

> Briefly defined therefore, Black Consciousness is the realization by the Black man of the need to rally together with his brother around the cause of operation—the blackness of their skin—and to operate as a group in order to rid themselves of the shackles that bind them to perpetual servitude. It seeks to demonstrate the lie that black is an aberration from the "normal" which is white . . . Black consciousness therefore, takes cognizance of the deliberateness of God's plan in creating black people black. It seeks to infuse the black community with a new-found pride in themselves, their efforts, their value systems, their culture, their religion and their outlook to life.[83]

Black Consciousness Movement had an impact in all facets of African community in South Africa including the Church. Black theology found an ally in the Black Consciousness Movement, for Biko endorsed the efforts of black theology.

> The bible must continually be shown to have something to say to the black man to keep him in his long journey towards realization of the self. This is the message implicit in "Black Theology." Black theology seeks to do away with spiritual poverty of the black people. It seeks to demonstrate the absurdity of the assumption by whites that "ancestor worship" was necessarily a superstition and that Christianity is a scientific religion. While basing itself on the Christian message, black theology seeks to show that Christianity is an adaptable religion that fits with the cultural situation of the people to whom it is imparted. Black theology seeks to depict Jesus as a fighting God who saw the exchange of Roman money—the oppressor's coinage—in His father's temple as so sacrilegious that it merited a violent reaction from Him—the Son of Man.[84]

The involvement of the Church in Black Consciousness Movement allowed black theology to reach the student population in the various universities. Through the University Christian Movement (UCM) in the 1960s, black theology became institutionalized in South Africa. The UCM sponsored seminars on black theology throughout universities and other institutions of higher learning. From these seminars came the first book on black theology in South Africa, *Essays in Black Theology*.

Black theology decodes the myth of *apartheid* with the aid of race as a hermeneutical key. Its method is informed by the scriptures and life of the Church. It is from an encounter with Jesus in the scriptures, prayer, meditation, and sacraments that black theology gets its cue on what to do as Tutu says, "the ultimate reference point is the man Jesus who is the Word of God par excellence."[85] He adds, "it is not our politics but our faith that inspires us."[86]

Liberation Themes

The economic and political situation of African countries in the post-colonial era has been the subject of theological discourse by some theologians in the independent states of Africa. Independence has brought national pride and revival of traditional values in most African countries, but the pre-independence question of selfhood still remains the problem. African countries have sunk into deep economic crisis. This is not necessarily because of lack of vision of the leaders, but the worsening of the world economy and the dependence relation into which the countries were programmed by the colonial masters. Dependence is a situation in which the trade economic cycle does not make a complete cycle. The turn, thus incomplete, causes unequal distribution of the trade benefits with one side having more than the other.

Given all the problems facing contemporary Africa, Ela asks: "How are we to re-state our faith and proclaim the gospel afresh in order to see the problems of Africa and its people with new eyes? How can we respond to pressures which are beginning to drive a wedge between town and village?" He further states: "If the Church wants to take part in African history today, it must recognize that at all levels of African society its identity is at stake. . . . If the Church is really the body of Christ crucified on Golgotha, it must be one with the men and women whose rights are denied, who are reduced to silence by state terrorism, threatens and intimidation; the Church must take up the condition of the people."[87]

The attempt to address a situation of dependence and other problems ensuing from it: poverty, disease, and political struggles, some African theologians have introduced another trend in African theology: liberation theology. The term "liberation theology" is of course borrowed from Latin America. It was first introduced in African theological discourse in 1976 at the first conference of Third World Theologians held in Dar-es-Salaam, Tanzania. It was the presence and contributions of Latin American theologians at the conference which made the liberation theme popular among some African theologians.[88] In the following year, José Chipendo, now Secretary General of AACC, urged delegates to the Pan-African Conference of Third World theologians, to develop a liberation approach.

African theologians realize that our countries are free but they are not

liberated.   We hear resounding sounds of our national anthems; we
rejoice seeing bright and colorful flags in the sky.   These are undeniable
symbols of our freedom but also a reminder of the unfinished task to
liberate Africa from ignorance, poverty, disease, ethnocentricism and
other "isms." We should not confuse freedom from liberation. Freedom
is exemption from external control; liberation is inner ability to handle
freedom constructively. In Africa we are familiar with colonial conditions
that created domination and institutionalized dependence. This situation
of dependence goes unabated. People in newly acquired power exploit
nationals who are weak; by the same token the new elite has its hand tied
because of the economic, political and military support they receive from
friends abroad.   A. Mahleka wrote: "We are no less dependent on
European traditions intellectually than we are economically."[89]

There are two main streams in Liberation Theology in Africa: one which
follows the method introduced by Latin American liberation theologians and
European political theologians, while the second approach appropriates the
national ideology of the respective countries of the theologian. The first group
of liberation theologians in Africa follow the approaches of Latin American
theologians and some political theologians in Europe, such as Jurgen
Moltmann. The second group has its advocates in both West and East Africa.
Names of some of the theologians in this group include Chukwudum B.
Okolo,[90] Zablon Nthamburi,[91] Jean-Marc Ela,[92] and bishop Bakole wa
Ilunga.[93] The task of liberation theology begins with a radical restructuring
of the Church so that the Gospel can be incarnated in African life.
Like their counterparts in Latin America, Okolo, Nthamburi, and bishop
Ilunga emphasize critical reflection on the concrete historical situation.
Nthamburi tends to pattern his method after the manner of Juan Luis
Segundo, he is guided by the scriptures in his analysis.[94] Okolo, on the other
hand, follows a marxist analysis of society.   Like his mentor, Gustavo
Gutierrez, Okolo does not seek to reject Christianity, but a break with the
oppressive past or status quo mentality. Okolo explains: "The problem does
not lie with Christianity but with the capitalistic and imperial culture out of
which it has spread to the countries of Africa and elsewhere."[95]
Magesa rejects both capitalism and European socialism as institution-
oriented. While affirming the redemptive power of African socialism, he
writes against it arguing that by being made absolute this person-oriented
philosophy runs the danger of becoming an idol.   He cautions against
absolutizing the person-centered philosophy of African society.   "African
Socialism is not an end in itself: it is not the Kingdom. Well pursued, it is at
best an excellent way towards the partial realization of the kingdom of God
here on earth. Everything here considered, our efforts here always remain
something like grouping in the dark, a painful journey through the desert

towards the promised land."[96]   Addressing the African Church on the question of liberation Magesa called for a moratorium on "financial assistance; personnel; liturgical and prayer books; theological treatises; orders and directions from abroad—everything" as moratorium as a way to true liberation of the Churches in Africa.[97]

Unlike all the liberation theologians mentioned above, Ela has followed Moltmann. This is evident in *African Cry*, chapters 3 and 5, but in his later works he shifted to a new approach, that of appropriating primary symbols. He argues that the issues facing the African Church today or the questions or relevance of faith have to be dealt with in light of a vast network of primary symbols in the world. For when the primary symbols are corrupted they distort people's value system and faith itself becomes false faith. Besides symbols, Ela urges fellow theologians to do "everything possible . . . to ensure that the Church acquires the instruments to analyze the current situation, and that it learns to read what it does in light of the gospel; everything possible needs to be done to prepare Christian intellectuals for the real problems of our society."[98]

Feminist Theology

A new and upcoming theology in Africa is by women theologians. African women suffer several forms of oppression: they are economically and sexually exploited, culturally dominated, and politically alienated. In society as in the Church, women are prevented from realizing their *umunthu*. The African woman embodies the oppression of all poor marginalized people of Africa. At a convention of African Christian Women at Accra, Ghana, (September 23-October 1, 1989), 70 women from 24 countries discussed the various forms and sources of their oppression. They all agreed that African customs and rituals exclude women from full participation in church and society. They asserted that the Church has failed them. Rosemary Edet expressed very well the feeling of the convention when she said:

The Christian proclamation of human liberation and the equality of men and women is indeed good news for women, but this teaching is more theoretical than practical. If it were practical, Christianity would have emancipated women from adverse rituals. I am not denying the fact that African women have benefitted from the Good News. What I am saying is that Christianity legalizes and reinforces the oppression of women and their subjugation to men in all aspects of life. The old adage that "women should be seen and not heard" is taken over by the Churches and given biblical foundation in the first letter to the Corinthians. This also affects ecclesial structures so that women are excluded from the ordained ministry and administrative roles of the Church and thus remain outside the Church. . . . The Churches continue to choose their leaders from the educated, predominantly male, middle classes. There are no women bishops. In local Churches, women are teachers who do not participate to any great extent in the Church's theological and political discussions, and whose views are not taken into account. Our Churches reject prostitutes, single mothers, and, in many Churches, women revolutionaries and intellectuals.[99]

In the Church women are looked down on or ignored despite the fact that women form a majority, are the backbone of the Church, and that the Church is referred to as female. In another article, Rosemary Edet and Bette Ekeya, say this reference to the Church in female terms, while the whole structure and hierarchy are predominantly male, is ironic. "No wonder the symbolism of birthing and the female womb-essence means very little in the Church. As a sacrament, both sign and cause of God's saving communion with creation, the Church must reflect in its own being both the being of God and of God's created world. Since God and Christ must be thought of as neither male nor female, so must the Church if in truth it is the body of Christ."[100] Since women are the most oppressed, their liberation will be the liberation of all Africa. "Africa will be great if African women are willing to make it great" says Loise Tappa, since the African woman

is oppressed by her African brother; she is oppressed by other women who are not African, she is oppressed by non-African men. Especially when the hierarchical scale on the international level is taken into account, the African woman is at the very bottom of the scale. She incarnates the mass of the poor and the oppressed. Thus I believe that when this woman has come to understand the message of liberation that Jesus bears, she will be able to take her brothers by the hand and lead them to the way of liberation that is ours.[101]

What is the way to liberation then? In her paper presented to the Continental Consultation on Theology from Third World Women's Perspective (EATWOT Women's Commission), Port Harcourt, Nigeria, August 19-23, 1986, Rosemary Nthamburi said the way to liberation is "to uncover all oppressive social structures which discriminate against women so that women can take their proper role alongside men in the society, and in the declaring of total liberation from all oppression. It should be an act of humanization."[102] Nthamburi says when women explore theology in Africa, their aim is "correcting the existing theology of liberation by rejecting the oppressive and sexist traditions that declare that they are socially, ecclesiastically and personally inferior. . . . They should contribute to the theology of liberation by adding the flavor of women liberation which should seek to bring about equality and partnership of men and women in Church and society."[103] Likewise, Dorothy Ramodibe, says there is a need for a new Church in which men and women participate as equals: "Women cannot build the Church with men, however, until men have been liberated to accept women." She adds,

> One of the tasks of this Church is to examine the symbols of Christianity and check to see if they are polluted by a male dominated culture. This means examining the Bible itself, theology, and Church history or traditions. It is important that women reread the Bible, because the Bible we have now has been edited with the influence of male domination. It is men who composed it, and it used male symbols.[104]

Teresa Okure says rereading Bible "demands that emphasis be placed on the vocation of woman as mother, God's privileged instrument for conceiving and bringing forth life."[105] The themes of motherhood and marriage are very central in womens theology in Africa; thus Okure says, "No sane woman, and certainly no African woman, would see anything belittling or derogatory of women in motherhood per se."[106] On this issue African women have a different opinion from the feminists in the West. The Ghana Convention mentioned above gave a lot of attention to motherhood, childbirth, and marriage, for if these particular experiences are brought to bear on theology, they will change the theological enterprise and consequently the nature and ministry of the Church. Musimbi Kanyoro says "Thus when I ask an African woman to affirm the cultural values embedded in motherhood I am not being blind to the unjust way in which culture portrays barrenness or the refusal of the culture to accept and accommodate single life. Rather I am simply affirming what is good in the culture, knowing that there is room to reject what is bad.[107]

Under marriage, African women theologians have also discussed polygamy from a biblical perspective and African culture. Women's views vary on this subject, some maintain there is no scriptural warrant for it, while others say Jesus did not condemn it either. Two illustrations will be enough. In her article "Un regard systématique sur le phénomène polygamie-polyandrie aujourd'hui," Louise Tappa makes the following observations on marriage in the Bible: (1) "Marriage is not a divine institution; it is rather an answer of man to his/her vocation to subdue the earth (Gen. 1:28)"; (2) Since marriage is a response of man, this response necessarily varies to the circumstances, "thus the various forms of marriage: polygamy, polyandry, group marriages, and marriages between two women." Therefore, (3) "The attitude of the Christian Churches towards polygamists is neither realistic nor theologically founded." Tappa argues both polygamy and monogamy existed in the time of Jesus, but he did not forbid either; what he taught against was divorce for "what God had joined together, let no man put assunder" (Matt. 19:6). She contends that it would be wrong to presume that these words applied only to monogamous marriages. Tappa concludes (4): "By preaching interdictions instead of leading people to take God's commandments to heart, the Church has chosen the easiest way." Jesus did not come to monogamize the polygamists; he did not replace one institution by the other, nor the one prohibition by the other. The role of the Church is to construct, rather than destroy, as was often the case with marriage.[108]

Anne Nasimiyu-Wasike is very much opposed to the views presented above. She argues that

> Monogamy emerges in the Old Testament as God's initial and final will for humanity. This is powerful and clear in the creation story (Gen. 2:18). The Genesis creation story is reechoed in the African myths of the origin of human life. Several African myths on human creation affirm that God created one woman and one man to begin the generation of human life on earth.[109]

She agrees with Tappa that there is no explicit commandment on monogamy or polygamy in the Bible, but "In many cases where polygamy is reported in the Old Testament, it is in a form of apology and criticism rather than exaltation. The authors of the Scriptures express a sense of regret and embarrassment as they narrate those events."[110]

African women theologians have done impressive critiques of interpretations of scripture and theology, especially in ecclesiology and christology. Their experience lead them to reject christological statements by male African theologians because the symbolism used by male theologians suggests that Christ is "nothing else but male." Elizabeth Amoah and Mercy Oduyoye say that "Though, in general, the women affirm the Christological position of the African men, at times they go beyond it or contradict it altogether. This can be gleaned not so much from the writings of African women as from the way they live and from their christianity—their very spirituality, their witness to what Christ means for their lives."[111] Women have developed several images of christology. Jesus is understood as a mother who removes obstacles, or as an elder brother, ancestor, great healer, and companion.

CONCLUSION

Since the origin of African theology, several approaches have emerged.

Delegates at the Pan African Conference of Third World Theologians
identified some of main movements in African theology as follows:

1. A theological approach which while admitting the inherit values in
traditional religions, sees in them a preparation for the Gospel;
2. A critical theology which comes from the Bible, the openness to
African realities, and the dialogue with non-African theologies;
3. Black theology in South Africa takes into consideration the experiences
of oppression and the struggle from liberation, and gets inspiration from
the Biblical faith as expressed by African language and categories as well
as the experience and reflections of Black North Americans.[112]

These are not the only movements in African theology. In our survey, we
have identified one more movement: African Liberation Theology. Through
the work of Ela and Boulaga, we see another approach in African theology
emerging. This approach seeks to critique the present situation through the
hermeneutic of symbols.

All these approaches seek to address problems faced by Africans in their
struggle to live an authentic Christian life. In other words, the burden of the
various approaches in African theology is to contend "against the same
principles and powers, from which Christ came to release humankind."[113]

What we see in the development of African theology is that once it emerged
there was no conscious effort to establish a method by which the socio-
political and economic African situation could be analyzed. The result was
that African theology did not prepare itself to address the situation that was
to unfold after independence. Black theology sought to make a move forward
but it only succeeded in pointing out the weakness of the earlier theological
approaches. African liberation theology, on the other hand, seeks to integrate
all what has been done in the other approaches in African theology, and at the
same time, search for ways to deal with dependence which is causing a lot of
hardship and misery in Africa. Here attempts are being made to understand
social-economic reality by following social analysis as a diagnostic process of
a given reality. This is still a foreign method, and it will not liberate African
theology and theologians.

One thing that has to be clear among African theologians is that Africa will
not be liberated by borrowing concepts from outside. Among some up and
coming African theologians, it has become a sign of academic enlightenment
or excellence to appeal to a Marxist theory of society. Intensive research has
yet to be done to find within Africa's own cultural system something that will
liberate the continent. Only when African theologians begin to draw from
their own resources shall they be truly free.

What is to be done? In answering this question I will give my own
theological method. I believe the way forward for African theology is to begin

with a critical examination of the situation to locate the symbol or symbols forming the way of life in a given context. There is always a basic symbol that mediates a people's vision of life. Once the symbol is located, the situation is again decoded to see how it draws on the people's vision of life as mediated by their symbol(s); or how the socio-political reality fails to reconcile itself with the people's vision. When a symbol fails to mediate a people's vision, it is because it has been distorted. Upon closer examination, symbols reveal where and how they have been falsified or misrepresented by those who have appropriated them. Once the misinterpretation or perversion has been unearthed, a reconstruction of society in light of the new understanding of the symbol follows. This new understanding is in fact a true understanding of the vision people have about themselves and their future.

Before making efforts towards reconstruction, symbols are to be grounded in cultural life and examined from a biblical point. The aim for examining a symbol in light of the biblical teachings is to find out how the symbol enriches Christian life and faith. The study of symbols is to precede biblical examination; it is to serve as a foundational moment in a theological process. This is a needed moment, for it is the moment which grounds theology in the life or aspirations of the people. These symbols are also grounded in the scriptures. Theology not grounded in the life and culture of the people becomes mere jargon.

In sum, I am arguing that a critical reading of a social situation and an interpretation of symbols mediating or distorting the way of life, as a moment in a theological process, may lead to an authentic Christian life. It is almost impossible to practice any form of ethics in a social system without a prior reflection on the reality of the system.

NOTES

1. The latest example of such works is by Gwinyai H. Muzorewa, *The Origins and Development of African Theology* (Maryknoll, N.Y.: Orbis Books, 1985). In the introduction he says he "can utilize only those materials in French, English and Shona," (p. 3) but he cites less than five works from Franco-phone Africa and none of the major theologians there is mentioned in the whole book!

2. *Revue Africaine du Clergé* (hereafter to be referred to as *RAC*), April 1983.

3. Gabriel M. Setiloane, "Theological Trends in Africa," *Missiolania*, 8 (1980): 47.

4. Gabriel M. Setiloane, *African Theology: An Introduction* (Johannesburg: Skotaville Publishers, 1988), 35.

5. John Mbiti, "The Biblical Basis for Present Trends in African Theology." ed. Appiah-kubi and Torres, *African Theology en route*, 84. See also Kwesi Dickson, *Theology in Africa*, 109.

6. I have argued against this theory in *Africa's Agenda: An African Critique of Liberalism and a Recapture of African Values*, chap. 5. (forthcoming).

7. Vincent Mulago, *L'Union vitale bantu, ou le principe de cohésion de la communauté chez les Bashi, les Banyarwanda et les Barundi* (Annali Lateranensi XX 1956), 61-263.

8. *la philosophie bantu-rwandaise de l'être* (Brussels, 1956). To this entry we may add "Le sacré paine, le sacré chrétien," *Aspects de la culture noire. Recherches et debates du Centre Catholique des Intellectuels Francais* (Paris, 1958), 126-145.

9. I have discussed negritude movement in *Africa's Agenda*, chap. 3.

10. A. Abble. *Des prêtres noirs s'interrogent* Coll. Rencontre, no. 47, (Paris: Cerf, 1956).

11. For the history of the concept see H. Rucker, *Africanishe Theologie, Darstellung und Dialog* (Innsbruck: Wien, 1985). See also John K. Agbeti, "African Theology: What is it?" *PA*, 5, (1972): 5-8; John S. Mbiti, "Some Current Concerns of African Theology," *The Expository Times*, March 1976, 176; K. Nsoki, "Genese de l'expression 'théologie africaine,'" *Telema*, (1979): 43; E. W. Fashole-Luke, "The Quest for African Christian Theology," *Scottish Journal of Theology*, 29 (1972): 159-175; *Manifeste des théologie du tiers-mode*, Paris: Édition du centre Lebret, 1976.

12. Among his many writings see *Un visage africain du christianisme*: *l'union vitale bantu face à l'unité vitale ecclésiale* (Paris: PA, 1965); "Le christiniasme face aux aspirations de l'ame bantu," *Antennes* (Louvain) (1962): 473-486; "Le probleme d'une théologie Africaine Revue a la Lumiere de Vatican 11," *RAC*, 24 (1969): 277-314; "Symbolisme dans les religions traditionelles africaines et sacramentalisme," *RAC* 27 (1972): 467-502; also in *Bulletin du Secreteriatus pro non-Christianis*, 18 (1971): 169-203.

13. Ngindu Mushete, "Unité et Pluralité de la Théologie?" *RCA* 22 (1967): 593-615; *La Théologie en Afrique* (Kinshasa: Faculté de Théologie Catholique, 1977); "The History of Theology in Africa: From Polemics to Critical Irenics" eds. Appiah-kubi and Torres, in *African Theology en route*, 23-35.

14. F. M. Lufuabulo, "Valeurs bantoues a christianiser," *Eglise Vivante*, 15 (1963): 357-364; *Orientation prechretienne de la conception bantoue de l'être* (Leopoldville, 1964); "Valeurs des religions africaines selon la Bible et selon Vatican 11," *RCA* 24 (1967): 318-341; Mentalité religieuse africaine et christianisme," *RCA* 22 (1967): 318-340.

15. "Debat sur théologie africaine," *RCA*, 15 (1960).

16. Tshishiku Tshibangu, "Vers une théologie de couleur?" *RCA*, 15 (1960).

17. *Ibid.*, 333f. See also "La Problèmatique d'une théologie Africaine," *RCA*, 4 (1968): 333-352. In an earlier work Tshibangu attempted to present a theological method in African theology, "Théologie Positive et Théologie Speculative" (Paris: Beatrice Nauwelaerts; Louvain: L'Universite, 1965). The question of theological method is carried on in his subsequent writings: *Le Propos d'une Théologie Africaine"* (Kinshasa: Faculté de Théologie Catholique, 1974); *"La Théologie Comme Science au XXeme Siecle* (Kinshasa: Presses Universite du Zaire, 1980). In this work Tshibangu seeks to relate the doctrine of revelation to person and society.

18. Tshibangu, *Vers une théologie de coulor Africaine*, 341.

19. A. Vanneste, "D'abord une vraie théologie," *RCA*, 15 (1960): 346. See also "Théologie univeselle et Théologie africain," *RCA*, 24 (1969); "Où en est le problème de la théologie africaine?" *Cultures et Development*, 6 (1974).

20. Vanneste, "vraie théologie," 346.

21. *Ibid.*, 349.

22. *Ibid.*

23. O. Bwimwenyi-Kweshi, *Discours théologique négro-africain. Problème des foundements* (Paris: Présence Africaine, 1981).

24. Bénézét Bujo, *African Theology in Its Social Context* (Maryknoll, N.Y.: Orbis Books, 1992). Other works include: "Kultur und Christentum in Afrika," *Neue Zeitschrift für Missionzieitschrift*, 32 (1976); "Africanische Theologie. Ruckblick auf eine Kontroverse," *Zeitschrift für Missionawissenschaft und Religionwissenschaft*, 61 (1977); "Welche Theologie braucht Afrika. Mit Inkuturation allein ist es nicht getan," *Herfer Korrespondenz*, 37 (1983); "Comment être religieux en Afrique aujourd'hui?" *Select*, 18 (1985); "L'apport africain à une conception de l'Eglise," *Sources*, (Fribourg), 11 (1985); "Des prêtres noirs s'interrogent. Une théologie issue de la négritude?" *Neue Zeitschrift für Missionzieitschrift*, 46 (1990); "Auf der Suche nach einer africanischen Christologie," eds. H. Demobowski und W. Grieve, *Der andere Christus. Christologie in Zeugnissen aus aller Welt*. (Erlagen: 1991).

25. V. Y. Mundimbe, *Entre les Eaux, Dieus un prêtres, la revolution*, 47.

26. See Agbeti, "African Theology: What is it?" *PA*, (1972): 5-8.

27. E. W. Fashole-Luke, "The Quest for African Christian Theologies," *Scottish Journal of Theology*, 29 (1972): 159-175; also in *Third World Theologies*, eds. G. H. Anderson and T. F. Stransky, (New York: Paulist Press; Grand Rapids, Mich.: Eerdmans, 1976), 135-150.

28. Kwesi A. Dickson, "Towards a Theologia Africana," *New Testament Christianity for Africa and the World*, eds. M. E. Glaswell and E. W. Fashole-Luke, In honor of Harry Sawyer (London: SPCK, 1974), 198-208; *Theology in Africa* (Maryknoll, N.Y.: Orbis Books, 1984).

29. Especially in his book *Towards an Indigenous Church* (London: Oxford University Press, 1965); also by the same author, *African Traditional Religion: A Definition* (London: SCM, 1973).

30. B. Kato, *Theological Pitfalls in Africa* (Kisumu, Kenya: Evangel Publishing House, 1975); "Black Theology and African Theology,"*Evangelical Review of Theology*, 1 (October 1977).

31. John S. Pobee, *Toward an African Theology* (Nashville, Tenn.: Abingdon, 1979).

32. Harry Sawyer, "The Basis for a Theology in Africa,"*International Review of Mission* (1963): 266-278; *Creative Evangelism: Towards a New Encounter with Africa* (London: Lutterworth, 1968); *God: Ancestor or Creator?* (London: Longman, 1970); "What is African Theology? A Case for Theological Africana" *Africa Theological Journal*, 4 (1971); "Salvation Viewed from the African Situation," *PA*, 5, no. 3 (1972): 16-23.

33. Gabriel Setiloane, "Confessing Christ Today,"*Journal of Theology for Southern Africa* 12 (September 1975); also "Christus heute bekenned: aus der afrikanishe Sicht von Mensch und Gemeinschaft," *Zeitschrift für Mission* 2, no. 1 (1976): 21-32; "Where are we in African Theology" eds. Appiah-kubi and Torres *African Theology*; "I am an African," eds. Gerald H. Anderson and Thomas F. Stransky *Third World Theologies*, 128-131;*The Image of God in the Sotho-Tswana* (Rotterdam, Netherlands: A. A. Balkema, 1976); "Theological Trends in African Theology,"*Missiolania*, 8 (1980).

34. John Mbiti "Some Current Concerns of African Theology," *The Expository Times*, March 1976, 168 n1. Also by the same author "Some Current Concerns of African Theology,"*African and Asian Contributions to Contemporary Theology: Report*, 6-17; "African Theology,"*All Africa Lutheran Consultation on Theology in the African Context* (Oct. 5-14, 1978), 33; "The Biblical Basis for the Present Trends in African Theology" ed. Appiah-kubi and Torres in *African Theology*, 83-94. Mbiti is one of the most prolific writers in African theology. Here we have cited only those works where he is directly dealing with the subject of theology.

35. Agbeti, "African Theology: What is it?" *PA*, 5, no. 3 (1972): 6.

36. Byang H. Kato, "Black Theology and African Theology,"*Evangelical Review of Theology*, 1 (Oct. 1977): 46. See also his *Theological Pitfalls in Africa* (Kisumu, Kenya: Evangel Publishing House, 1975).

37. *Ibid.*, 45.

38. This review is in *Polycom*, 1 (April 1978): 62ff.

39. For further explanation see the encyclical *Humani Generis*, A.A.S.,32, 1950, 567-578.

40. Charles Nyamiti, *African Theology, Its Nature, Problems and Methods*. Gaba Pastoral Papers 19 (Eldoret, Kenya: Gaba Publications, 1971); *The Scope of African Theology*. Gaba Pastoral Papers no. 30 (Eldoret, Kenya:

Gaba Publications, 1973). Responding to criticism concerning his methodology he wrote, "An African Theology Dependent on Western Counterparts," *African Ecclesiastical Review*, 17 (May 1975): 141-147; *African Tradition and the Christian God*. Spearhead no. 49 (Eldoret, Kenya: 1977). Carrying on the project of adaptation, that is, focusing on revelation, Nyamiti has published *Jesus Christ as Our Ancestor. Christology from an African Perspective* (Harare, Zimbabwe: Mambo Press, 1986).

41. Charles Nyamiti, "Some Items on African Christian Theism," *African Christian Studies*, 8, no. 4 (December 1992): 1-32.

42. Ngindu Mushete, "The History of Theology in Africa," eds. Appiah-kubi and Torres, in *African Theology en route*, 28.

43. *Ibid.*, 33.

44. *Ibid.*, 29.

45. *Ibid.*, 27.

46. AACC, *Drumbeats from Kampala*, (London: Lutterworth, 1963). For more discussion on the problem of content and direction in African Theology see also AACC, *Engagement: Abidjan 1969*, Nairobi: AACC.

47. E. Bolaji Idowu, *African Traditional Religion: A Definition* (London: S.C.M., 1973), xi.

48. Pobee, *African Theology*, 22.

49. Sinde Sempore, "Conditions of the Theological Service in Africa: Preliminary Reflections," ed. Fashole-Luke in *Christianity in Independent Africa*, 518.

50. *Ibid.*

51. John Kurewa, "The Meaning of African Theology," *Journal of Theology for Southern Africa*, 11 (1975): 37.

52. John Mbiti, "Christianity and African Culture: A Review," *Evangelical Review of Theology*, 3, no. 2 (October 1979): 183, 187, 195.

53. For examples of such biblical works see Mbiti "The Biblical Basis for Present Trends in African theology" eds. Appiah-Kubi and Torres in *African Theology en route*, 87-88.

54. K. E. M. Mgojo, "Church and Africanization," *Hammering Swords into Ploughshares: Essays in Honor of Archbishop Mpilo Desmond Tutu*, eds. Buti Tlhagale and Itumeleng Mosala (Grand Rapids, Mich.: Eerdmans Publishing Co.; Trenton, N.J.: Africa World Press, 1986), 112-113.

55. Gabriel Setiloane, in Tlhagale and Mosala, *Ibid.*, 76.

56. *Ibid.*, 78.

57. *Ibid.*, 77.

58. For arguments see Allan Boesak, "Coming in out of the Wildness," eds. Sergion Torres and Virginia Fabella, in *The Emergent Gospel: Theology from the Developing World* (Maryknoll, N.Y.: Orbis Books, 1978), 82-83.

59. Manas Buthelezi, "Toward Indigenous Theology in South Africa,"*Ibid.*, 61.

60. Setiloane, "Trends in African Theology,"*Missiolania*, 50.

61. Desmond Tutu, "Black Theology and African theology: Soul Mates or Antagonists," *Journal of Religious Thought*, (Fall-Winter 1975): 32-33.

62. Desmond M. Tutu, *Hope and Suffering* (Grand Rapids, Mich.: Eerdmans Publishing Co., 1984), 75.

63. Desmond Tutu, "Black Theology/African Theology- Soul Mates or Antagonists?" *Black Theology: A Documentary History 1966-1979*, Eds. Gayraud Wilmore and James Cone (Maryknoll, N.Y.: Orbis Books, 1979), 490.

64. Gabriel M. Setiloane, "Where are we in African Theology,"eds. Appiah-Kubi and Torres, in *African Theology en route*, 65.

65. Gabriel Setiloane, "Theological Trends in Africa,"*Missiolania*, 8 (1980): 52.

66. *Ibid.*

67. Bonganjalo Goba, "The Task of Black Theological Education in South Africa," *Journal of Theology for Southern Africa*, 21 (March 1978): 20, 21.

68. Goba, *An Agenda for Black Theology: Hermeneutics for Social Change* (Johannesburg: Skotaville Publishers, 1988), 14, 15.

69. Benjamin Witbooi, "Liminality, Christianity and the *Khoikhoi* Tribes" eds. Tlhagale and Mosala in *Hammering Swords into Ploughshares*, 108.

70. Dickson, *Theology in African* , 137-138.

71. Buthelezi, "An African or Black theology" ed. M. Motlhabi in *Essays on Black Theology* (Johannesburg: University Christian Movement Publication, 1972), 7. This also appears under the title "Toward Indigenous Theology in South Africa," ed. Torres and Fabella in *Emergent Gospel*, 74.

72. Allan Boesak, "Liberation Theology in South Africa" eds. Appiah-Kubi and Torres, in *African Theology en route*, 173.

73. Tutu, *Hope and Suffering*, 77.

74. Tutu, *Hope and Suffering*, 76.

75. Manas Buthelezi, "An African Theology or Black Theology," ed. Motlhabi in *Essays on Black Theology*, 7-8. Also edited by Basel Moore as *Black Theology: The South African Voice* (London: Hurst, 1973).

76. Allan Boesak, "Coming in Out of the Wildness," *The Emergent Gospel* (Maryknoll, N.Y.: Orbis Books, 1978), 80.

77. *Ibid.*

78. Boesak, "Liberation Theology in South Africa," 170.

79. K.E.M. Mgojo, "Prolegomenon to the Study of Black Theology,"*Journal for Southern African Theology*, 21 (December 1973): 28.

80. Allan Boesak, *Farewell to Innocence: A Socio-Ethical Study on Black Theology and Power* (Johannesburg: Ravan, 1976; Maryknoll, N.Y.: Orbis Books, 1977), 13.

81. Tutu, *Hope and Suffering*, 26-27.

82. See Moore, *Black Theology: The South African Voice*.

83. Steve Biko, *I Write What I Like* (San Francisco: Harper and Row, 1986), 49. The words also appear under the title "Black consciousness and the Quest for a True Humanity," ed. M. Motlhabi in *Essays in Black Theology*, 21.

84. *Ibid.*, 31-32.

85. Tutu, "The Theology of Liberation in South Africa," eds. Appiah-kubi and Torres in *African Theology en route*, 165.

86. *Ibid.*, 168.

87. Ela, *From Charity to Liberation*, 3, 18.

88. See Enrique Dussel, "The Political and Ecclesial Context of Liberation Theology in Latin America," eds. Torres and Fabella in *Emergent Gospel*, 175-192; also in the same book see Gustavo Gutiérrez, "Two Theological Perspectives: Liberation Theology and Progressivist Theology," especially 240-251.

89. José Chipendo, "Theological Options in Africa Today" eds. Appiah-kubi and Torres in *African Theology en route*, 67.

90. His works include, "Diminished Man and Theology: a Third World Perspective," *AFER* , 1976; *Marxian and Christian Ethics*. Spearhead (Eldoret, Kenya: Gaba Publications 1978); *The Church and Signs of Times* . Spearhead (Eldoret, Kenya: Gaba Publications, 1978).

91. See his article, "African theology as a Theology of Liberation," *AFER* , 1980.

92. Ela has written more than most of the liberation theologians. His main works include: *Voice le temps des heritiers:enlises d'Afrique et voies* (with Rene Lunean, Christiane Ngenda-kuriyo) preface Vincent Cosmao, 1984; *Ma foi d'Africain*, preface d'Achille Mbembe, postpreface Vincent Cosmao (Paris: Editions Karthla, 1985). We have already cited *From Charity to Liberation* and *My Faith as an African*.

93. Bishop Bakole wa Ilunga, *Paths of Liberation: A Third World Spirituality* (Maryknoll, N.Y.: Orbis Books, 1986).

94. See Nthamburi, "African Theology as Liberation Theology," 281-282.

95. Okolo, *Marxian and Christian Analysis*, 86-87.

96. L. Magesa, *The Church and Liberation in Africa,* "Spearhead (Eldoret, Kenya: Gaba Publications, 1976), 26-27.

97. Magesa, *The Church*, 30.

98. Ela, *From Charity to Liberation*, 20.

99. Rosemary N. Edet, "Christianity and African Women Rituals," *The Will to Arise: Women Tradition and the Church in Africa*, eds. Mercy Amba Oduyoye and Musimbi R. A. Kanyoro, (Maryknoll, N.Y.: Orbis Books, 1992), 35, 37-38.

100. Rosemary Edet and Bette Ekeya, "Church Women of Africa: A Theological Community," *With Passion and Compassion: Third World Women Doing Theology*, eds. Mercy Amba Oduyoye and Virginia Fabella, (Maryknoll, N.Y.: Orbis Books, 1989), 8.

101. Loise Tappa, "The Christ-Event: A Protestant Perspective," *Ibid.*, 33.

102. Rosemary Nthamburi, "On the Possibility for a New Image for an African Woman," *African Theological Journal*, 10, no. 1 (1987): 110.

103. *Ibid.*, 107-108.

104. Dorothy Ramodibe, "Women and Men Building Together the Church in Africa," *With Passion and Compassion*, 19.

105. *Ibid.*

106. *Ibid.*, 55.

107. Musimbi Kanyoro, "What is in a name?" *Women Lutheran World Federation*, 30 (1988): 6.

108. Louise Kumandjek Tappa, "Un regard systématique sur le phénomène polygamie-polyandrie aujourd'hui," *La Polygamie et lÉglise* (1982): 87-98.

109. Anne Nasimiyu-Wasike, "Polygamy: A Feminist Critique," *The Will to Arise*, 107.

110. *Ibid.*, 109.

111. Elizabeth Amoah and Mercy Oduyoye, "The Christ for African Women," *With Passion and Compassion*, 43.

112. *Pan African Conference of Third World Theologians Communique*.

113. Observation of the delegates to the consultation "Black Identity and Solidarity: The Role of the Church as a Medium for Social Change," held in Dar-es-Salaam, Tanzania (August 1971). For details of the consultation see E. E. Mshana, "The Challenge of Black Theology," *African Theological Journal*, 5 (December 1972): 19-30. Here the quoted by Cornish Roger, "Pan African and the Black Church: A Search for Solidarity," *Christian Century*, LXXXVIII, (November 17, 1971): 1347.

Bibliography

Abble, A. *Des prêtres noirs s'interrogent* Coll. Rencontre, no. 47, Paris: Cerf, 1956.

Achebe, Chinua. *Things Fall Apart*. London: Heinemann, 1962.

_____. *Arrow of God*. London: Heinemann, 1976.

Agbeti, John. "African Theology: What is it?" *Présence Africaine*, 5, no. 3 (1972).

All Africa Conference of Churches. *Engagement: Abidjan 1969*. Nairobi: AACC, 1970.

_____. *Drumbeats from Kampala*. London: Lutterworth, 1963.

_____. *Newsletter*, 11, no. 3 (1976).

Appiah-kubi, Kofi. "Indigenous African Churches: Signs of Authenticity," *African Theology en Route*. Edited by Appiah-kubi and Sergio Torres. Maryknoll, N.Y.: Orbis Books, 1979.

Apter, David. *Pan Africanism*. New York: Praeger, 1968.

Arethae, Martyrium. *Acta Santorium*, Oct, X.

Arkell, A. J., ed. *A History of the Sudan to 1821*. London: Oxford University Press, 1961.

Asante, Molefi Kete. *Afrocentricity*. New rev. ed. Trenton, N.J.: Africa World Press, 1988.

_____. *The Afrocentric Idea*. Philadelphia, Pa: Temple University Press, 1987.

_____. *Kemet, Afrocentricity and Knowledge*. Trenton, N.J.: Africa World Press, 1990.

Athanasius. *Apologia ad Constanitum*. Patrologiae Cursus Completus, Series Graeca vol. xxv. Edited by J. P. Migne. Paris: Venit apud editorem, 1857-66.

_____. *Oratio de Incarnatione*. Patrologiae Cursus Completus, Series Graeca, vol. xxv. Edited by J. P. Migne. Paris: Venit apud editorem, 1857-66.

Augustine. *Sermons*. Patrologiae Cursus Completus, Series Latina. Edited by

J. P. Migne. Paris: Venit apud editorem, 1849.

_____. *Epistle*. Patrologiae Cursus Completus, Series Latina. Edited by J. P. Migne. Paris: Venit apud editorem, 1849.

Baker, Samuel W. "The Races of the Nile Basin," *Transactions of the Ethnological Society of London*, n.s. v., 1867.

Bandawe, Lewis. *Memoirs of a Malawian*. Edited by B. Pachai. Blantyre: Christian Literature Association of Malawi, 1971.

Barrett, David B. *Schism and Renewal in Africa: An Analysis of Six Thousand Contemporary Religious Movements*. Nairobi: Oxford University Press, 1968.

_____, ed. *African Initiatives in Religion*. Nairobi: East Africa Publishing House, 1971.

Barros, Da Asia. *1st. Decade. Records of South-Eastern Africa*. Vol. 6. Translated by G. M. Theal. Oxford: Claredon Press, 1900.

Benveniste, Emile. *Problems in General Linguistics*. Translated by Mary Elizabeth Meek. Miami, Fl.: University Press of Miami, 1971.

Beti, Mongo. *The Poor Christ of Bomba*. London: Heinemann, 1971.

Biko, Steve. *I Write What I Like*. San Francisco, Ca.: Harper and Row, 1986.

Bimwenyi-Kweshi, O. *Discourrs théologique négro-africain Problème des foundements*. Paris: Présence Africaine, 1981.

Blyden, E. W. "A Vindication of the African Race," *Liberia's Offering*. New York: G. A. Gray, 1862.

_____. *Selected Letters of Edward Wilmot Blyden*. Edited by Hollis R. Lynch. New York: KTO Press, 1978.

Boesak, Allan. "Coming in Out of the Wilderness," *The Emergent Gospel: Theology from the Developing World*. Edited by Sergio Torres and Virginia Fabella. Maryknoll, N.Y.: Orbis Books, 1978.

_____. *Farewell to Innocence: A Socio-Ethical Study on Black Theology and Black Power*. Johannesburg: Ravan, 1976; Maryknoll, N.Y.: Orbis Books, 1977.

_____. "Liberation Theology in South Africa," *African Theology en Route*. Edited by Appiah-kubi and Torres. Maryknoll, N.Y.: Orbis Books, 1979.

_____. *Black and Reformed: Apartheid, Liberation and the Calvinist Tradition*. Johannesburg: Skotaville Publishers, 1984; Maryknoll, N.Y.: Orbis Books, 1984.

Boulaga, F. Eboussi. *Christianity Without Fetishes: An African Critique and Recapture of Christianity.* Translated by Robert R. Barr. Maryknoll, N.Y.: Orbis Books, 1984.

_____. "La démission," *Spiritus*, no. 56 (May-August 1974).

Buchanan, Scott, ed. with introduction. *The Portable Plato*. New York: Penguin Books, 1981.

Buchheit, Vinzenz. "Rufinus von Aquileja als Falscher des Adamantiosdilogs," *Byzantinische Zeitschrift*, 51 (1958).

Budge, E. W. H. *The Queen of Sheba and her Only Son Menyelik*. London: Oxford University Press, 1922.

_____. *The Book of the Saints of Ethiopian Church*. Vols. 1 and 6. Cambridge: Cambridge University Press, 1928.

Buerkle, Horst. "Patterns of Sermons from Various Parts of Africa," *African Initiatives in Religion*. Edited by David Barrett. Nairobi: East African Publishing House, 1971.

Buhlmann, Walbert. *The Coming of the Third Church*. Maryknoll, N.Y.: Orbis Books, 1977.

Bujo, Bénézét. *African Theology in Its Social Context*. Translated by John O'Donohue. Maryknoll, N.Y.: Orbis books, 1992.

_____. "Des prêtres noirs s'interrogent. Une théologie issue de la négritude?" *Neae Zeitschrift für Missionzieitschrift*, 46 (1990).

_____. "Auf der Suche nach einer africanischen Christologie," *Der andere Christus. Christologie in Zeugnissen aus aller Welt*. Edited by H. Demobowski and W. Grieve. Erlangen: Verlag, 1991.

_____. "Kultur und Christentum in Afrika. Bemerkung zu einem Aufsatz," *Neue Zeitschrift für Missionzieitschrift*, 32 (1976).

_____. "Africanische Theologie. Ruckblick auf eine Kontroverse," *Zeitschrift für Missionawissenscaft Religionwissenshaft*, 61 (1977).

_____. "Welche Theologie braucht Afrika. Mit Inkuturation allein ist es nicht getan," *Herfer Korrespondenz*, 37 (1983).

_____. "Commentre religieux en Afrique aujourd'hui?" *Select*, 18 (1985).

_____. "L'apport africain à une conception de l'Eglise," *Sources*, 11 (1985).

Burton, Richard F. *A Mission to Gelele, King of Dahome*. Vol. 2 London: Tinsley Brothers, 1864.

Buthelezi, Manas. "Toward Indigenous Theology in South Africa," *The Emergent Gospel*. Edited by Sergio Torres and V. Fabella. Maryknoll, N.Y.: Orbis Books, 1978.

_____. "An African Theology or Black Theology," *Essays on Black Theology*. Edited by M. Motlhabi. Johannesburg: University Christian Movement Publication, 1972.

Bwimwenyi-Kweshi, O. *Discours théologies négro-africain. Problème des foundements*. Paris: Présence Africaine, 1981.

Chalmers, J. A. *Tiyo Soga: A Page of South African Mission Work*. Lovedale, South Africa: Lovedale Press, 1857.

Chamberlin, D. *Some Letters from Livingstone*. London: Oxford Universities Press, 1940.

Clement. *Stromateis*, 1. *Ante-Nicean Fathers*. Grand Rapids, Mich.: Eerdemans, 1973.

Colvin, Tom. *Christ's Work in Free Africa*. Glasgow: Iona Community, 1964.

Cone, James. *My Soul Looks Back*. Nashville, Tenn.: Abingdon Press, 1982.

_____, and Gayraud Wilmore, eds. *Black Theology: A Documentary History*,

1966-1979. Maryknoll, N.Y.: Orbis Books, 1982.

Cornevin, R. and M. Cornevin. *Historie de l'Afrique des Origines a la 2e. Fuerre Modialle.* Paris: Petite Bibliotheque Payot, 1964.

Coxill, H. Walkin, and Sir Kenneth Grub. *World Christian Handbook.* London: Lutterworth Press, 1968.

Crane, William H. "The Kimbanguist Church and the Search for Authentic Catholicity," *Christian Century,* LXXXVII: vol. 22, June 3, 1970.

Cross, F. L. *Oxford Dictionary of Church History.* London: Oxford University Press, 1958.

Cugoano, Ottabah. *Thoughts and Sentiments on the Evil and Wicked Traffic of Slavery and Commerce of the Human Speci: Humbly Submitted to the Inhabitants of Great Britain.* London: s.n., 1787.

Cyril. *Epistle iv. Patrologia Series Graeca.* LXXVII. Edited by J.P. Migne. Paris: Venit apud editorem, 1857-66.

Dallmayr, Fred R. and Thomas A. MacCarthy, eds. *Understanding and Social Inquiry.* Notre Dame, Ind.: University of Notre Dame Press, 1977.

Dames, Mansel Longworth, trans. *The Book of Duarte Barbosa.* 2 vols. London: Hakluyt Society, 1918.

Dampier-Whetham William, Cecil. *A History of Science and Its Relation with Philosophy and Religion.* Cambridge; New York: Cambridge University Press, 1929.

Daneel, Marthinius L. "Charismatic Healing in African Independent Churches," *Theological Evangelica,* 16, no. 3, (August, 1983).

_____. *Aksum, Richerche di topographia generale.* Roma: Potificium Institutum biblicum, 1938.

Declaration of Belief of the African National Church, 1928. *Constitution of the African National Church as approved by the Chief Secretary, Zomba: Nyasaland, 1928.*

de Villard, U. Monneret. *Storia della Nubia cristiana.* Rome: Potificium Institutum biblicum, 1938.

Dickson, Kwesi A. *Uncompleted Mission: Christianity and Exclusivism.* Maryknoll, N.Y.: Orbis Books, 1991.

_____. *Theology in Africa.* Maryknoll, N.Y.: Orbis Books, 1984.

_____. "Towards a Theologia Africana," *New Testament Christianity for Africa and the World.* Edited by M. E. Glaswell and E. W. Fashole-Luke. In honor of Harry Saywer. London: SPCK, 1974.

_____, and P. Ellingworth, eds. *Biblical Revelation and African Beliefs.* London: Lutterworth, 1969.

Diop, Chiekh Anta. *The African Origin of Civilization: Myth or Reality.* Edited and translated by Mercer Cook. Westport, N.Y.: Lawrence Hill and Co., 1974.

Domingo, Charles. "To the Pastors and Evangelists, Seventh Day Historical Society, 1911," *Sources for the Study of Religion in Malawi.* Reproduced as *Collected Papers* no. 9, December 1983. Chancellor College, University of Malawi.

Drake, St. Clair. *The Redemption of Africa and Black Religion*. Chicago, Ill.: Third World Press, 1970.

Dussel, Enrique. "The Political and Ecclesial Context of Liberation Theology in Latin America," *The Emergent Gospel*. Edited by Torres and Fabella. Maryknoll, N.Y.: Orbis Books, 1978.

Echewa, T. Obinkaram. *The Land's Lord*. London: Heinemann, 1976.

Ecumenical Press Service, June 20, 1974.

Edet, Rosemary. "Christianity and African Women Rituals," *The Will to Arise: Women Tradition and the Church in Africa*. Edited by Mercy Oduyoye and Musimbi R. A. Kanyoro. Maryknoll, N.Y.: Orbis Books, 1992.

_____, and Bette Ekeya. "Church Women of Africa: A Theological Community," *With Passion and Compassion: Third World Women Doing Theology*. Edited by Mercy Amba Oduyoye and Virginia Fabella. Maryknoll, N.Y.: Orbis Books, 1989.

Ela, Jean-Marc. *From Charity to Liberation*. London: Catholic Institute for International Relations, 1984.

_____. *My Faith as an African*. Translated by John P. Brown and Sussan Perry. Maryknoll, N.Y.: Orbis, 1988; London: Geoffrey Chapman, 1989.

_____. *African Cry*. Translated by Robert Barr. Maryknoll, N.Y.: Orbis Books, 1986.

_____, Rene Lunean, and Christiane Ngenda-kuriyo. Preface by Vincent Cosmao. *Voice le temps des heritiers: enlises d'Afrique et voies*. Paris: 1984.

Elias, Norbert. *The Civilizing Process: The Development of Manners*. New York: Urizen Books, 1977.

Equiano, Olaudah. *Equiano's Travel*. London: Heinemann, 1967.

Erivwo, S. U. "Review of Kato's Theological Pitfalls," *Polycom*, 1, no. 1, (April 1978).

Eusebius. *Ecclesiastical History*. Vols. 1 and 4. Translated by K. Lake. London: Loeb Classical Library, 1927.

_____. *Church History: Life of Sonstantine the Great and, Oration in Praise of Constantine*. New York: Scribner and Sons, 1925.

Evans-Pritchard, E.E. *The Institutions of Primitive Society*. Oxford: Basil Blackwell, 1954.

_____. *Theories of Primitive Religion*. Oxford: Claredon Press, 1965.

Fashole-Luke, Edward W. "The Quest for African Christian Theologies," *Scottish Journal of Theology*, 29 (1972).

_____. *Manifeste des theologiens du Tiers-Mode*. Paris: Édition du Centre Lebret, 1976.

_____. "The Quest for African Theologies," *Third World Theologies*. Edited by G.H. Anderson and T.F. Stransky. New York: Paulist Press; Grand

Rapids, Mich.: William Eerdmans, 1976.

_____, Richard Gray, Adrian Hastings, and Godwin Tassie, eds. *Christianity in Independent Africa*. Bloomington, Ind.: Indiana University Press; London: Rex Collings, 1978.

Foster, John. *Church History: The First Advance A.D. 29-500.* London: SPCK, 1972.

Fraser, Donald. "The Opportunity in Pagan Africa." Address made to an Ecumenical Conference held in Nashville, Tennessee, February 28 - March 4, 1906.

_____. *New Africa*. London: Edinburgh House Press, 1927.

Freeman-Grenville, G. S. P. *East African Coast, Select Documents from the First to the Earlier Nineteenth Century*. Oxford: Claredon Press, 1962.

Frend, W. H. C. *The Early Church*. London: Hodder and Stoughton, 1971.

Gadamer, Hans-Georg. *Truth and Method*. New York: Crossroad, 1982.

Garvey, Amy Jacques, ed. *The Philosophy and Opinions of Marcus Garvey*. Edited by Mclelland and Stewart. New edition with a new preface by Hollis R. Lynch. New York: Atheneum, 1986.

Geddes, Michael. *The Church History of Ethiopia*. London: Rich Chiswell, 1825.

Gerth, H. H., and Wright C. Mills, trans. and ed., with introduction. *From Max Weber: Essays in Sociology*. New York: Oxford University Press, 1980 Reprint.

Gibb, H. A. R. *Ibn Battuta: Travels in Asia and Africa*. London: Hakluyt Society, 1929.

Goba, Bonganjalo. "The Task of Black Theological Education in South Africa," *Journal of Theology for Southern Africa*, 21 (March 1978).

_____. *An Agenda for Black theology: Hermeneutics for Social Change*. Johannesburg: Skotaville Publishers, 1988.

Gollmer, C. A. "On African Symbolic Messages," *Journal of the Anthropological Institute*, XIV, 1985.

Gollock, G. A. *Sons of Africa*. London: Student Christian Movement, 1928.

Gregg, R. G. and D. E. Groth. *Early Arianism: A View of Salvation*. Philadelphia: Fortress, 1981.

Groves, C. P. *The Planting Christianity in Africa 1840-1954* Vol. 1. London: Lutterworth Press, 1948.

Gutiérrez, Gustavo. *A Theology of Liberation: History Politics and Salvation*. Edited and translated by Sister Caridad Inda and John Eagleson. Maryknoll, N.Y.: Orbis Books, 1973.

Haliburton, G. M. *The Prophet Harris.* London: Longman, 1971.

Harnack, Adolf von. *The Mission and Expansion of Christianity in the First Three Centuries*. Vol. 2, New York: G. B. Putman's Sons, 1905.

_____. *Geschichte der altchristilichen literature* Reprint. Leipzig: J. C. Hinrichs Verlag, 1958.

Harris, Joseph. "Introduction to the African Diaspora," *Emerging Themes of African History*. Edited by T. O. Ranger. Nairobi: East Africa Publishing House, 1968.

Harris, Rendel, ed. *Acta Scilitanorum*. Cambridge: Cambridge University Press, 1891.

Hassing, Per. "Christian Theology in Africa," *Religion and Life*, xl, no. 4 (Winter 1971).

Hastings, Adrian. *African Christianity.* New York: Seabury; London: Geoffrey Champman, 1976.

_____. *A History of African Christianity 1950-75.* Cambridge: Cambridge University Press, 1979.

Hegel, George F. *Philosophy of Right*. Translated by T. M. Knox, with notes. London and New York: Oxford University Press, 1967.

_____. *The Philosophy of History*. Translated by Sibree, a new introduction by C. J. Friedrich, New York: Dover, 1956.

Hetherwick, Alexander. *The Gospel and the African*. Edinburgh: T. & T. Clark, 1932.

_____. *The Romance of Blantyre: How Livingstone's Dream Came True*. Fife, Scotland: Lassodie Press, n.d.

Hobbes, Thomas. *Leviathan*. Edited by Michael Oakeshott, with introduction by Richard S. Peters, New York: Macmillan Publishing Co., 1962.

Hollis, Lynch R. *Edward Wilmot Blyden: Pan-Negro Patriot 1832-1912* New York: Oxford University Press, 1970.

Hopkins, Paul. *What Next in Mission*. Philadelphia: Westminster Press, 1977.

Hourtart, Francis, and Andre Rousseau. *The Church and Revolution*. Maryknoll, N.Y.: Orbis Books, 1971.

Humani Generis, A. A. S., 32, 1950.

Hume, David. *Essay and Treatise*. Dublin: J. Williams, 1779.

_____. *On Human Nature and the Understanding*. Edited by Antony Flew, with introduction. New York: Collier Macmillan Publishers, 1962.

Ibn Battuta, Muhammad ibn Abudullah. *Tuhfat al-Muzzar fi Ghar àih al-Ansar wa 'Adj àih al-Astar*. Translated by H. A. R. Gibb. London: Hakluyt Society, 1929.

Idowu, E. Boulaji. *Towards an Indigenous Church*. London: Oxford University Press, 1965.

_____. *African Traditional Religion: A Definition*. London: SCM, 1973.

Jacobs, Slyvia M., ed. *Black Americans and the Missionary Movement in Africa*. Westport, Conn.: Greenwood Press, 1982.

Jaritz, E. "Uber Bahmen auf Billardtischen-Oder: Eine Mathematische Untersuchung von Ideogrammen Angolanischer Herkunft," *Mathematische-Statistiche Sektion*, Research Centre A-8010, Graz, Austria, 1983.

Johnson, Walter R. "The African-American Presence in Central and Southern Africa, 1880-1905,"*Journal of African Affairs*. 4, no. 1 (Jan. 1979).

Jones, A. H. M. and Elizabeth Monroe. *A History of Ethiopia*. Oxford: Claredon Press, 1962.

Jones, Thomas Jesse, ed. *Education in Africa: A Study of West, South and Equatorial Africa by Africa Education*. London: Phelps Stokes Foundation, 1921; New York: Oxford University Press, 1962.

_____, ed. *Education in Africa: A Study of East, Central and South by Second Africa Education Commission*. London: Phelps Stokes Foundation, 1925; New York: Oxford University Press, 1962.

Jules-Rosette, Bennetta, ed. *The New Religions of Africa*. Forward by James W. Fernandez. Norwood, N.J.: Ablex Publishing Corporation, 1979.

Jumbam, Kenjo. *The White Man of God*. London: Heinemann, 1980.

Kagame, Alex. *la philosophie bantu-rwandaise de l'être*. Brussels, 1956.

_____. "Le sacré paine, le sacré chretien," *Aspects de la culture noire*. Recherches et debates du Centre Catholique des Intellectuels Francais. Paris, 1958.

Kameeta, Zephania. *Why O Lord: Psalms and Sermons from Namibia*. Philadelphia: Fortress Press, 1986.

Kant, Immanuel. *Prolegomena to any Future Metaphysics which will be able to come forth as Science (1783)*. Translated by Mahaffy-Carus. New York: Library of Arts, H. W. Sams, 1950.

Kanyoro, Musimbi. "What is in a Name?" *Women Lutheran World Federation*, 30 (1988).

Karenga, Maulana, and H. Carrauthers. *The proceeding of Selected of the proceeding of the First and Second conference of the Association for the Study of Classical Civilization*, Feb. 24-26, 1984 (6224 AFE) Los Angeles, and March 1-3, 1985 (6225 AFE) Chicago.

_____. *Africa Kemet and the African World View: Research Rescue and Restoration*. Los Angeles, Ca.: University of Sankore Press, 1986.

Kato, Byang H. *Theological Pitfalls in Africa*. Kisumu, Kenya: Evangel Publishing House, 1975.

_____. "Black Theology and African Theology," *Evangelical Review of Theology*, 1 (Oct. 1977).

Kaunda, Kenneth, and Colin Morris. *A Humanist in Africa*. Nashville, Tenn.: Abingdon Press, 1966.

Kendall, R. Elliot. "On the Sending of Missionaries: A Call for Restraint," *International Review of Missions*. 64, no. 253 (January 1975).

Kent, R. K. "Palmares: an African State in Brazil,"*Journal of African History*, vi, no. 2 (1965).

Kessler, David. *The Falashas: The Forgotten Jews of Ethiopia*. New York: Schocken Books, 1985.

Kibanda, M. "L'écreiture dans la civilisation Kongo: Problemes theoriques et methodologiques," *Revue de Linguistique Theorique et Appliquee*, (Janvier 1985).

Kirwan, L. P. "A Contemporary Account of the Conversion of the Sudan to Christianity," *Sudan Notes and Records*, xx (1937).

Kubik, G. "African Graphic Systems: A Reassessment," *mitteilungan der Anthropologischen Gesellsscraft in Wien*, 114 and 115 (1984-1988).

Küng, Hans. *The Church*. New York: Doubleday, 1976.

Kurewa, John. "The Meaning of African Theology," *Journal of Theology for Southern Africa*, 11 (1975).

Lagos Weekly Record, February 24, 1917.

Lamb, David. *The Africans*. New York: Random House, 1984.

Latourette K. S. *A History of the Expansion of Christianity*. Vol. 2. Grand Rapids, Mich.: Zondervan, 1953.

Leslau, Wolf. *Countumes et croyances des Falachas (Juifs d'Abyssinie)*. Université de Paris, Travaux memoires de l'Institut d'Ethnologie, n. LXI. Paris: 1957.

Levy-Bruhl, Lucien. *Primitive Mentality*. Translated by L. A. Clare. London: Allen and Unwin, 1923.

Llyod, A. B. *Apolo of the Pygmy Forest*. London: Claredon, 1923.

Locke, John. *The Reasonableness of Christianity with a Discourse of Miracles and Part of A Third Letter Concerning Toleration*. Edited by I. T. Ramsey. Stanford, Ca: Stanford University Press, 1958.

Lufuabulo, F. M. "Valeurs bantoues a christianiser," *Englise Vivante*, 15 (1963).
_____. *Orientation prechretienne de la conception bantoue de l'être*. Léopoldville (Kinshasa): Centre d'Etudes Pastorales, 1964.
_____. Valeurs des religions africaines selon la Bible et selon Vatican 11," *Revue du Clergé Africaine*, 24 (1967).
_____. Mentalité religieuse africaine et christianisme," *Revue du Clergé Africaine*, 22 (1967).

Lyimo, Camilus. "Quest for Relevant Theology: Towards An Ujamaa Theology," *African Ecclesiastical Review*, 3 (1976).

Magesa, Laurentine. *The Church and Liberation in Africa*. Spearhead, no. 44. Eldoret, Kenya: Gaba Publications, 1976.

Mapuranga, M. M. "Dr. Thorne's Unsuccessful Attempt at Setting a Black Colony in Malawi, 1894-1923, "*Malawi Journal of Social Science*. 5 (1976).

Martin, John. "They Have Grown - And On Their Own," *International Review of Mission*, 72 (Oct. 1963).

Matecheta, Harry. *Blantyre Mission: Nkhani ya Ciyambi Cace*. Blantyre, Malawi: Hetherwick Press, 1949.

Mbinda, John Samuel Mutiso. "Liberation and Mission in Africa." Address presented at the IV IAMS Conference at Maryknoll, New York, 21-26 August, 1978.

_____. "Towards A Theology of Harambee," *African Ecclesiastical Revue,* 1978.

Mbiti, John Samuel. *African Religions and Philosophy.* New York: Doubleday and Co., 1970.

_____. "An African Views American Black Theology,"*Worldview,* 17 (August 1974).

_____. "Some Current Concerns of African Theology,"*African and Asian Contributions to Contemporary Theology: Report.* Edited by John S. Mbiti. Geneva: Bossey, 1976. Also in *The Expository Times* , March 1976.

_____. "African Theology,"All Africa Lutheran Consultation on Theology in the African Context, October 5-14, 1978.

_____. "Christianity and African Culture: A Review,"*Evangelical Review of Theology,* 3, no. 2 (October 1979).

_____. "The Biblical Basis for Present Trends in African Theology,"*African Theology en Route.* Edited by Appiah-Kubi and Torres. Maryknoll, N.Y.: Orbis Books, 1979.

MacAlpine, A. G. "The Missionary and the Native Church." Unpublished letter: Edinburgh University Library, Manuscripts.

McCracken, John. "The Nineteenth Century in Malawi," *Aspects of Central African History.* Edited by T. O. Ranger. Evanston, Ill.: Northwestern University Press, 1968.

_____. *Politics and Christianity in Malawi 1875-1940: The Impact of the Livingstonia Mission in Northern Province.* London: Cambridge University Press, 1977.

McCrindle. *The Christian Topography of Cosmas Indicopleustes.* Cambridge: Cambridge University Press, 1909.

McMinn, R. D. "A Devoted African Pastor," *Other Lands* , July 1936.

Meir, August. *Negro Thought in America.* Ann Arbor, Mich.: University of Michigan Press, 1963.

Memorandum submitted to the Bledisloe Commission in April 1938 by the International Missionary Council of Nyasaland.

Mercer, Samuel A. "The Falashas," *Aethiops,* 3 (1930).

Mgojo, K. E. M. "Church and Africanization," *Hammering Swords into Ploughshares: Essays in Honor of Archbishop Mpilo Desmond Tutu.* Edited by Buti Tlhagale and Itumeleng Mosala, Grand Rapids, Mich.: William Eerdmans Publishing Co.; Trenton, N.J.: Africa World Press, Inc., 1986.

_____. "Prolegomenon to the Study of Black Theology,"*Journal for Southern African Theology,* 21 (December 1973).

Moore, Basel, ed. *Black Theology: The South African Voice.* London: Hurst, 1973. Also published as *The Challenge of Black Theology in South Africa.* Atlanta, Ga.: John Knox Press, 1974.

Mosala, Itumeleng J. "Ethics of the Economic Principles: Church and Secular

Involvement," *Turning Swords in Ploughshares.* Edited by Tlhagale and Mosala. Grand Rapids, Mich.: William Eerdmans, 1986.

_____. *Biblical Hermeneutics and Black in South Africa.* Grand Rapids, Mich.: William Eerdmans Publishing Co., 1989.

Mshana, E. E. "The Challenge of Black Theology," *African Theological Journal,* 5 (December 1972).

Mulago, Vincent. "Le christiniasme face aux aspirations de l'ame bantu," *Antennes,* Louvain, 1962.

_____. *Un visage africain du christianisme: l'union vitale bantu face à l'unitè vitale ecclesiale.* Paris: Présence Africaine, 1965.

_____. "Le problème d'une théologie Africaine Revu à la Lumière de Vatican 11," *Revue du Clergé Africaine,* 24 (1969).

_____. "Symbolisme dans les religions traditionelles africaines et sacramentalisme," *Revue du Clergé Africaine,* 27 (1972); also in *Bulletin du Secreteriatus pro non-Christianis,* 18 (1971).

Mumba, Levi. "The Native Idea of the Divine Being," *Vyaro na Vyaro,* 15 (June 1923).

_____. "Religion of My Fathers," *International Review of Mission,* 19 (1930).

Mundimbe, V. Y. *The Invention of Africa: Gnosis, Philosophy, and the Order of Knowledge.* Bloomington, Ind.: Indiana University Press; London: James Currey, 1988.

Munonye, John. *The Only Son.* London: Heinmann, 1966.

Mushete, Ngindu. "Unité et Pluralité de la Théologie?" *Revue du Clergé Africaine,* 22 (1967).

_____. *La Théologie en Afrique, d'Hier et Aujourd'hiu.* Kinshasa: Faculté de Théologie Catholique, 1977.

_____. "The History of Theology in Africa: From Polemics to Critical Irenics," *African Theology en Route.* Edited by Appiah-kubi and Torres. Maryknoll, N.Y.: Orbis Books, 1979.

Muzorewa, Gwinyai H. *The Origins and Development of African Theology.* Maryknoll, N.Y.: Orbis Books, 1985.

Mveng, Englebert. *Black African Art as Cosmic Liturgy and Religious Language.* 2d ed. Yaoundé CLE, 1974.

Mwasi, Yesaya. Z. *My Essential and Paramount Reasons for Working Independently.* Sources for the Study of Religion in Malawi, no. 2, 1979.

Mwoleka, Christopher. "Trinity and Community" *African Ecclesiastical Review,* 4 (July 1975).

Nascimento, Abdias do. "Quilombismo: The African Brazilian Road to Socialism," *African Culture: The Rhythm of Unity.* Edited by Molefi Kete Asante and Kariam Welsh Asante. Trenton, N.J.: Africa World Press, 1990.

Neander, August. *General History of the Christian Religion and Church.* 5 vols. Translated by Josephy Torrey. New York: Hurd and Houghton, 1871.

Neil, Stephen. *A History of Christian Missions*. Middlesex: Penguin, 1973.

New Black Friars, January 1984.

Niangoran-Bouah, B. *The Akan World of Gold Weights: Abstract Design Weights*. Abidjan: Les Nouvelles Editions, 1984.

Nicolas, Archbishop. *Church's Revival: Emancipation from 1600 Years' Guardianship: Free Church in Free State*. Cairo, Egypt. Distributed by the Prime Minister's Library, Addis Ababa.

Njoya, Timothy Murere. *Human Dignity and National Identity: Essential for Social Ethics*. Nairobi: Jemisik Cultural Books, 1987.

Nkrumah, Kwame. Speech at the Conference of Independent African States. Accra, Ghana, April 15, 1958.

Nsoki, K. "Genese de l'expression 'théologie africaine'," *Telema: Revue de réflexion et créatiivté chrétiennes en Afrique*, (1979).

Nthamburi, Rosemary. "On the Possibility of a New Image for an African Woman," *Voices from the Third World*, 10, no. 1 (1987).

Nthamburi, Zablon. "African theology as a Theology of Liberation," *African Ecclesiastical Review*, 1980.

Nthara, S. *Mbiri ya Achewa*. Zomba and Lusaka, Northern Rhodesia: Nyasaland Literature Bureau, 1949.

Nyamiti, Charles. *African Theology, Its Nature, Problems and Methods*. Eldoret, Kenya: Gaba Publications, 1971.

_____. *The Scope of African Theology*. Eldoret, Kenya: Gaba Publications, 1973.

_____. "An African Theology Dependent on Western Counterparts," *African Ecclesiastical Review*, 17, no. 4 (May 1975).

_____. *Jesus Christ as Our Ancestor*. Harare, Zimbabwe: Mambo Press, 1986.

_____. "Some Items on African Christian Theism," *African Christian Studies*, 8, no. 4 (December 1992).

Nyerere, Julius K. *Freedom and Socialism*. Dar-es-Salaam; London: Oxford University Press, 1968.

_____. *"Is Poverty the Real Problem?"* Address given to Maryknoll Sister's General Chapter, New York in 1970. Extracts, Indian Social Institute. Banglore, India.

Nzekwa, Onoura. *Blade Among Boys*. London: Heinemann, 1971.

O'Leary, D. L. *The Ethiopian Church: Historical Notes on the Church of Abyssinia*. London: SPCK, 1936.

Obijole, Olubayo. "South African Liberation Theologies of Boesak and Tutu- A Critical Evaluation," *African Theological Journal*, 16, no. 3 (1987).

Okigbo, Christopher. *Labyrinths with Path of Thunder*. London: Heinemann, 1971.

Okolo, Chukwudum B. "Diminished Man and Theology: a Third World Perspective," *African Ecclesiastical Review*, 1976.

_____. *Marxian and Christian Ethics*. Spearhead, no. 55. Eldoret, Kenya:

Gaba Publications, 1978.

_____. *The Church and Signs of Times*. Spearhead. Eldoret, Kenya: Gaba Publications, 1978.

Oliver, Roland. *The Missionary Factor in East Africa*. London: Longman, Green and Co., 1952.

_____, and J. D. Fage, *A Short History of Africa*. 5th ed. New York: Penguin Books, 1975.

Oruke, Theresa. "Women in the Bible," Edited by Virginia Fabella and Mercy Amba Oduyoye. *With Passion and Compassion: Third World Women Doing Theology*. Maryknoll, N.Y.: Orbis Books, 1989.

Pan African Conference of Third World Theologians: Communique .

Parratt, J. K., ed. "Y. Z. Mwasi and the Origins of the Blackman's Church," *Journal of Religion in Africa*, IX, fasc. 3 (1979).

Parrinder, Geoffrey. "Learning from Other Faiths," *Expository Times*, 1972.

Pirouet, M. Louise. *Black Evangelists: The Spread of Christianity in Uganda 1891-1914* London: Rex Collings, 1978.

Pobee, John S. *Toward an African Theology*. Nashville, Tenn.: Abingdon, 1979.

Popkin, Richard H. "Hume's Racism," *The Philosophical Forum*, ix, nos. 2-3, (1977-78).

Proceedings of the Church Missionary Society, 1916/1917.

Rabinow, Paul, and William M. Sullivan, eds. *Interpretive Social Sciences: A Reader*. Berkeley and Los Angeles, Ca.: University of California Press, 1979.

Ralston, Richard D. "American Episodes in the Making of an African Leader: A Study Case of Alfred B. Xuma (1893-1962)," *International Journal of Historical Studies*, 6, no. 1 (1973).

Ramodibe, Dorothy. "Women and Men building the Church Together in Africa," *With Passion and Compassion: Third World Women Doing Theology*. Edited by Virginia Fabella and Mercy Oduyoye Maryknoll, N.Y.: Orbis Books, 1989.

Ranger, T. O., ed. *Emerging Themes of African History*. Nairobi: East African Publishing House, 1968.

Report of the Tuskegee Institute Task Force on its Visit to the Republic of South Africa, September 25, 1874.

Robinson, John A. T. *Honest to God*. London: SCM, 1963.

Roger, Cornish. "Pan African and the Black Church: A Search for Solidarity," *Christian Century*, LXXXVIII, no. 46 (November 17, 1971).

Ross, David A. "The Career of Domingo Martinez in the Bight of Benin 1833-64," *Journal of African History*, vi, no. 1 (1965).

Rossini, C. Conti. *La Storia d'Etiopia*. Milan: A. Lucinni, 1928.

Rufinus. *Historia Ecclesiastica*. Patrologiae Curcus Completus, Series Latina, vol. XX1. Edited by J. P. Migne. Paris: Venit apud editorem, 1849-66.

Salih, Abu. *Churches and Monasteries of Egypt and the Neighboring Countries.*
    Translated by B. T. A. Evetts, with notes by Alfred J. Butler. Oxford:
    Claredon Press, 1895.

Sanneh, Lamin. *West African Christianity: The Religious Impact.* New York:
    Orbis books, 1983.

Sawyer, Harry. "The Basis for a Theology in Africa," *International Review of
    Mission*, 1963.

_____. *Creative Evangelism: Towards a New Encounter with Africa.* London:
    Lutterworth, 1968.

_____. *God: Ancestor or Creator?* London: Longman, 1970.

_____. "What is African Theology? A Case for Theologica Africana," *Africa
    Theological Journal*, 4 (1971).

_____. "Salvation Viewed from the African Situation," *Presence Africaine.* 5,
    no. 3 (1972).

Schaff, Philip. *History of the Christian Church* vol. 3. Reprint. Grand Rapids,
    Mich.: Eerdmans, 1987.

Schoffeleers, J. M. "Symbolic and Social Aspects of Spirit Worship among the
    Mang'anja," a Ph.D. dissertation presented to Oxford University, 1968.

_____. "The Beginnings of Life," *Vision of Malawi*, 3, no. 4 (Dec. 1972).

_____, and A. A. Roscoe. *The Land of Fire: Oral Literature from Malawi.*
    Limbe: Popular Publications; Lilongwe: Likuni Press and Publishing
    House, 1985.

Seaver, George. *David Livingstone: His Life and Letters.* New York: Harper
    and Row, 1957.

Sellassie, Sergew Hable. *The Ancient and Medieval History of Ethiopia to 1270.*
    Addis Ababa, Ethiopia: United Printers, 1972.

Sempore, Sinde. "Conditions of the Theological Service in Africa: Preliminary
    Reflections," *Christianity in Independent Africa.* Edited by Fashole-Luke,
    et al. Bloomington: Indiana University Press, 1979.

Setiloane, Gabriel. "I am an African," *Mission Trends No 3: Third World
    Theologies.* Edited by Gerald H. Anderson and Thomas F. Stransky.
    New York: Paulist Press, 1976.

_____. "Confessing Christ Today," *Journal of Theology for Southern Africa*, 12
    (September 1975); also in "Christus heute bekenned: aus der afrikanishe
    Sicht von Mensch und Gemeinschaft," *Zeitschrift für Mission*, 2, no. 1
    (1976).

_____. "Where are we in African Theology," *African Theology en Route.*
    Edited by Kofi Appiah-kubi and Sergio Torres. Maryknoll, N.Y.: Orbis,
    1979.

_____. *The Image of God in the Sotho-Tswana.* Rotterdam, Netherlands: A.
    A. Balkema, 1976.

_____. "Theological Trends in African Theology," *Missiolania*, 8 (1980).

_____. *African Theology: An Introduction.* Johannesburg: Skotaville

Publishers, 1988.

Shepherd, R. H. W. *Lovedale, South Africa: The Story of a Century 1841-1941.* Lovedale: Lovedale Press, 1941.

Shepperson, George, and Tom Price. *The Independent African.* Edinburgh: Edinburgh University Press, 1959.

_____. "The African Abroad or the African Diaspora," *Emerging Themes in African History.* Edited by T. O. Ranger. Nairobi: East Africa Publishing House, 1968.

_____. "Notes on Negro American Influences on the Emergence of African Nationalism," *Journal of African History,* 1, no. 2 (1960).

Shorter, Aylward. *African Culture and the Christian Church: An Introduction to Social And Pastoral Anthropology.* London: Geoffrey Chapman, 1973.

Sindima, Harvey J. *The Legacy of Independent Churches in Malawi.* Lewiston, N.Y.: Edwin Mellen Press, 1992.

_____. *Africa's Agenda: An African Critique of Liberalism and a Recapture of African Values* (forthcoming).

_____. *The Gospel According to the Marginalize: A Survey of Liberation Theologies* (forthcoming).

_____. *Christianity and Political Crisis in Africa* (forthcoming).

_____. "Community of Life," *The Ecumenical Review,* 41, no. 4 (October 1989); also in Charles Birch, David Eakin, and Jay MacDaniel. *Theologies for the Liberation of Life: Contemporary Approaches to Ecology Theology,* as "Community of Life: African Understanding of Creation." Maryknoll, N.Y.: Orbis Books, 1990.

_____. "A General Survey of Independent Churches in Malawi 1900-1976," *All Africa Conference of Churches Bulletin,* 1977.

_____. "Africa's Christian Heritage: Some Notes on the Ethiopian Church," *Africa Theological Journal,* 2, no. 2 (1991).

Slade, R. *English Speaking Missions in the Congo Independent State.* Brussels: Academie Royale Des Sciences Coloniales. n.d.

Smith, E. W. *African Ideas of God.* London: Edinburgh House Press, 1961.

Socrates. *Historia Eccllestica.* Imprint. Oxford: Claredon Press, 1969.

Sofala, 'Zulu, "The Theater in the Search for African Authenticity," *African Theology en Route.* Edited by Appiah-kubi and Torres. Maryknoll, N.Y.: Orbis, 1979.

Spencer, Herbert. *On Social Evolution.* Edited by J. D. Y. Peel. Chicago: Chicago University Press, 1972.

Sundkler, Bengt G. M. *Bantu Prophets in South Africa.* 2d ed. London: Oxford University Press, 1961.

Symposium of Episcopal Conference of Africa and Madagascar, *Seeking Gospel Justice in Africa.* Spearhead, no. 69, 1981.

Tamrat, Taddesse. *Church and State in Ethiopia 1270-1527.* London: Oxford University Press, 1972.

Tappa, Louise. "Un regard systématique sur le phénomène polygamie-polyandrie aujour'hui," *La Polygamie et l'Église* (1982).

_____. "The Christ-Event: A Protestant Perspective," *With Passion and Compassion: Third World Women Doing Theology*, Edited by Mercy Amba Oduyoye and Virginia Fabella. Maryknoll, N.Y.: Orbis Books, 1989.

Tassie, G. O. M. A Ph.D. dissertation presented to the University of Aberdeen, 1969.

Tertullian, *Apology*, 50. 14. Ante-Nicean Fathers, Grand Rapids, Mich.: Eerdmans, 1973.

_____. *De Exhortatione Castitatis*, 10. Ante-Nicean Fathers. Grand Rapids, Mich.: Eerdmans, 1973.

_____. *De Baptismo*, 8 and 15. Ante-Nicean Fathers. Grand Rapids, Mich.: Eerdmans, 1973.

_____. *De Test.amin*. 6. Ante-Nicean Fathers. Grand Rapids, Mich.: Eerdmans.

Thompson, Virginia, and Richard Adolff. *French West Africa*. Stanford, Ca.: Stanford University Press, 1967.

Thuku, Harry. *An Autobiography*. Nairobi: Oxford University Press, 1970.

Tillich, Paul. *A History of Christian Thought: From its Judaic and Hellenistic Origins to Existentialism*. Edited by Carl E. Braaten. New York: Simon and Schuster, 1968.

Tshibangu, Tshishiku. *Théologie Positive et Théologie Speculative*. Paris: Beatrice Nauwelaerts, Louvain: L'Universite, 1965.

_____. "La Problématique d'une théologie Africaine," *Revue du Clergé Africaine*, 4 (1968).

_____. *La Théologie Comme Science au XXeme Siecle*. Kinshasa: Presses Universite, 1956.

_____. *Le Propos d'une Théologie Africaine*. Kinshasa: Faculté de Théologie Catholique, 1974.

Turner, Harold W. "Prophets and Politics: a Nigerian Test-Case," *The Bulletin of the Society for African Church History*, 11, no. 1 (1965).

Tutu, Desmond M. "Black Theology and African Theology: Soul Mates or Antagonists," *Journal of Religious Thought*, Fall-Winter 1975. Also in *Black Theology: A Documentary History 1966-1979.* Edited by Gayraud Wilmore and James Cone. Maryknoll, N.Y.: Orbis Books, 1979.

_____. "Whether African Theology," *Christianity in Independent Africa*. Edited by Edward Fashole-Luke, Adrian Hastings and Godwin Tassie. Bloomington, Ind.: Indiana University Press; London: Rex Collings, 1978.

_____. "The Theology of Liberation in South Africa," *African Theology en Route*. Edited by Appiah-kubi and Torres. Maryknoll, N.Y.: Orbis Books, 1979.

_____. *Hope and Suffering*. Johannesburg: Skotaville Publishers; Grand

Rapids, Mich.: Eerdmans Publishing Co., 1984.

Tylor, Edward B. *Religion in Primitive Culture,* Introduction by Paul Radin. Gloucester, Mass.: Peter Smith, 1970.

Tzadua, Abba Paulos. *The Fetha Nägäst, the Law of the Kings.* Addis Ababa: 1968.

Ukpong, Justin S. *African Theologies Now: A Profile.* Spearhead, no. 80, 1984.

Vanneste, A. "Debat sur théologie africaine," *Revue du Clergé Africaine,* 15 (1960).

_____. "Théologie univeselle et Théologie africain," *Revue du Clergé Africaine,* 24 (1969).

_____. Où en est le problème de la théologie africaine?" *Cultures et Development,* 6 (1974).

Verger, Pierre. *Bahia and the West Coast Trade (1549-1851)* Ibadan, Nigeria: University Press, 1964.

Voice of Missions, August 1895.

wa Ilunga, Bakole. *Paths of Liberation: A Third World Spirituality.* Maryknoll, N.Y.: Orbis Books, 1986.

Wa Thiong'o, Ngugi. *Decolonizing the Mind: The Politics of Language in African Literature.* Nairobi: Heinemann, 1986.

_____. *The River Between.* London: Heinemann, 1965.

Washington, Booker T. *Up From Slavery.* New York: Doubleday and Company, 1963.

Weber, Max. *The Methodology of the Social Sciences.* Translated by Edward A. Shils and Henry A. Finch, with a forward by Edward Shils. New York: The Free Press, 1949.

_____. *The Sociology of Religion.* Translated by Ephraim Fischoff, introduction by Talcott Parsons. Boston: Beacon Press, 1964.

Webster, J. B. "The Bible and the Plough," *Journal of Historical Society of Nigeria,* 2, no. 4 (December 1963).

West, Martin. *Bishops and Prophets in a Black City.* Cape Town, South Africa: David Philip, 1965.

Why Not Be Fair? London: Federal High Commissioner, n.d.

Williams, Walter L. "The Afro-American Presence in Central and Southern Africa, 1880-1905,"*Journal of African Affairs,* 4, no. 1 (January 1979).

_____. *Black Americans and the Evangelization of Africa 1877-1900.* Madison, Wis.: University of Wisconsin Press, 1982.

Wilmore, Gayraud, and James Cone. eds. *Black Theology: A Documentary History 1966-1979.* Maryknoll, N.Y.: Orbis Books, 1979.

Wilson, Bryan, ed. *Rationality.* London: Basil Blackwell, 1970.

Winch, Peter. "Understanding a Primitive People," *American Philosophical Quarterly,* 1 (1964).

Witbooi, Benjamin. "Liminality, Christianity and the Khoikhoi Tribes," *Hammering Swords into Ploughshares.* Edited by Tlhagale and Mosala.

Grand Rapids, Mich.: William Eerdmans Publishing Co.; Trenton, N.J.:
Africa World Press, 1986.

World Council of Churches: Faith and Order Commission: "Giving Account
of the Hope in us." Report of the Yaound é Faith and Order Seminar,
1974.

_____. "Uniting in Hope," *Report of World Council of Churches Faith and
Order Consultation, Accra, 1974.* Geneva: World Council of Churches,
1975.

Index

About the Author

HARVEY J. SINDIMA is currently Assistant Professor of Philosophy and Religion at Colgate University in Hamilton, New York. He is the author of *The Legacy of Scottish Missionaries in Malawi* (1992).